"Empathetic, rigorous, erudite, funny, generous, and surprising, *The Magician's Book* is easily the best book ever written about C. S. Lewis. Miller draws sound and dazzling connections among the details of his life and literary inspirations, which ranged from medieval epics to the Victorian forerunners of modern fantasy."

— Michael Joseph Gross, *Los Angeles Times*

"A thorough and thoroughly engrossing look at one reader's lifetime love affair with Narnia. You need not be a C. S. Lewis fan or aficionado to enjoy Miller's book, though a few of your own affairs with imaginary places and people probably help. Smart, meticulous, and altogether delightful."

— Karen Joy Fowler, author of *The Jane Austen Book Club*

"A journey of great pleasure — Miller is a wise, down-to-earth, and often funny narrator. The result is one of the best books about stories and their power that I have ever read."

— Mary Ann Gwinn, *Seattle Times*

"Of all the critics writing today, I trust Laura Miller the most, because her peerless critical intelligence and extraordinary erudition are in perfect balance with her love of books and her deep sympathy for writers. Reading her thrilling new book about C. S. Lewis and his Narnia series is like sitting down with the smartest and least tendentious person you know and dishing your favorite books. I came away from this book feeling thoroughly informed, entertained, and inspired." — James Hynes, author of *The Lecturer's Tale* and *Next*

"Truly original." — Katherine A. Powers, *Boston Globe*

"A tribute to the power and depth of story and imagination, and to the pure joy of reading. Though the grown critic realized how the magician does his tricks, something of the childhood magic remains." — Lacey Galbraith, *BookPage*

"An engrossing examination of the importance of children's literature.... *The Magician's Book* is a beautiful and thoughtful journey back to why we read." — Danielle Trussoni, *People*

"An agreeable and insightful book.... Miller's sometimes affectionate, sometimes analytical book will delight both skeptics and true believers." — Michael Cart, *Booklist*

"It is refreshing to come across an author who shows us how to talk about the books we love.... She also moves us beyond childhood, revealing that the books we loved as children can continue to quicken and expand our imaginations, especially when we have a guide like this one to help us understand the miracle of how Lewis produced the intoxicating and addictive Chronicles of Narnia."
— Maria Tatar, *Bookforum*

"Miller is particularly interested in how and why we read — what we take from books but also what we bring to them ... and gives us piquant glimpses of her past and present selves."
— Kerry Fried, *Newsday*

"In a braided narrative Miller weaves together details about the life of C. S. Lewis, her personal journey with his books, and astute observations about how children and adults read.... Anyone who believes in the power of literature will want to savor *The Magician's Book*. In the end you feel as if you have had a stimulating literary conversation with a group of very smart and savvy friends."
—Anita Silvey, author of *100 Best Books for Children*

the Magician's Book

of picking up the Chronicles of Narnia again, forty-five years after I first fell in love with it, too."

— Anne Lamott, author of *Grace (Eventually)*

"A powerful meditation on 'the schism between childhood and adult reading.'"
— *The New Yorker*

"Miller's book is itself a welcome bit of magic: part reader's log, part biography, part literary criticism. She relates much that is familiar about Lewis's life and a little that is less well known. . . . Miller has learned much from Lewis, not least a bracingly colloquial, honest, intimate tone."
— Gregory Maguire, *New York Times Book Review*

"A lucid and vibrant tale."
— Rebecca Traister, Salon.com

"Along with her fascinating insights into the world of Narnia and the mind that conjured it, Miller provides one of the best explanations I have ever read about why so-called children's literature is so inimitably affecting. This book is both a wonderful antechamber to Lewis's wardrobe portal and a convincing attempt to rescue Aslan from the Christian imagination and embed him where he has always belonged — the human imagination."
— Tom Bissell, author of *The Father of All Things*

"Reading *The Magician's Book* is like revisiting the enchanting realm of Narnia on the arm of a local. . . . Miller's quest charts the divine magic of the imagination, why and how the books of our youth mold our souls. Miller has created a rare and beautiful beast: a book with the head of a critique, the body of a bibliography, and the heart of a memoir. By recapturing Narnia, she redeems our passion and allows readers to rediscover the wonder of first love. That's some trick."
— Elissa Schappell, *Vanity Fair*

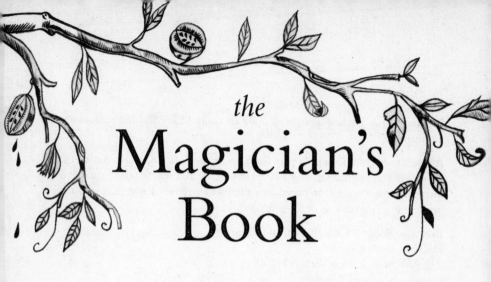

the Magician's Book

A SKEPTIC'S ADVENTURES *in* NARNIA

LAURA MILLER

BACK BAY BOOKS

Little, Brown and Company

New York   Boston   London

Back Bay Books / Little, Brown and Company
Hachette Book Group
237 Park Avenue, New York, NY 10017
www.hachettebookgroup.com

Originally published in hardcover by Little, Brown and Company, December 2008
First Back Bay paperback edition, December 2009

Back Bay Books is an imprint of Little, Brown and Company. The Back Bay Books name and logo are trademarks of Hachette Book Group, Inc.

Rebecca Traister's conversation with Laura Miller, which appears in the Reading Group Guide at the back of this book, was originally posted at Salon.com on December 6, 2008. Copyright © 2008 Salon Media Group, Inc. Reprinted with permission.

Library of Congress Cataloging-in-Publication Data
Miller, Laura.
    The magician's book : a skeptic's adventures in Narnia / Laura Miller.— 1st ed.
      p. cm.
    Includes index.
    ISBN 978-0-316-01763-3 (hc) / 978-0-316-01765-7 (pb)
    1. Lewis, C. S. (Clive Staples), 1898–1963—Criticism and interpretation. 2. Lewis, C. S. (Clive Staples), 1898–1963. Chronicles of Narnia. 3. Lewis, C. S. (Clive Staples), 1898–1963—Appreciation. 4. Lewis, C. S. (Clive Staples), 1898–1963—Influence. 5. Children's stories, English—History and criticism. 6. Fantasy fiction, English—History and criticism. 7. Narnia (Imaginary place) 8. Books and reading. I. Title.
    PR6023.E926C53627 2008
    823'.912—DC22   2008020629

10 9 8 7 6 5 4 3 2 1

RRD-IN

Designed by Greta D. Sibley

Printed in the United States of America

For Wilanne Belden

On the next page she came to a spell "for the refreshment of the spirit." The pictures were fewer here but very beautiful. And what Lucy found herself reading was more like a story than a spell. It went on for three pages and before she had read to the bottom of the page she had forgotten that she was reading at all. She was living in the story as if it were real, and all the pictures were real too. When she had got to the third page and come to the end, she said, "That is the loveliest story I've ever read or ever shall read in my whole life. Oh, I wish I could have gone on reading it for ten years. At least I'll read it over again."

But here part of the magic of the Book came into play. You couldn't turn back. The right-hand pages, the ones ahead, could be turned; the left-hand pages could not.

"Oh, what a shame!" said Lucy. "I do so want to read it again. Well, at least I must remember it. Let's see ... it was about ... about ... oh dear, it's all fading away again. And even this last page is going blank. This is a very queer book. How can I have forgotten? It was about a cup and a sword and a tree and a green hill. I know that much. But I can't remember and what shall I do?"

And she never could remember; and ever since that day what Lucy means by a good story is a story which reminds her of the forgotten story in the Magician's Book.

—C. S. Lewis, *The Voyage of the Dawn Treader*

CONTENTS

Part Three

Songs of Experience

The Magician's Book

Introduction

In one of the most vivid memories from my childhood, nothing happens. On a clear, sunny day, I'm standing near a curb in the quiet suburban California neighborhood where my family lives, and I'm wishing, with every bit of my self, for two things. First, I want a place I've read about in a book to really exist, and second, I want to be able to go there. I want this so much I'm pretty sure the misery of not getting it will kill me. For the rest of my life, I will never want anything quite so much again.

The place I longed to visit was Narnia, the setting for a series of children's novels by C. S. Lewis. There are things about these books that I, at age nine, did not yet understand and did not even realize were there to be understood. My relationship to Narnia would turn out to be as rocky as any love affair, a story of enchantment, betrayal, estrangement, and reunion. A few years after the day I'm remembering, when I discovered some of the more obvious "secret" meanings in C. S. Lewis's children's books, I felt tricked, and for a long time I avoided even thinking about Narnia.

Eventually, warily, after I became someone who reads books and writes about them for a living, I decided to revisit the Chronicles of Narnia. I was thinking about origins. I'd been given an assignment: describe the single book that had most influenced me, that had changed my life. I could have written about *Jane Eyre,* the first "grown up" novel with which I fiercely identified as a teenager, or Dante's *Divine Comedy,* the first literary monument that was made to breathe and bleed and yield up its splendor to me by a gifted professor. That's the sort of title most writers would choose when presented with this question. If you've ever read one of those articles that asks notable people to list their favorite books, you may have been impressed or daunted to see them pick Proust or Thomas Mann or James Joyce. You might even feel sheepish about the fact that you reread *Pride and Prejudice* or *The Lord of the Rings* or *The Catcher in the Rye* or *Gone With the Wind* every couple of years with so much pleasure. Perhaps, like me, you're even a little suspicious of their claims, because we all know that the books we've loved best are seldom the ones we esteem the most highly—or the ones we'd most like other people to think we read over and over again.

I vowed to be scrupulously honest about this assignment, and that meant acknowledging that the most momentous passage in my reading life came when I was in second grade. A teacher I idolized handed me a copy—her copy—of *The Lion, the Witch and the Wardrobe.* It was this book that made a reader out of me. It showed me how I could tumble through a hole in the world I knew and into another, better one, a world fresher, more brightly colored, more exhilarating, more fully felt than my own. This revelation really did make a new person out of me. I reread *The Lion, the Witch and the Wardrobe* and its six sequels countless times. I became one of those children who haunt libraries, checking out the maximum number of titles every week, scouring the shelves for signs that this one or that one would spirit me away to a place almost as marvelous as Narnia. I was notorious at school for sneaking a library book into my lap during class and becoming so mesmerized by it that I wouldn't hear the teacher when she called my name. I read through recess and lunch hours, deaf and blind to whatever was going on around me.

This aspect of my story isn't unusual, although I did have the good fortune to find a way to make a living writing about books. Still, being a literary critic isn't really very much like being a ten-year-old girl, dead to the world in the corner of a playground as she turns the pages of *The Dark Is Rising.* A critic has to write as well as read, and while the process of writing about a book can reveal things you'd never get from simply reading it, it can also make reading a less immediate and visceral experience. I began the long task of learning how to read in this new way not long after I first discovered Narnia.

A lot of people remember the bliss of their earliest reading with a pang; their current encounters with books offer no more than faint echoes of what they once felt. I've heard friends and strangers talk about the days when they, too, would submerge themselves in a story, surfacing only to eat and deal with the minimal daily business of childhood. They wonder why they don't get as much out of books now. If you dig deep to the roots of what makes someone a reader, you'll usually find the desire to recapture that old spell. But as we get older we acquire another set of reasons for picking up a book: because reading is "good for you," for example, or because it was assigned by a teacher. People read to fend off the boredom of long flights, to find out what kinds of books get published nowadays, to stay abreast of what's new, to catch up on what they should have learned in school, to hold their own at a cocktail party, to be able to say they've read *Moby Dick.*

No wonder we pine for the days when we read only for ourselves. Many years after I first opened *The Lion, the Witch and the Wardrobe,* I learned that C. S. Lewis, too, was a literary critic, and that he, too, was interested in readerly pleasure. He had the eccentric notion that the delight people take in a book might give us some clue as to its worth. In a slender volume entitled *An Experiment in Criticism,* one of the best books about reading I have ever found,

Lewis suggested that the literary preferences of children are significant because "children are indifferent to literary fashions. What we see in them is not a specifically childish taste, but simply a normal and perennial human taste, temporarily atrophied in their elders by a fashion."

But the schism between childhood and adult reading can't be entirely written off to vanity and trendiness. Although I miss the childhood experience of being engulfed by a story, I would not willingly surrender my adult ability to recognize when a writer is taking me someplace I don't want to go. In my early teens, I discovered what is instantly obvious to any adult reader: that the Chronicles of Narnia are filled with Christian symbolism and that *The Lion, the Witch and the Wardrobe* offers a parallel account of the Passion of Christ. I'd been raised as a Catholic, but what faith I'd had was never based on anything more than the fact that children tend to believe whatever adults tell them. As soon as I acquired any independence of thought, I drifted away from the Church and what I saw as its endless proscriptions and requirements, its guilt-mongering and tedious rituals.

So I was horrified to discover that the Chronicles of Narnia, the joy of my childhood and the cornerstone of my imaginative life, were really just the doctrines of the Church in disguise. I looked back at my favorite book and found it appallingly transfigured. Of *course,* the self-sacrifice of Aslan to compensate for the treachery of Edmund was exactly like the crucifixion of Christ to pay off the sins of mankind! How *could* I have missed that? I felt angry and humiliated because I had been fooled.

Part of the purpose of learning to read critically is to alert us to an author's hidden intentions and unconscious biases. Once you realize that a good story has the power to deceive you, it's impossible to wholeheartedly embrace the ignorance that is always a part of innocence. I was sorry, very sorry, to lose Narnia, but I always would have chosen to know the truth.

For reasons like these, most of us, somewhere along the line, are taught to read with an intellectual distance. At school, we graduate from simple book reports to writing essays in which we're expected to ferret out the symbols and themes of stories we once might have believed to be the stuff of actual life. We learn who authors are and how to detect what they're really up to. But that's not the end of the judgments we learn to apply. Later still, we will realize that some books are in better taste than others, and that our own favorites might not number among the acknowledged best.

The critic Clive James has written with chagrin of what he eloquently calls "the radiant books of our youth"; his boyhood enthusiasm for Arthur Conan Doyle's fiction embarrasses him now. Fifty years later, he still remembers the "heft" of a volume entitled *The Complete Professor Challenger Stories*—remembers it so clearly, in fact, that he thinks of it every time he picks up a book of the same weight. Yet when James reads Doyle now, he finds only a rummage sale of callow, long-discarded fantasies, "superseded daydreams of glamour, sex, bravery and deductive brilliance," which "are always funny when they are not shameful."

The novelist Graham Greene is another who marveled at the now-alien world of his boyhood reading. "Perhaps it is only in childhood that books have any deep influence on our lives," he wrote. "In later life we admire, we are entertained, we may modify some views we already hold, but we are more likely to find in books merely a confirmation of what is in our minds already.... But in childhood all books are books of divination, telling us about the future." The books we happen to latch onto as children help to furnish our imagination and, to a certain degree, our identity. But if we return to them as adults, we sometimes find, as Clive James did, that the décor is garish or uncomfortable. It's not a place to which we'd care to invite our friends.

Ever since I reread *The Lion, the Witch and the Wardrobe* for that assignment over a decade ago, the Chronicles of Narnia have presented me with a puzzle, one that would eventually prompt me to write this book. When I finally came back to Narnia, I found that, for me, it had not lost its power or beauty, or at least not entirely. Although I am a little bit abashed about this, I am not like Clive James; the radiant books of my youth still seem radiant to me. Yet there are aspects of Narnia I can no longer embrace with the childish credulity that Greene describes. Then again, I *am* like James in that I'm sometimes dismayed by the prejudices and narrow-mindedness of the Chronicles' author, and in a way I am also like Greene, in that I reread these books partly to find what is already in my mind. Nevertheless, what I dislike about Narnia no longer eclipses what I love about it, and the contents of my own mind still have the capacity to surprise me when I study them carefully enough.

What I am not, however, is a Christian; for all the countless times I have reread Lewis's books, they have never succeeded in converting me. This, to many casual observers, no doubt makes my continuing enjoyment of the Chronicles perplexing. Most of the critics and scholars who pay any kind of sustained attention to Lewis's work are Christians themselves, and their faith is the motivation for that attention. To everyone else, Lewis is an apologist for the Christian faith, and that is the only kind of meaning that could ever be found in anything he wrote. The Chronicles are merely religious "allegory" (the term most often—and erroneously—used to describe them in the general-interest press) and about as interesting to the nonbeliever as a cruise ship sales brochure is to a man determined never to leave dry land.

Besides, the Chronicles are children's fiction. They belong to a class of literature that, in the opinion of many, doesn't merit serious critical consideration. I can see how James or Greene might agree with this point of view: the former finds that the ugly old lamp no longer produces a genie when rubbed and the latter realizes he has nothing left to wish for. Nevertheless, I go on thinking that there is something significant in the Chronicles of Narnia, something more or less apart from their thinly concealed theological messages. I'm unwilling to resign myself to accepting a fathomless gap in the early part of my life, between the reader I was as a child and the reader I am now.

Lewis himself liked to read children's books occasionally, both the ones he'd loved as a child growing up in Ireland in the early twentieth century, and others that he discovered later; Kenneth Grahame's *The Wind in the Willows* was a particular favorite. "A children's story which is enjoyed only by children is a bad children's story," he once remarked. Lewis was an Oxford don, a bachelor pushing fifty who had very little real-world experience with children, when he wrote *The Lion, the Witch and the Wardrobe*. Unlike his good friend J. R. R. Tolkien, who told an early version of *The Hobbit* to his children, Lewis had to rely on memories of his own childhood tastes while writing his books. Evidently, those memories lay close to hand; his facility at writing for children has ever since offered his biographers cause to describe him as a man who never entirely grew up.

Lewis always maintained that he chose to write a "fairy tale" because he had something to say which could only be expressed in this way. He didn't offer much detail as to what that something was, but he did once write that he had fallen in love "with the form itself: its brevity; its severe restraints on description; its flexible traditionalism; its inflexible hostility to all analysis, digression, reflections, and 'gas.'" To my mind, these are all ways of describing one variety of good writing, whether for adults or children, and when the Chronicles are well written—which is often—the quality is not age-dependent. Lewis, however, would have found nothing remarkable in this fact, for he also insisted that "fairy tales" (a term he used to include writings that we'd call "fantasy" today) were not meant only for children. Although the Chronicles were patently intended for young readers, they partake of literary traditions that are as old as the act of storytelling itself.

There is yet another reason to devote the kind of attention to the Chronicles that critics ordinarily reserve for the works of writers

like Flaubert or F. Scott Fitzgerald, and it may be the most persuasive of all. In *An Experiment in Criticism,* Lewis floats the idea that
we can determine how good a book is by how it is read. This was
an offbeat notion at a time when most critics judged a book by how
it was written, and it would become an irrelevant one a few years
later, when deciding how "good" a book was would seem immaterial to most academics. But Lewis—who was, above all else, a passionate, omnivorous, and generous reader—thought that this might
be the best way to appreciate a book's worth, especially since he
regarded the literary mandarins of his day as slaves to pernicious
intellectual fads.

A hater of progress, newfanglement, and vulgarity, Lewis was not
a notably tolerant man, but reading brought out the populist in him.
He worked out a set of criteria for identifying truly "literary" readers; their ranks include people who reread books, those who savor
what they read for more than just the plot, and those for whom the
first encounter with a favorite book is an "experience so momentous that only experiences of love, religion, or bereavement can furnish
a standard of comparison. Their whole consciousness is changed.
They have become what they were not before."

Nothing on this list dictates what *type* of book the literary
reader ought to prefer; it is the quality of the attention brought to
it that matters. There is an uncharacteristic radicalism to Lewis's
further suggestion that if we can find "even one reader to whom
the cheap little book with its double columns and the lurid daub
on its cover had been a lifelong delight, who had read and reread
it, who would notice, and object, if a single word were changed,
then, however little we could see in it ourselves and however it
was despised by our friends and colleagues, we should not dare
to put it beyond the pale."

He is, among other things, describing the way certain children
read certain books, with a fervor that can inspire mystification and
awe in their adult counterparts. Such experiences *can't* be merely

ephemeral, meaningless, but they often seem entirely inaccessible when we look back on them years later. This, at least, is what Clive James felt upon returning to Professor Challenger, and so he was forced to dismiss the whole situation as merely comical. Still, how could he have failed to be formed as a man and as a reader by Doyle's adventure yarns? We would not expect any other overwhelming emotional experience from his childhood to have left him untouched. Today, James is a gifted, witty critic. Perhaps there is more to Professor Challenger than meets the eye.

The relationship between book and reader is intimate, at best a kind of love affair, and first loves are famously tenacious. A first love teaches you how to be with another human being by choice, rather than out of the imperative of blood ties. If we are lucky, our first love shows us how to negotiate the paradox of entering into a union with someone who remains fundamentally unknowable. First love is a momentous step in our emotional education, and in many ways, it shapes us forever.

The meeting of author and reader has a similar soul-shaping potential. The author who can make a world for a reader — make him believe that the people, places, and events he describes are, if anything, truer than his real, immediate surroundings — that author is someone with a mighty power indeed. Who can forget the first time they experienced this sensation? Who can doubt that every literary encounter they have afterward must somehow be colored by it? If we weigh the significance of a book by the effect it has on its readers, then the great children's books suddenly turn up very high on the list.

I've titled this book after a passage in my current favorite among the Chronicles of Narnia, *The Voyage of the Dawn Treader*. It's the part where Lucy, who has reluctantly agreed to enter the house of an invisible magician, slips into his study in order to read a spell out of his great book. She finds a couple of charms that intrigue and tempt her, and then she arrives at something special, a spell that is "like a story" but that disappears as she reads it, and soon vanishes even from her memory.

Perhaps Lewis is alluding here to the fleeting enchantment of childhood reading. But that's not all this passage is about. He also had the idea that certain stories run deep in human nature, deeper than the individual books that tell them, deeper even than words themselves. He tried to tap into that kind of story in his fiction, and he achieved this in his children's books better than anywhere else. The peculiarly heady effect of the Chronicles on young readers is testimony to his success. Francis Spufford, author of the memoir *The Child That Books Built,* writes of feeling that Lewis "had anticipated what would delight me with an almost unearthly intimacy," in stories that became "the inevitable expressions of my longing." The Chronicles have bewitched millions of children of vastly different backgrounds in just this way since they were first published in the 1950s.

Lucy can't remember any more from the story than "a cup and a sword and a tree and a green hill," but that doesn't mean she isn't able to recognize it when she meets it again, even when it appears in a different form. "Ever since that day," the narrator continues, "what Lucy means by a good story is a story that reminds her of the forgotten story in the Magician's Book." I've read a lot of great literature since the day my second-grade teacher handed me a clothbound copy of *The Lion, the Witch and the Wardrobe.* I've read both towering masterpieces and less exalted novels that, when it comes to felicity of craftsmanship, thoroughly trounce any of Lewis's fiction. But none of these is my Magician's Book, the story to which all other stories must be compared. *The Lion, the Witch and the Wardrobe,* my introduction to Narnia, is that book for me, not merely because of its form or style or historical significance, but because of how it made me feel, which is at heart the fundamental question with any work of fiction. In the right light, *The Lion, the Witch and the Wardrobe* will always be the best book I've ever read.

Why is this so? Many of the answers lie with its author, a man whom the critic William Empson (ideologically unsympathetic to Lewis in almost every way) characterized as "the best read man of his generation, one who read everything and remembered everything he read." Much of this reading, and many of Lewis's own life experiences, make themselves felt in the Chronicles, as we would expect of any writer striving to bring his full talent to the task. He did not think any less of the work because it was intended for children, or any less of his readers because they were young. Lewis was cognizant of reading, the moment when the words of the writer mingle with the mind of the reader, as a kind of duet, with the reader bringing as much, in her own way, to the union as the writer. Here, from *An Experiment in Criticism,* is a remarkable description of the act of reading:

> [If the] dance is devised by a master, the rests and movements, the quickenings and slowings, the easier and the more arduous passages, will come exactly as we need them; we shall be deliciously surprised by the satisfaction of wants we were not aware of till they were satisfied. We shall end up just tired enough and not too tired, and "on the right note." It would have been unbearable if it had ended a moment sooner—or later—or in any different way. Looking back on the whole performance, we shall feel that we have been led through a pattern or arrangement of activities which our nature cried out for.... The relaxation, the slight (agreeable) weariness, the banishment of all our fidgets, at the close of a great work all proclaim that it has done us good.

Dance is the metaphor he chooses and, as Yeats observed, it is impossible to distinguish the dancer from the dance. Accordingly, if I want to write about the meanings of Narnia, then one aspect of the story must be personal; Lewis's children's fiction played an important role in my early life, so much so that I could never be the least bit objective about it. Some of what I have to say can only be demonstrated by my own experiences. Therefore, to quote Lewis again, "I must here be autobiographical for the sake of being evidential." Literary value *is* personal, after all, because somebody — a person — needs to experience it as a reader for it to exist at all.

But my history with Narnia is not idiosyncratic, and so I've also occasionally included interviews I conducted with writers and people who responded to my first essay about *The Lion, the Witch and the Wardrobe,* published on Salon.com. Conversations with other readers have always been essential to the growth of my own literary understanding, and I suspect this is true for most other critics as well. But for some reason convention has dictated that we seldom mention these exchanges when writing about books. I've tried to correct that omission here.

In the concluding volume of the Chronicles, *The Last Battle,* Lewis wrote of a place that "was far larger than it seemed from the outside." Although this book will wend its way through the life and thoughts of Lewis and his friends (especially his close friend and colleague J. R. R. Tolkien), my own life and thoughts, the memories and feelings of other readers, the history and literature of Britain and of Ireland and the mythical taproots of humanity, all of this, in the end, is contained in seven children's novels. These books are far larger than they seem from the outside, and *The Magician's Book* is an attempt to explore some of their interior terrain. There is one major thematic province, however, that I will do no more than fly over: Lewis's Christianity. Many, many other writers have dealt exhaustively with this aspect of Lewis's work, to the point of obscuring other elements in the Chronicles, the ones that appeal to me. Lewis's theological writings don't interest me much, and while religion is an unavoidable subject when considering Narnia, my goal has been to illuminate its other, unsung dimensions, especially the deep roots of the Chronicles in the universal experiences of childhood and in English literature.

I am no longer young, and I can't read the Chronicles the way I once did, with the same absolute belief. Some of what I find there still moves me profoundly, but other bits now grate and disturb. I began *The Magician's Book* hoping to explain not only why but *how* it is still possible for me to love these books, despite the biases and small-mindedness they sometimes display, despite often feeling that I wouldn't have much liked the man who wrote them, despite the proselytizing that most adults assume is their only real content.

I don't believe that my appreciation amounts to mere nostalgia or a yearning for my own lost innocence. At the very least, that would be a betrayal of the child I once was. *She* would have had no patience with such mopey sentimentality; one of the reasons she prized the Chronicles was her belief (correct, I still think) that they educated her on the nature of evil as well as good, and that she was the better for it. I like to think that in the end, I've kept faith with her.

A Note on the Order of the Chronicles of Narnia

The Chronicles of Narnia have been numbered by their publishers in two different orders. The first, and the order in which I originally read them, is the order of their publication: *The Lion, the Witch and the Wardrobe; Prince Caspian; The Voyage of the Dawn Treader; The Silver Chair; The Horse and His Boy; The Magician's Nephew;* and *The Last Battle.* In recent years, citing a letter C. S. Lewis wrote to a child in 1957, Lewis's estate (which is managed by his stepson, Douglas Gresham) has specified that the books be numbered according to the chronological sequence of the fictional events they describe: *The Magician's Nephew; The Lion, the Witch and the Wardrobe; The Horse and His Boy; Prince Caspian; The Voyage of the Dawn Treader; The Silver Chair; The Last Battle.* Feelings run high on this matter. Lewis expressed the intention of one day going back to the Chronicles to correct various problems, and perhaps he would have revised them to make the current order more consistent with the content of the books themselves. However, he never got around to this, and as is, some lines in *The Lion, the Witch and the Wardrobe* don't make much sense if you presume that its readers are already familiar with *The Magician's Nephew.*

Most of the people I've talked with about Narnia are old enough to have read the books in the original order and, like me, they can't imagine discovering them in any other sequence, for reasons of art as well as logic. I remain unconvinced that Lewis himself had any definite opinions on the proper order in which to read the Chronicles (he was probably just being kind to his young correspondent), and even if he did, I would still recommend that they be read in the original configuration. Accordingly, throughout this book, I will discuss all seven books as if the original ordering still prevailed.

Part One

Songs of Innocence

CHAPTER ONE

The Light in the Forest

Long before I learned of *The Lion, the Witch and the Wardrobe,* before it was even written, a twelve-year-old girl named Wilanne Belden walked two miles once a week to the library in Cleveland Heights, Ohio, to check out the maximum quantity of five books. It was the Depression, and buying any book was a luxury. The deal Wilanne's parents struck with her was that if she checked out the same title from the library three times, and read it from cover to cover each time, she could have a copy of her own.

This arrangement worked well enough until Wilanne discovered what would become her favorite book, J. R. R. Tolkien's *The Hobbit* (then in its first edition, before even Tolkien himself knew the significance of Bilbo Baggins's magic ring). *The Hobbit* is long for a children's book, and by the time she had read it three times, it had gone out of stock in bookstores. Buying a copy was no longer an option. So Wilanne decided to make her own, checking the book out of the library over and over again, typing up a couple dozen pages at a time using two fingers on the family's manual typewriter. She got as far as page 107 before the book returned to the stores.

There is no reader more devoted than a bookish child who has found the story that suits her perfectly. Thirty years later, Wilanne would turn me into one of those children when she handed me a slim hardcover bound in gray fabric with the image of a little stag stamped on the front, and said, "I think you'll like this one." It was her copy; she'd had the book for a while, but I was the first of her second-grade students that she'd tried it on. "You were a child who needed to read C. S. Lewis," she said firmly when, not long ago, I asked her why.

"How did you know? How can you tell something like that?"

"I can't explain. It's just one of those things that happens."

Even today, this intuition strikes me as slightly supernatural, in the same way that Narnia seemed to emerge, by some miracle, out of my own unspoken self. "When you brought the book back," Wilanne remembered as we sat in her cozy apartment, surrounded by books, knitting, and cats, "You told me, and this I have always remembered, that you didn't know that there were other people who had the kind of imagination that you did."

Wilanne and I were not, I think, unhappy children. I grew up in a comfortable American home, in a big, intact family, with a lawyer father and a homemaker mom, and she still remembers feeling fortunate that her father had a steady job when so many others didn't. But we were neither of us, I suspect, entirely satisfied with that.

"You were automatically one of *my* kids," Wilanne said when I asked her what she remembered about first meeting me forty years ago. By this, she means one of those children "interested in the imagination and in the relationship between the real and the unreal. They are entirely capable of telling the difference between truth and falsehood, but they prefer the falsehood occasionally." Nothing exciting had ever happened to me, was how I saw it, and I was convinced that nothing exciting ever could, as long as I was stuck in a world of station wagons and jump rope, backyard swim classes and spelling tests. Then Mrs. Belden handed me a book.

I've read *The Lion, the Witch and the Wardrobe* so often since then that I no longer have a distinct recollection of the first time. What was it like to be genuinely *surprised* when Lucy Pevensie's fingertips brushed against branches instead of fur coats as she first walked through the wardrobe and into the snowy woods? That sensation is lost to me. What remains is a dim recollection of how life was shaped before I knew about Narnia, and a more distinct sense of what it was like afterward. I had found a new world, which at the same time felt like a place I'd always known existed. It wouldn't have occurred to me to be wistful about the fact that I'd never read this perfect book for the first time again. All I wanted was more.

Do the children who prefer books set in the real, ordinary, work-aday world ever read as obsessively as those who would much rather be transported into other worlds entirely? Once I began to confer with other people who had loved the Chronicles as children, I kept hearing stories, like my own, of countless, intoxicated rereadings. "I would read other books, of course," wrote the novelist Neil Gaiman, "but in my heart I knew that I read them only because there wasn't an infinite number of Narnia books." Later, when I had the chance to talk with him about the Chronicles in person, he told me, "The weird thing about the Narnia books for me was that mostly they seemed true. There was a level on which I was absolutely willing at age six, age seven, to accept them as a profound and real truth. Un-questioned, there was definitely a Narnia. This stuff had happened. These were reports from a real place."

Most of us persuaded our parents to buy us boxed sets of all seven Chronicles, but I also saved up my allowance and occasional small cash gifts from relatives to buy a hardcover copy of *The Lion, the Witch and the Wardrobe,* one of the few times in my life I've ever succumbed to the collector's impulse. If I hadn't been able to obtain a copy of the book, I have no doubt that I, too, would have resorted to typing up one of my own. This was not about obtaining a posses-sion, but about securing a portal. I was not yet capable of thinking about it in this way, but I'd been enthralled by the most elementary of readerly metaphors: A little girl opens the hinged door of some commonplace piece of household furniture and steps through it into another world. I opened the hinged cover of a book and did the same.

Why did I fall so hard and so completely, and why was a land of fauns and centaurs and talking animals so exactly what I wanted to read about? Not long ago, a friend told me about her nine-year-old daughter's infatuation with Narnia. My friend had grown up loving historical novels about "prairie girls," and while she didn't disapprove of her daughter's appetite for fantasy, it baffled her. "I just don't get it," she complained.

If you had asked me at the same age why I liked *The Lion, the Witch and the Wardrobe* better than, say, *Little Women* or any other story that was about lives more like my own, I wouldn't have been able to answer; it seemed crazy to prefer anything else. The best analogy I can make is a corny one, to the film version of *The Wizard of Oz* and that famous moment when Dorothy ventures out of the drab, black-and-white farmhouse that's carried her all the way from drab, black-and-white Kansas and into the Technicolor of Oz. Who in her right mind would poke her head out for just a sec, then slam the door shut, and shout, "Take me back to Kansas"?

Once upon a time, people used to label the kind of book I would come to crave — the kind "with magic," as I usually thought of it — as escapist. Consequently, readers with this taste often have a chip on their shoulders. Lewis, who enjoyed the occasional H. Rider Haggard adventure or H. G. Wells novel in addition to Anglo-Saxon epics and medieval allegories, wrote several essays defending science fiction and "fairy tales" from the scornful advocates of stringent realism. I, on the other hand, came up in the age of metafiction, postmodernism, and magic realism; realism no longer commands all the prestige. Lewis's arguments on behalf of fantastic literature feel a bit superfluous to me. Still, I can hazily remember, long ago, having adults — librarians, friends' parents — suggest to me that I liked books "with magic" because I wanted to escape from a reality that, by implication, I lacked the gumption to face. Perhaps this still happens, say, to kids who obsess about Harry Potter. Or perhaps adults are now so thankful to see children reading that they don't quibble with the books they choose.

Did I use storybooks to get away from my life? Of course I did, but probably no more so than the kids who chose *Harriet the Spy* instead of books about dragons and witches. (For the record, I read and liked *Harriet the Spy,* too.) Insofar as they are stories at all, all stories are escapes from life; all stories are unrealistic, or at least all of the good ones are. Life, unlike stories, has no theme, no formal unity, and (to unbelievers, at least) no readily apparent meaning. That's why we *want* stories. No art form can hope to exactly reproduce the sensations that make up being alive, but that's OK: life, after all, is what we *already* have. From art, we want something different, something with a shape and a purpose. Any departure a story might make from real-world laws against talking animals and flying carpets seems relatively inconsequential compared to this first, great leap away from reality. Perhaps that's why humanity's oldest stories are full of outlandish events and supernatural beings; the idea that a story must somehow mimic actual everyday experience would probably have seemed daft to the first tellers. Why even bother to tell a story about something so commonplace?

There were particular fantastic elements that drew me to Narnia at that age, and they were not always what people associate with fairy tales. I disliked princesses and any other female whose chief occupation was waiting around to be rescued, but I also had no great interest in knights, swords, and combat. The Chronicles, which are relatively free of such elements, spoke to me across a spectrum of yearning. The youngest part of my child self loved Narnia's talking animals. The girl I was fast growing into fiercely seized upon the idea of possessing an entire, secret world of my own. And the seeds of the adult I would become reveled in the autonomy of Lewis's child heroes and the adventures that awaited them once they escaped the wearying bonds of grown-up supervision.

CHAPTER TWO

Animal-Land

One of the first stories I found both true and terribly sad is a chapter that comes in the middle of P. L. Travers's *Mary Poppins,* an interlude devoted to the infant twins, John and Barbara Banks, in their nursery. (Jane and Michael, the older and better-known Banks siblings, have gone off to a party.) The twins can understand the language of the sunlight, the wind, and a cheeky starling who perches on the windowsill, but they are horrified when the bird informs them that they will soon forget all of this. "There never was a human being that remembered after the age of one — at the very latest — except, of course, Her." (This "Great Exception," as the starling calls her, is Mary Poppins, of course.) "You'll hear all right," Mary Poppins tells John and Barbara, "but you won't understand."

This news makes the babies cry, which brings their mother bustling into the nursery; she blames the fuss on teething. When she tries to soothe John and Barbara by saying that everything will be all right after their teeth come in, they only cry harder. "It won't be all right, it will be all wrong," Barbara protests. "I don't want teeth!" screams John. But, of course, their mother can't understand them any better than she can understand the wind or the starling.

It's at age one that we acquire our first words. This story, which made me so melancholy as a girl, is, among other things, about the price we pay for language, for the ability to tell our mothers that it's not our teeth that are upsetting us but something else. It alludes to what we have given up to be understood by her and all the other adults, our lost brotherhood with the rest of creation. Words are what separate us from the animals, or as Travers would have it, from the elements themselves, from everything that can simply be without the scrim of consciousness intervening.

In an early, abandoned version of *The Magician's Nephew,* Lewis experimented with a similar theme. He has the story's boy hero, Digory, able to understand the language of animals and trees until Polly, the little girl who lives next door to him in London, persuades him to cut off a branch from the big oak in his garden. In Lewis's tale, the separation is literal, physical, and violent, a sin against nature itself. Travers makes the more eloquent choice; to become ourselves, to be human, we must necessarily set ourselves apart.

In Narnia, this mournful rift is healed; there, people can talk to animals, to trees, and sometimes even to rivers (as happens in *Prince Caspian*). Human beings have longed to communicate with the universe since time immemorial—a profound, mystical longing. Tolkien described it as one of the two "primordial desires" behind fairy tales (after the desire to "survey the depths of space and time"); we want to "hold communion with other living things." But since children are literalists and materialists, not mystics, their love for animals, and for stories about people who can talk to animals, is seldom understood as a manifestation of this desire.

To say that, as a child, I—and my brothers and sisters and most of our friends—loved animals would be an understatement; much of the time we wanted to *be* animals. Take us to a park or some place with a rambling yard, and we'd immediately begin mapping out the territory for one of our elaborate games of make-believe. At first, we pretended to be various woodland fauna, inspired by the Old Mother West Wind books by Thornton Burgess, a series our mother read to us. At home, one of us would clamber up onto the roof of our ranch house (via the top bar of the swing set) to play the eagle who came swooping down to pounce on the squirrels and chipmunks below. Later, after *The Lion, the Witch and the Wardrobe* introduced me to classical mythology, we invented a game we called "mythical creatures," and played at being griffins, unicorns, and winged horses.

This preoccupation with animals starts early. Two friends of mine, toddler twins named Corinne and Desmond, began pointing at themselves and saying "This is a puppy" almost as soon as they learned to talk. As time goes by and the impossibility of such imaginings becomes obvious, the ache for contact with the animal world grows more desperate. By age seven, when I first read *The Lion, the Witch and the Wardrobe,* I longed for some better rapport with the family cats and the neighborhood dogs, with any kind of beast, really. Animals seemed like relatives left behind in the Old Country, except that the growing expanse that separated us wasn't a physical ocean but a cognitive one. They stood on the dock, getting ever smaller, while we children watched from the deck, on the way to a new, supposedly better way of being in the world, haunted by the image of what we were losing.

Animals, like infants, belong to the vast nation of those who communicate without words, through gesture, expression, scent, sound, and touch. Children are immigrants from that nation and, like most recent immigrants, still have a mental foothold on the abandoned shore. I believed, probably correctly, that I understood animals better and cared about them more than the adults around me. I could still faintly remember what it was to be like a beast, before language complicated things. But I didn't appreciate the inverse relationship between the individual self I was building out of the new words I acquired every day and the inarticulate world that moved away from me as my identity gained definition.

Watching Corinne and Desmond grow up, I have noticed another drawback to learning to talk: speaking also ushers in the stage at which grown-ups stop doing anything you want just to make you stop crying. It's only when you can ask for something with words that people expect you to understand "no." So age one also marks the beginning of our entry into human society proper, where compromise is the price of admission. Many adults—and especially the authors of great children's books—view growing up as a kind of tragedy whose casualties include innocence and the capacity for wholehearted make-believe. But kissing Puff the Magic Dragon good-bye happens later, on the brink of prepubescence. Travers, in her chapter on poor John and Barbara Banks, seems to be saying that even the smallest children have *already* suffered a heartbreaking separation, before they leave their cribs.

When I first read William Wordsworth's "Ode: Intimations of Immortality from Recollections of Early Childhood," with its lines about birth as the beginning of an exile from heaven, I thought of John and Barbara:

> Our birth is but a sleep and a forgetting:
> The Soul that rises with us, our life's Star,
>   Hath had elsewhere its setting,
>   And cometh from afar:
>   Not in entire forgetfulness,
>   And not in utter nakedness,
> But trailing clouds of glory do we come
>   From God, who is our home:
> Heaven lies about us in our infancy!
> Shades of the prison-house begin to close
>   Upon the growing Boy...

Wordsworth surely didn't mean to include language among the shades of the "prison-house" that close in upon "the growing Boy"; poetry, after all, was a kind of religion to the Romantics. Yet incarceration was also the metaphor that occurred to the philosopher Friedrich Nietzsche when he called words and grammar a "prison-house of language." Some poststructuralist philosophers would go on to insist that our thought is so shaped by language that the only reality we can ever know is entirely constructed of it. We live in a hall of mirrors, and the mirrors are made of words.

Words, furthermore, introduce us to our most implacable enemy: time. Developmental psychologists believe that memory begins with the learning of language; to speak (or more accurately, to understand speech, since most children can comprehend before they can articulate) is to remember. With memory comes the capacity to dwell on the past and to anticipate the future; without memory, how could we know our lives and our selves? And without knowing these things, how could we own them? But as Travers's mournful little parable would have it, to speak is also to forget—to forget what it is not to remember, to forget what it feels like to live the way animals do, in a perpetual now, unaware of death and outside of time.

I can't shake the feeling that even if children don't cognitively grasp the miraculous tragedy of consciousness, they nevertheless feel the aftershocks of the journey they've made. Animals inhabit the world of raw experience we've left behind; animals are the people of our lost homeland. To a child, an animal seems like a compatriot. The attachments that I had to the animals I knew were every bit as powerful as my feelings toward, say, my siblings (and less ambivalent, too, since I wasn't competing with the family cats for my parents' attention or a bigger share of the french fries). It's true that some adults still feel this way about their pets, and if you ask them why, the explanation often has to do with the transparency of animals' affection, their sincerity, which also turns out to be connected to their lack of language. Animals can't speak, ergo, they can't lie.

Yet the most cherished creatures in children's fantasy are *talking* animals. If we have mixed feelings about the gifts of language and consciousness, we have no intention of surrendering them. Instead, we want to bring animals along with us, into the solitude of self-knowledge, perhaps hoping that they'll make it a less lonely place for us. Children are more likely than adults to fantasize about talking beasts because kids don't have the logical faculties to see that giving animals the power of speech would surely spoil everything we like about them. Children still think they can finesse the difference, that the breach between the one animal who speaks and all the others who cannot will at last be closed, or at least bridged.

Talking animals were one of the things I loved most about the Chronicles as a child, but over the years that aspect of the books has lost its old allure. Once I would have given anything to join the Pevensie siblings at the round dinner table in Mr. and Mrs. Beaver's snug little house, trading stories about Aslan and eating potatoes and freshly caught trout. What I now like about animals—their lack of self-consciousness—I know to be intimately bound up in their speechlessness. As a little girl, I suspected them of having inner lives much like my own, if only they could (or would) tell me about it; now, I recognize that their charm lies in their lack of such secret thoughts. If my neighbor's cat, my friend's dog, the squirrel who sometimes treks along my fire escape, peering in on me while I'm reading on my sofa, could speak, would they really have anything to say that they can't already communicate well enough in their usual way: by purring, snuffling, wagging, chittering?

The denizens of Narnia were not the first talking beasts C. S. Lewis invented. As a little boy, growing up in Belfast at the beginning of the twentieth century, he dreamed up an imaginary kingdom he called "Animal-Land," where he could "combine my two chief literary pleasures—'dressed animals' and 'knights in armor.'" His older brother, Warren (nicknamed Warnie), wanted to join in but preferred such modern paraphernalia as trains and steamships. So Animal-Land grew to encompass both a semilegendary past full of contests between armored mice and ferocious cats, and a present linked to Warnie's own fantasyland, called "India," in which the same sorts of creatures—frogs and rabbits—stood around in waistcoats, puffing on pipes and discussing parliamentary politics. Warnie and Jack (as Clive Staples Lewis was nicknamed) called this amalgamation "Boxen." Jack immediately set about writing a history of the place to cover the years intervening between his stories and Warnie's, and this in turn entailed drawing up maps of trade routes and railway lines, as well as sketching pictures of all the principal characters.

Lewis regarded the elaboration of Boxen to be his earliest training as a novelist. However, in *Surprised by Joy,* he warned readers that these boyhood writings were "astonishingly prosaic." Animal-Land, he wrote, had no similarities to Narnia "except for the anthropomorphic beasts." It was a place, he insisted, entirely lacking in "wonder." The publication in 1986 of *Boxen: The Imaginary World of the Young C. S. Lewis,* a collection of these maps, drawings, histories, and stories, shows this to be an accurate assessment; the book is deadly dull. Its characters — irresponsible kings and concerned prime ministers — behave much like Lewis's father, Albert, a prominent solicitor, and his politically active friends, the only adults Jack and Warnie had had a chance to observe. There's something absurd about inventing an elaborate fantasy world in which you merely replicate the tedium of the world around you, but Boxen stands as a case in point: it's a lot harder than it looks to tap into the enchantments of childhood. Even an actual child, it seems, isn't necessarily up to the job.

Stories about talking animals are not, of course, solely the province of children's literature. Folklore — which is made by and for adults — has its share of them, too, but it always uses talking beasts didactically, to personify a particular principle or trait: the wily fox, the fearsome wolf, the methodical tortoise. The animals of fable and fairy tale are used to signify an identity that is simple and unchanging. Take the scorpion who breaks his promise by stinging the frog who has agreed to carry him across a river; when asked how he could betray his rescuer, he replies, "It's my nature." People repeat this parable as a way of asserting that a thief is always a thief, and a liar is always a liar, so it's best not to trust either one. A leopard never changes his spots, goes the saying, but it's meant as a knock on a certain kind of human being, not on leopards themselves. (Why *should* they change their spots?) When it comes to people who behave badly, who indulge their lowest impulses, character is animalistic: inborn, inherent, and fixed.

Adults rarely tell each other real stories (as opposed to fables and parables) about animal characters because the adult notion of a good story—especially now, a few hundred years into the history of the novel—demands psychological change, enlightenment, growth. When a contemporary novel with animal characters appears—Richard Adams's *Watership Down,* for example—even if in most ways it meets the criteria of adult fiction, its moorings there are never secure. Chances are it will drift, sooner or later, to the children's bookshelves. Stories that expect us to invest ourselves in the thoughts and fates and personalities of animals, stories like *The Wind in the Willows,* are obviously for kids.

Children freely and delightedly identify with the characters in animal stories, often more easily than they identify with child characters. Children's authors know that what insults an adult reader —being likened to an animal—delights a young one. Robert McCloskey's celebrated picture book *Blueberries for Sal,* for example, is simply an extended conceit on the similarities between the small child Sal and Little Bear—to the degree that at one point the two youngsters accidentally swap mothers. Curious George is ostensibly a mischievous monkey, but his most devoted readers recognize that he is also a wayward three-year-old.

And in Narnia, even God is an animal. Although as a girl I adored Aslan, he is another part of the Chronicles that no longer moves me as it once did. This is only partly because I now see, all too clearly, the theological strings and levers behind Lewis's stagecraft; the great lion seems less a character than a creaking device. I also stopped loving Aslan because I have since grown into the autonomy I was only

tentatively experimenting with at seven. The kind of story in which
a distant, parental presence hovers behind the scenes, ready to step
in and save the day at the moment when hope seems lost—a narrative safety net of sorts—now annoys rather than comforts me. I
no longer need this device in the same way that I no longer need
to hold someone's hand while crossing the street.

Still, being able to navigate traffic on your own doesn't keep you
from wanting to hold somebody's hand every once in a while, if for
different reasons. Holding hands feels nice, and this is one aspect of
Aslan that has retained its charm for me. Unlike the God I was raised
to worship, he is a god you can touch, and a god who asks to be
touched physically in his darkest hour. "Lay your hands on my mane
so that I can feel you are there and let us walk like that," he says to
Lucy and Susan as he goes to his execution at the stone table. After
he has been killed, the weeping girls come to kiss "his cold face"
and stroke "his beautiful fur," in a far more raw and tangible evoca-
tion of grief than anything in the New Testament. Then, after Aslan
has been resurrected, the girls climb onto his "warm, golden back,"
bury their hands in his mane, and go for a breathless cross-country
ride through a Narnia you can almost taste, thanks to one of Lewis's
most exhilarating descriptions:

Have you ever had a gallop on a horse? Think of that; and
then take away the heavy noise of the hoofs and the jingle of
the bits and imagine instead the almost noiseless padding of
the great paws. Then imagine instead of the black or gray or
chestnut back of the horse the soft roughness of golden fur,
and the mane flying back in the wind. And then imagine you
are going about twice as fast as the fastest racehorse. But this
is a mount that doesn't need to be guided and never grows
tired. He rushes on and on, never missing his footing, never
hesitating, threading his way with perfect skill between tree
trunks, jumping over bush and briar and the smaller streams,

wading the larger, swimming the largest of all. And you are
riding not on a road nor in the park nor even on the downs,
but right across Narnia, in spring, down solemn avenues of
beech and across sunny glades of oak, through wild orchards
of snow-white cherry trees, past roaring waterfalls and mossy
rocks and echoing caverns, up windy slopes alight with gorse
bushes, and across the shoulders of heathery mountains and
along giddy ridges and down, down, down again into wild
valleys and out into acres of blue flowers.

Traditional Christian iconography is filled with a mangled eroticism: the half-naked, suffering body of Christ hanging from the
cross, the woman humbly drying his feet with her own hair, the
graphic torments of martyrs displayed in centuries of religious
art—all of it warped by a pervasive ambivalence about sexuality.
(This ambivalence, incidentally, and whatever wishful thinkers might
say to the contrary, is not limited to Judeo-Christian religions.) Nowhere among these images do you find the plain, untrammeled joy
in being alive that Lewis captures in Lucy and Susan's "romp" with
Aslan. The scene is blissfully sensual. It ends with all three "rolled
over together in a happy laughing heap of fur and arms and legs." It
would be hard to imagine the two girls sharing the same intimacy
with a god in the form of a man—or, rather, it's imaginable, but
only with uncomfortable undertones.

"Animal" is a word sometimes used as a synonym for "carnal,"
and not in a good way, but Lucy and Susan's desire to touch Aslan,
and Aslan's desire to be touched by them, is carnal without ambivalence because he is an *actual* animal. Like most adults of his time and
place (or adults of most times and places, for that matter), Lewis had
mixed feelings about sex, but in this scene, at least, he escapes into a
pure delight in physicality that's almost, but not quite, erotic. And although I myself am ambivalent about having to use the word "pure"
to characterize that delight—or worse yet, the word "innocent,"

which I've so far managed to avoid—there is no other adjective for it. Even if I would prefer not to think that sexuality *contaminates* experiences, I have to admit that ambivalence about sexuality does just that. Lucy and Susan's romp with Aslan is as much pleasure as you can have in a body without sex—that is, without sex and the ambivalence that comes with it.

It's also transcendent. "Whether it was more like playing with a thunderstorm or playing with a kitten, Lucy could never make up her mind," Lewis writes. What Susan and Lucy are tumbling around with on Narnia's springy turf is something titanic and formidable, not just their own carnality with all its dormant, unpredictable potential, but a divinity who has just unleashed snowbound Narnia into the rampant vitality of spring. Yet if you're going to romp with a thunderstorm, what better form could it take than a gigantic kitten? Play and youth, too, are forces of nature.

When I read picture books to my toddler friends, Corinne and Desmond, they like to sidle up close to me. Their little fingers creep under my watchband and twine around my thumbs like the ivy that, under Aslan's direction in *Prince Caspian,* pulls down all the manmade structures in Narnia. The twins can't sit still; they have to fiddle with locks of my hair, climb onto my shoulders and into my lap. I usually wind up with a foot in my solar plexus and a head blocking my view of the book I'm supposed to be reading. They make me feel like a patient old dog, beset by puppies, my ears chewed on and paws squashed. I suppose they'll only be able to get away with behaving like this for a few more years, when, inevitably, self-consciousness will set in. Except, of course, with animals, who have only ever had this way of showing their love.

CHAPTER THREE

The Secret Garden

Discovering Narnia felt like a breathtaking expansion of the boundaries of my world, yet it was also an intensely private event. "You were so excited you couldn't talk about it," Wilanne Belden recalled. "I tried, but you sort of clammed up. I knew how important it was to you, but I think you thought that if you talked about it, it would get away."

A friend of mine recalls having solemn discussions with his childhood cohorts about what they'd do if they ever got to Narnia or Middle-earth, but this youthful collegiality seems to be the exception. One woman, who had just described her grammar school to me as a place where "magical things happened" and "we were allowed to let our imaginations really run," couldn't say whether her classmates had also liked the Narnia books. As for myself, I didn't know anyone else who'd read them, and to the best of my recollection I never urged them on my friends or siblings. There was Mrs. Belden, of course, but her role in initiating me had a priestly aspect—I expected to be led by her, not to befriend her—and I was a congregation of one. Even with the high priestess, I played it pretty close to my chest.

Like a lot of children from large families, I was preoccupied with getting and maintaining some small, inviolable portion of privacy.

The advantage of Narnia was that it was a whole world I could have all to myself. C. S. Lewis's childhood had its fortified aspect, as well. Jack had a friend in Warnie, the brother to whom he remained close for the rest of his life, but from the start their bond was predicated on excluding adults. "We stood foursquare against the common enemy," Lewis wrote in his memoir, *Surprised by Joy*. Their mother, Flora, died when Jack was nine; it was a loss he referred to sparingly afterward. Their father, Albert, had lost his own father a few weeks before that, and seems to have briefly fallen apart after the death of his wife. Lewis's biographers (himself included) universally regard what happened next—the temperamental Albert's efforts to seek comfort from his sons rather than to comfort them, and his occasional outbursts of what Jack called "unjust" behavior—as a mistake that resulted in a long estrangement.

At least, that's the theory, a theory that jibes with the commonplace, quasi-Freudian notion that a single traumatic event can cause lasting changes in the ecology of a relationship. It's also one of those notions that treats life as more of a narrative than it actually is. In real life, a well-balanced relationship can regain its footing pretty well, even after a severe knock. It's in the nature of human beings (especially young, adaptable ones) to get over things when given half a chance. I suspect that if the makings of real intimacy had ever existed between Albert and his sons, it probably would have revived in the years after Flora's death, however badly he behaved just afterward. What really alienated the two brothers from their father was something less momentous—something with fewer of the dramatic qualities of a good excuse.

The autobiographical writings of both Jack and Warnie portray Albert as a well-intentioned but irritating man. Behind his back, the boys complained about him constantly and mocked his many foibles. They invented a nickname for him, the P'daytabird, and wrote each other letters grumbling about the "rows after tea and penitentiary strolls in the garden" that dominated their home life when he was around. When Jack was an undergraduate, he described Albert to a friend as "one for whom I have little affection and whose society has for many years given me much discomfort and no pleasure." This, as Lewis seems acutely aware in *Surprised by Joy,* was unkind and looks especially bad in retrospect; Albert's peculiarities were hardly the caliber of sin that merits rejection by one's own children.

Lewis's most distinguished biographer, A. N. Wilson, regards the boys' coolness toward their father as a personal failing, at least on Jack's part. He characterizes the portrait of Albert in *Surprised by Joy* as "devastatingly cruel" and Jack's resentment of his financial dependence on his father during his early Oxford years as amounting to a "venomous" hostility; Albert's own diary confirms that he sometimes felt mistreated and disrespected by Jack. Yet in Jack and Warnie's defense, consider how much easier it is to reconcile with a charming friend who has wronged you once (if seriously) than it is to get along with someone who aggravates you three times an hour every single hour you spend with him. People like this are not any more endurable because they're technically harmless or mean well.

Wilson argues, plausibly, that guilt over how he'd behaved toward Albert would haunt Jack for the rest of his life; "I treated my own father abominably," Lewis once wrote to a friend after Albert's death in 1929, "and no sin in my whole life now seems to be so serious." No doubt Lewis learned to value patience and forbearance in his later years because he knew all too well how difficult it can be to summon both. In his adulthood, when he would be sorely tested in this department, Lewis's Christianity gave him a moral framework in which to place all the small annoyances of difficult relationships. Indulging a querulous person's unreasonable little demands and eccentricities could then be transfigured in Lewis's mind into a cross to bear, a hair shirt, an opportunity to demonstrate that his faith had humbled him.

I have more sympathy for the young Lewis (and his brother) than Lewis had for himself—more than Wilson has, too. In their memoirs,

Warnie and Jack both try repeatedly to capture the particular manner that Albert had of vexing them; you can sense their frustration at not being able to get it right, at failing to convey just how bad things could be. Their grievances do sound minor, but they're revealing all the same. In a memoir that was later condensed to serve as the introduction to a volume of his brother's letters, Warnie explained why Jack avoided inviting Arthur Greeves, the boy who lived across the street and who would become a lifelong friend, into their family home:

> My father would certainly have welcomed his son's friend very cordially, but not for a moment would it have occurred to him that the two boys might want to talk together, alone. No: he would have joined them, inescapably, for a good talk about books, doing nine-tenths of the talking himself, eulogizing his own favorites without regard to their interests. Two bored and frustrated youths would have been subjected to long readings from Macaulay's essays, Burke's speeches, and the like, and my father would have gone to bed satisfied that he had given them a literary evening far more interesting than they could have contrived for themselves.

Albert Lewis was, furthermore, perpetually anxious and prone to hysteria, particularly about money. He did not hide this from his children. In *Surprised by Joy*, Lewis writes of how seriously he had once taken his father's frequent, melodramatic talk of the poorhouse: "All security seemed to be taken from me; there was no solid ground beneath my feet." Albert was exaggerating, but until Jack grew old enough to understand that these panicky warnings were mere "rhetoric," he believed them, and was terrified that his family would soon be begging on the street.

Albert, although essentially kindhearted, didn't really listen to Jack or Warnie, usually got whatever they told him about themselves wrong, and then could never be persuaded that he had misunderstood them. (This imperviousness occasionally became a serious problem, as when he sent the boys to a small boarding school run by a sadistic headmaster who eventually had to be institutionalized.) When they were all at home, he insisted that his sons be, in Lewis's words, "as closely bound to his presence as if the three of us had been chained together," whereupon his own peculiar habits and endless, overwrought lectures monopolized everything they did or talked about. "The theory," Lewis wrote, "was that we lived together more like three brothers than like a father and two sons." The reality, of course, was that Albert failed to become a virtual brother and neglected to behave like the father he actually was. Small wonder, then, that Lewis also wrote, "I thought Monday morning, when he went back to his work, the brightest jewel of the week."

In modern parlance, we'd say Albert had boundary issues. His heart was in the right place, but he exposed his children to his raw grief, confusion, and fear when they were too young to be anything but frightened by it. He couldn't grasp that they had thoughts or lives of their own, and so he never gathered that at times, he must necessarily be excluded from both, emotionally and physically. Even as an adult, Jack never entered his father's house without first checking his pockets for anything he would prefer to keep private; Albert would go through them as casually as he'd enter his sons' rooms without knocking. And thus, in Jack, "a habit of concealment" was formed. Unless you've had a parent of this sort, it's hard to communicate how powerfully the sensation of perpetual intrusion shapes a child's character or how fiercely an adolescent is likely to rebel against it.

Any habit of concealment inevitably leads to the division of one's life and personality into compartments, and this, I believe, is a signal trait of the bookish child. "I am telling the story of two lives," Lewis wrote of his early teens in *Surprised by Joy*, meaning that the outer story, set in the series of hateful boarding schools he attended after his mother's death, must be contrasted with an inner story, contemporaneous with the first. In the inner story, Lewis reveled in "a period of ecstasy" fed by his discovery of classical and Norse mythology and his independent explorations of English literature and the Northern Irish countryside. At home, he soldiered through the weary hours with his father, and when Albert went to work, he would happily devise elaborate sagas set in the imaginary world he shared with Warnie. Best of all, on those rare, cherished occasions when he had the house to himself, he enjoyed the "complete satisfaction" of "a deeper solitude than I had ever known."

Like many great readers, Lewis regarded his time alone as his real life. By the age of nine—the same age at which I was thinking that my hunger for Narnia might kill me—he, too, was "living almost entirely in my imagination; or at least…the imaginative experience of those years now seems to me more important than anything else." Like Lewis's, my material life often seemed to be nothing more than the drab and shadowy interludes between the hours when I could read and retreat to an interior realm furnished with the fabulous treasure I had scavenged from hundreds of books. I sometimes wonder if this kind of inward-turning, inward-dwelling, probably unhealthy temperament is acquired or inherited. Did tumbling into Lewis's own imagined world at such an impressionable age imprint me with some of his traits? Or did I perhaps get my dreaming ways from my father, who liked nothing better than to escape the rumpus of family life and work alone in his garden?

Gardens speak to people of this solitary temperament. Even those of us who don't tend the real ones find the idea of gardens, especially walled ones, evocative. In *Surprised by Joy*, Lewis recalls his first experience of true "beauty," which appeared in the unlikely form of the lid of a cookie tin that his brother had filled with bits of moss and twigs to create a miniature garden. "What the real garden had failed to do," Lewis writes, "the toy garden did. It made me aware of nature—not, indeed, as a storehouse of forms and colors but as something cool, dewy, fresh, exuberant." Gardens are man-made concentrations of the natural world, places where nature is trained to seem more itself than it is when left to its own devices. In a way, the artificiality of gardens is like the artificiality of stories, which take the components of life and arrange them into forms that intensify and order them, saturating them with meaning.

In *The Magician's Nephew,* the Chronicles' Creation story, Aslan sends the boy Digory on a quest to a walled garden in the mountains far to the west of the newly made land of Narnia. Digory has been given the task of bringing back a single apple from a tree that grows there, and although Aslan hasn't told him not to taste the apples himself, an inscription on the gate admonishes all visitors to "Take of my fruit for others" only. There are, of course, the obviously biblical connotations to this walled garden at the beginning of the world, with its semiforbidden fruit. But Digory is no Adam; he has committed his transgression *before* he arrives at the garden's gate. He has already unwittingly introduced an evil into Narnia—the sorceress Jadis, who will one day become the White Witch in *The Lion, the Witch and the Wardrobe.* Aslan sets him the task of fetching the apple as a form of expiation.

Digory's friend Polly has come along for most of the journey, and the two children travel on the back of Fledge, a talking winged horse. Polly and Fledge are stalwart companions, but at the entrance to the garden they instinctively hang back. "You never saw a place which was so obviously private," the narrator explains. "You could see at a glance that it belonged to someone else." It's all right for Digory to go inside, but not the others. Like all of the most magical places in the Narnia books, the garden is very quiet; even the fountain at its center makes "only the faintest sound." Jadis, however, has snuck in before Digory, and he spots her there, gorging herself on plundered apples. (I never forgot the "horrid stain" their juice leaves around her mouth, and sometimes I wonder if that's why my most vivid recollection of Madame Bovary is of her mouth stained by the poison she swallows at the end of the novel.)

Jadis does try to tempt Digory to steal one of these magical, life-giving apples for his gravely ill mother, but unlike Satan she botches the job. This scene touches on the central tragedy of Lewis's childhood, the death of his own mother from cancer when he was not much older than Digory. The witch invokes Digory's grief and fear not because she sympathizes (having killed her own sister in an imperial power struggle, presumably she's immune to such feelings), but because she knows that his love for his mother is his greatest weakness. Digory hesitates to follow her suggestion for a few reasons: because he instinctively trusts Aslan, because he does not want to break his promise, and because he believes that his mother herself wouldn't approve of him stealing and then lying about it.

Jadis marshals persuasive counterarguments against all of these reservations, but what trips her up is her underestimation of Digory's affection for Polly, of the power of friendship, a type of love Lewis considered underrated. Thinking that Digory is worried about getting caught, she tells him that he can easily cover his tracks by ditching Polly up in the mountains. In the pinch, Digory rebuffs her, not out of simple obedience to Aslan's orders, but out of disgust at the "meanness" of the witch's suggestion that he abandon his friend. Suddenly he perceives everything she's said as "false and hollow." The selfish, vainglorious evil she represents advocates more than just rebellion against God—she has subscribed to a radical disconnection from humanity. Symbolically, she has already demonstrated her disregard for natural feeling by violating the garden.

As a metaphor, the garden in *The Magician's Nephew* has less in common with Eden than it does with the walled gardens that appear in the medieval courtly romances that Lewis wrote about in *The Allegory of Love,* his first great scholarly work, published in 1936. He came to Oxford from Belfast when he was in his late teens, and apart from a stint in the army during World War I, he never really left it. *The Allegory of Love,* an examination of the evolution of the form of allegory from the epics of late antiquity to the chivalric poems of the Middle Ages, made his academic reputation. It was in medieval literature, more than in scripture, that Lewis's imagination lived and breathed. As arcane as its subject might seem to contemporary readers, for Lewis *The Allegory of Love* was an extension of his childhood enthusiasm for "knights in armor," an enthusiasm that lasted all his life, beginning with the creaky historical novels of Sir Arthur Conan Doyle, and threading through the Arthurian works of Tennyson, Thomas Malory, William Morris, and Edmund Spenser.

Lewis adhered to a very particular, almost technical definition of allegory, so when critics later called *The Lion, the Witch and the Wardrobe* allegorical (or, for that matter, suggested that *The Lord of the Rings* was an allegory for World War II), he took great pains to correct their error. He had a point—only someone who has a pretty feeble grasp of allegory would mistake *The Lion, the Witch and the Wardrobe* for one. Some of the book's elements are *symbolic,* but that is not the same thing. None of the characters in *The Lion, the Witch and the Wardrobe* are given labels like Despair or Prudence, nor can they be simply equated with such abstractions, like the figures in a strict allegory, such as John Bunyan's *Pilgrim's Progress.*

Still, the mistake is understandable. Why would most modern readers know anything much about allegory? Today the form is usually derided, rarely read, and never practiced, unless you count the allegories in political cartoons, where a gluttonous hog might appear with the letters "IRS" stamped on its side. *The Pilgrim's Progress* is probably the only true allegory contemporary readers have ever heard of, let alone read. As a result, our ability to recognize allegories and to appreciate the best of them has withered away.

Nevertheless, Lewis was a medievalist at heart, and if none of the Narnia books are actual allegories, they are infused with a related affinity for emblems, pageants, and layered symbolism. This was the way his imagination worked, by constructing a series of meaning-drenched images. Lewis didn't deny that *The Lion, the Witch and the Wardrobe* was allegory because he disliked the form (as Tolkien claimed to); to the contrary, he thought allegory was unjustly disdained. He believed modern readers required training to read it properly. If they could learn, at least temporarily, to think like the medievals, they would finally grasp allegory's distinctive, if antiquated beauty. Then it might give as much pleasure to the average educated reader as it had given to him.

One of the allegories Lewis most admired was *The Romance of the Rose,* a thirteenth-century French poem begun but not finished by Guillaume de Lorris and completed (to Lewis's mind in an inferior fashion) by Jean de Meun. The story concerns a young courtier engaged in the delicate process of winning a lady's love (symbolized by the rose of the title) in accordance with the elaborate protocols of chivalry. His opponents in this quest include figures named Shame and Fear; his chief ally is called Bialacoil, a term, Lewis explains, that is not quite the same as the chivalric principle of courtesy, but fairly similar.

If you check the entry for *The Romance of the Rose* in *The Norton Anthology of English Literature,* you will be told that the lover's personified enemies stand for the "personal and social restraints standing against his advances." Lewis felt that this sort of all-too-common, slapdash interpretation of allegorical figures — describing them as merely "standing for" something else — missed the point. If, while reading *The Romance of the Rose,* we see Shame and Fear as no more than broad abstractions (much like the statue symbolizing Justice mounted over many a courtroom), we miss the richness of a medieval allegory, and its intimacy. What we must first remember, Lewis argued, is that the friendly and hostile figures the lover meets are contained *within* the lady he loves. "Her character," he wrote, "is distributed among personifications."

What made allegory powerful, and in Lewis's eyes "realistic," is that it was a sophisticated way of representing the inner lives of human beings at the time the great allegories like *The Romance of the Rose* were written. Though we now take for granted the notion of

Jadis, the invader, tries to manipulate Digory's fear not just of losing his mother, but of being culpable for that loss. "What would your mother think if she knew that you *could* have taken her pain away and given her back her life and saved your Father's heart from being broken, and that you *wouldn't?*" she taunts. She knows exactly which is the sorest spot to press because she has trespassed on territory where no one but Digory (besides Aslan) has the right to tread. Climbing the walls and eating the apples turns her skin "deadly white, white as salt," an indication that she has lost whatever humanity had remained in her and has become something else, a voice in Digory's head, his own worst impulses, the eternal Tempter. She is now allegorical. While the garden in *The Magician's Nephew* bears a certain resemblance to the biblical Eden, it is even more evocative as an emblem of the self.

This moment, the moment of Digory's choice, is the most emotionally naked depiction Lewis ever wrote of his feelings about Flora Lewis's death. In *Surprised by Joy,* he describes the loss with a faded sorrow, as the moment when "all settled happiness, all that was tranquil and reliable, disappeared from my life....It was sea and islands now; the great continent had sunk like Atlantis." He also recalls trying to will himself into a belief that prayer could either cure or, finally, resurrect her. *Surprised by Joy,* a memoir intended to explain the circumstances of Lewis's conversion, handles this early spiritual disappointment cursorily. Lewis claims, unconvincingly, that the futility of his boyhood prayers (and the unspoken likelihood that he blamed their failure on his own insufficient faith) had "no religious importance." A few years later, however, the teenage Lewis would come to regard himself as an unbeliever.

Digory keeps his promise to Narnia's god, and in the end is rewarded by Aslan with a second apple, which does cure his mother. Not only is the great catastrophe of Lewis's early life averted in his fiction; so, too, is the foundering of his own faith. The fact that the image of a dying mother crops up in a book he wrote over forty years later suggests that, not surprisingly, Lewis never entirely recovered from this loss. Yet apart from the few pages that he devotes to his mother's death in *Surprised by Joy*, it wasn't a topic he mentioned much. He became notorious among his adult friends for his reluctance to enter into any conversation at all about his personal life, particularly his intimate relationships. In *Surprised by Joy*, Lewis recalls how he loathed the "fuss and flummery" of Flora's funeral, which, he believed, instituted his lifelong "distaste for all that is public," but "public" for him seemed to include even confidences shared with good friends. The best of friends, like Polly, knew not to intrude where they had not been invited.

Gardens make a particularly good image of the self for a writer, because while a garden can be cultivated and enjoyed privately, it can also yield fruit that can be shared with others. It can be watered with books and music and pictures. It can serve as a retreat from the world for an hour or two. It is also a place where you can spend days puttering away like my father, weeding flower beds, tying up vines, re-laying little paths. Lewis's own inner self—fed by Arthurian legends, Norse myths, Wagnerian opera, the Celtic folktales he heard from the family's maid, the countryside around Belfast that he explored on foot and bicycle, the poetry he discovered on his own and through his family's library—was like a walled garden, lavishly tended and well guarded. A handful of people (Warnie and Arthur Greeves, the boy across the street) were occasionally invited inside, but in every such place there is some fruit that must not be picked, and an inner garden that no one else can ever enter.

CHAPTER FOUR

Boxcar Children

It wouldn't be truthful to say that the only books I liked as a child were fantasy stories, although those were my favorites, and I became adept at sniffing them out, often with as little as a title and cover art to go by. I did read books like Laura Ingalls Wilder's *Little House on the Prairie* and a Newbury Medal winner by Scott O'Dell called *Island of the Blue Dolphins,* about a Native American girl who is left behind on an island when her tribe is evacuated. The Wilder books were enjoyable if not riveting, but *Island of the Blue Dolphins* had real power. With its detailed descriptions of the girl learning how to make weapons to hunt with, to find fresh water, to dry meat, and to fend off the island's wild dogs, it fascinated me. I persuaded a neighborhood friend to set up a "camp" in a corner of her backyard, where we crouched, pretending to be Indian hunters, draping slices of raw bacon over strings suspended between a couple of shrubs and calculating how much trouble we were likely to get into if we lit a fire to cook them over.

Both *Little House on the Prairie* and *Island of the Blue Dolphins* took what I considered to be a laudable interest in the nuts and bolts of survival in other times and places; I remember the maple-syrup-making scenes from the Wilder books more vividly than anything else. However, *Island of the Blue Dolphins* had one great advantage over *Little House on the Prairie:* no parents. A few years ago, while I was working on an essay about the boom in "problem novels"—fiction for young people centering on a trauma or an issue like drug addiction or rape—my editor reminisced about reading *Island of the Blue Dolphins* as a girl, too. "I can't believe they give a book like that to children," she remarked. "It's about being abandoned by your family! What could be more disturbing?" I was startled; it had never occurred to me before that the novel described a terrifying scenario, although the girl's situation was occasionally desperate. I didn't see her as abandoned. To my child's mind, she was liberated.

If you had asked me then what I liked so much about the Narnia books—or E. Nesbit's *Five Children and It* or Edward Eager's *Half Magic* series, among other favorites—I would eventually discover, I probably would have told you it was the magic. Reading them now, what I notice is the absence or irrelevance of parents. Mothers and fathers play, at best, a very minor supporting role in the Nesbit and Eager books. Sometimes beloved adults are sick or otherwise troubled and need to be rescued. Otherwise, if they're around at all, they just get in the way.

The parents of the four Pevensie children, who have sent them off to stay in an old house in the country "because of the air-raids," go nearly unmentioned in *The Lion, the Witch and the Wardrobe.* (Early in the story, Edmund accuses Susan of "trying to talk like Mother," and he does not mean it appreciatively.) When the children arrive at Professor Kirk's house, they never speak of the war that brought them there or of missing their parents; instead they go on excitedly about all the animals they hope to find in the countryside ("Badgers!" "Foxes!" "Rabbits!"). "This is going to be perfectly splendid," Peter announces, without a hint of ambivalence. People who see the novel's story as precipitated by trauma (the bombings, separation) are misreading it, as adults are prone to do.

It's often been said of a certain kind of children's book that the author has to get rid of one or both parents before anything interesting can happen. Nancy Drew has a father but no mother because no self-respecting mother would allow her teenage daughter to gallivant around in a blue roadster, chasing criminals. (A fond father can be gotten around, and apparently even coaxed into springing for the roadster.) Nancy's mother is simply *gone,* and apparently unmourned, because Nancy exists in a fictional fantasy world where a missing mother is not missed.

While this isn't very plausible, it is understandable. In the great enterprise of growing up, a child's imagination practices the painless, surgical removal of an attachment that, however essential it may be at the moment, will sooner or later have to be left behind. The same child (myself, for example) who finds imagining her parents' deaths heart-freezingly scary will also fantasize about the exciting escapade of being left entirely to her own devices. In her memoir, *Welcome to Lizard Motel,* the educator Barbara Feinberg describes leading a children's creativity workshop whose participants liked pretending they were orphans, though not, one little girl clarified, "the sad part of orphans."

Had anyone quizzed me further about the kinds of books I liked, I would have said that I wanted to read about adventures, and those didn't happen when parents were around. The presence of Mother and Father guaranteed that children were stuck being children. Without their parents, Narnia's young visitors finally get the chance to try out all the practical knowledge they've acquired over their years of reading what Lewis, in *The Voyage of the Dawn Treader,* refers to as "the right books."

The Pevensies know all about jungle explorers and buccaneers and questing knights, and they can keep their heads in a crisis; they belong to a long tradition in British fiction of what the novelist and critic Colin Greenland calls "competent children." I admired both their wherewithal and the delicacy of their scruples in a scene from *The Lion, the Witch and the Wardrobe* in which all four of the siblings have finally made it through the wardrobe and debate what to do next. They decide to put on the fur coats from the wardrobe before venturing on into the snowy woods, reasoning that because they're not actually taking the coats *out* of the wardrobe, they won't be stealing them.

The second Chronicle, *Prince Caspian,* of which a goodly portion is a wilderness adventure yarn, begins with the Pevensies magically yanked back into Narnia and stranded on a desert island. They are made castaways without the preliminary grief of a shipwreck, but as usual they're not at a loss. I was especially impressed when Peter announced to his thirsty siblings, "If there are streams they're bound to come down to the sea, and if we walk along the beach we're bound to come to them." I stowed that tip away for the future. As the oldest child in my own tribe of brothers and sisters, I thought this was exactly the sort of thing I ought to know in the event of an emergency—though how, exactly, we might be lucky enough to get shipwrecked together I didn't consider. Likewise, Susan keeps the two younger children from abandoning their hot, heavy shoes after a wade in the surf because "we shall want them if we're still here when night comes and it gets cold," and Edmund suggests exploring the woods: "Hermits and Knights Errant and people like that always manage to live somehow if they're in a forest. They find roots and berries and things."

Later in *Prince Caspian,* under the influence of the Narnian air, the Pevensies will begin to recall all of the skills—archery, sword fighting, the composition of a formal challenge to single combat—they acquired in *The Lion, the Witch and the Wardrobe,* during their time as kings and queens. At first, however, their points of reference are strictly literary. From Defoe and Stevenson, possibly Walter Scott, and any number of less exalted authors, they have acquired this idea of adventure, and they don't consider themselves to be excluded from it simply because they're children. Play has girded them for action, and initially Narnia itself has to be distinguished from a game of make-believe. "We can pretend we are Arctic explorers," suggests

Lucy in *The Lion, the Witch and the Wardrobe,* as the siblings set off through the woods. "This is going to be exciting enough without pretending," Peter points out. Narnia is a place so thrilling that you can finally stop imagining you're somewhere better. It is the place where adventures are transformed from something you read about in books to something you actually get to do.

Still, the Pevensies never stop reading adventure stories in our world just because they have experienced real, live adventures in Narnia. Practically speaking, reading the wrong books would leave them unprepared, making them the kind of children who wouldn't know that you should kick off your shoes if you happen to fall into deep water with your clothes on, as Lucy does at the beginning of *The Voyage of the Dawn Treader.* The Chronicles are full of such advice, some of it very useful, even if in the first book Lewis archly parodied the mother-hen tone of other children's authors by repeatedly warning of the dangers of shutting oneself up in a wardrobe. In *The Silver Chair,* we learn that midday is a better time to sneak out of a house than the night (you look less suspicious if you get caught) and that a good way to keep your companions from realizing you're afraid is to say nothing at all; otherwise, your quavering voice will probably give you away.

The Chronicles, then, become the same kind of adventurers' handbooks that stand their own characters in good stead. I can remember thinking that I'd gotten plenty of invaluable information from them, although strictly speaking most of it was only helpful if you also happened to be a character in an adventure story. Eustace Scrubb, in the early chapters of *The Voyage of the Dawn Treader,* manages to get himself turned into a dragon largely because the books he has read have "a lot to say about exports and imports and governments and drains, but they were weak on dragons." Eustace's prosaic taste in reading matter is of a piece with more serious personal failings, of course. His selfishness and sloth also lead him to the dragon's lair, and only an ordeal will give him back his humanity.

For some adults, "Narnia" has become shorthand for an excessively, impossibly safe fantasyland. In the novel *Special Topics in Calamity Physics* by Marisha Pessl, a character out of the young heroine's past telephones from a posh sanitarium she describes as "a Narnia kind of place," by which she means an artificially sustained shelter that bears no resemblance to the real world. But however cozy the land of Narnia might look from the vantage of adulthood, now that memory has mingled it with nostalgia for childhood itself, it is not especially secure. The place seems to be under perpetual threat, and the course of action required to save it is invariably difficult, physically as well as psychically.

I, for one, didn't experience the Chronicles as a retreat into an orderly playpen populated by sweet-talking animals and a kind, cuddly godhead. I was, of course, being sheltered by the traditional conventions of children's stories, in which the good are rewarded, the evil defeated, and the ending is at least partially happy. But getting to that happy ending was no picnic; along with the child heroes, I vicariously slogged through trackless forests and snowy wastes, took up arms against monsters, and wrangled with menacing adults. I was stirred by how much was expected of the Pevensies. I wanted to be challenged in the same way. I wanted to be asked to give my all for a cause I could be sure was worthy. (And even at that tender age, I had an inkling that finding such a cause would be the hardest part of the quest.)

Not all of these sentiments are entirely admirable, but they do represent a mezzanine between the dependency of childhood and the autonomy of adulthood. They're an imaginative projection, not (quite) a real wish, and Lewis takes some care to remind his readers of the distinction. As Jill, Eustace, and Puddleglum enjoy a brief, easy stretch on the moors at the beginning of *The Silver Chair,* Jill announces that she might just enjoy adventures after all, to which Puddleglum responds, "We haven't had any yet." Later on, Jill will get the opportunity to observe that "when, in books, people live on what they shoot, it never tells you what a long, smelly, messy job it is plucking and cleaning dead birds, and how cold it makes your fingers." The sort of experience that makes for a good story is seldom a comfy one.

"Adventure," then, is what might otherwise be called a hardship if it were attempted in a different spirit. Turning a difficult task or a perilous journey into an adventure is largely a matter of telling yourself the right story about it, which is one thing that Lewis's child characters have learned from reading "the right books." This is surely the oldest of the many tasks that stories are called upon to perform. The honor that propels the warriors of *The Iliad* is bestowed in the form of stories, accounts of bravery first passed on by fellow soldiers and later recited by poets long after the hero himself is dead. When Shakespeare's Henry V rallies his men before the Battle of Agincourt, he tells them that their courage on Saint Crispin's Day will soon be legendary, offering them a kind of immortality:

> This story shall the good man teach his son;
> And Crispin Crispian shall ne'er go by,
> From this day to the ending of the world,
> But we in it shall be remembered.

"This is War. This is what Homer wrote about," was what Lewis himself thought one afternoon in November 1917 at the beginning of his only encounter with real, life-and-death adventure in France. A bullet had just whined past him, and even then, his mind turned toward books. Afterward, he would write even less about the war than he did about his mother's death. In *Surprised by Joy*, he explains that the period is "too cut off from the rest of my experience and often seems to have happened to someone else. It is even in a way unimportant." This remark comes just after a sentence that describes, with excruciating vividness, the horrors of the trenches: "the frights, the cold, the smell of H.E. [human excrement], the horribly smashed men still moving like half-crushed beetles, the sitting or standing corpses, the landscape of sheer earth without a blade of grass, the boots worn day and night till they seemed to grow to your feet."

Passing references made in the years that followed suggest that the war stuck with Lewis more than he let on. He was lucky enough to sustain a minor wound fairly early in his stint (the shrapnel remained in his shoulder for the rest of his days), and that probably saved his life. The following year, he makes reference, in a letter to his father, of suffering from "nightmares — or rather the same nightmare over and over again. Nearly every one has it." In 1925, again writing to his father, he recounts a walk with Warnie, during which they overheard a battery practicing nearby, the first gunfire he'd heard since returning from France. His own response startled him: "It seemed much louder and more sinister and generally unpleasant than I had expected." Later still, he would gratefully note "the stamp of the war" on Hugo Dyson, a new friend, and in one of his few surviving letters to Tolkien, he praises *The Lord of the Rings* for capturing "so much of our joint life, so much of the war," which otherwise seemed to be slipping out of immediate memory.

The lives Lewis and Tolkien led might appear sheltered at first glance, but in this respect they endured more than almost anyone in my own circle ever will; middle-class American intellectuals in recent years have seldom gone to war. Tolkien, in a preface to *The Lord of the Rings,* wrote that by 1918, when he turned twenty-six, all but one of his closest friends had been killed. The formative trials of his youth, and Lewis's, the almost incommunicable agonies of the trenches, have become increasingly alien to their readers, who are gradually losing even the ability to understand that they don't understand them. All the same, although I was only a little girl who knew nothing of real violence, I recognized the ring of truth in Peter's battle with the wolf in *The Lion, the Witch and the Wardrobe:*

All this happened too quickly for Peter to think at all — he had just time to duck down and plunge his sword, as hard as he could, between the brute's forelegs into its heart. Then came a horrible, confused moment like something in a nightmare. He was tugging and pulling and the Wolf seemed to be neither alive nor dead, and its bared teeth knocked against his forehead, and everything was blood and heat and hair. A moment later he found that the monster lay dead and he had drawn his sword out of it and was straightening his back and rubbing the sweat off his face and out of his eyes. He felt tired all over.

Aslan knights Peter after this messy victory (admonishing him, "Never forget to wipe your sword"—more practical advice!) and gives him the nickname Wolf's-Bane. Peter has not only rescued Susan from the wolf; he has entered a heroic narrative and acquired a title. Lewis dreaded war (especially as his brother became a career officer in the Royal Army Service Corps and was recalled to active duty during World War II), but the literature he studied showed it to be a continuing fact of human existence. He firmly believed that sometimes war was necessary. Religion explains why—sometimes we must be willing to sacrifice ourselves for a greater good—but stories show us *how.* Stories are what make heroes. You can only become a hero by participating in a story, and stories bestow meaning on what might otherwise look like raw suffering and waste.

This, of course, is not always a virtue. You can get people to do a lot of difficult, unpleasant, and dangerous things by convincing them that someday a golden story will be spun out of the straw of their mortal lives. Many of these things are not worth doing, and not all Christians agree with Lewis's views on war. But war is not the only enterprise that requires courage, energy, and will. Another is the perilous adventure of growing up.

CHAPTER FIVE

Something Wicked
This Way Comes

At age seven, I believed that I knew sermonizing when I saw it, and I loathed no book more on this count than *Elsie Dinsmore*. Martha Finley's 1867 novel had been pressed on me by my grandmother, who, incredibly, claimed to have enjoyed it in her youth. The title character is a weepy Goody Two-shoes, mistreated by her stepmother yet responding with an unflagging, inhuman sweetness and docility that the reader is obviously meant to admire and emulate. Later in the narrative, Elsie even manages to get into a ludicrous doctrinal dispute with her adored father, who orders her to read a secular book aloud to him on his sickbed; it is Sunday and Elsie believes that Sabbath reading should be reserved for the Bible or some other appropriately pious literature.

Despite hating it so thoroughly, I read *Elsie Dinsmore* all the way through. Part of my reason for persisting with the book was to marvel at the sort of hogwash adults expected me to swallow, and to congratulate myself on knowing better. This was my first taste of the righteous indignation of the abused reader, that strangely pleasurable outrage we experience when we recognize that an author has broken an important trust. As every critic knows, readers relish a negative review, and not simply out of spite. Seeing an author punished by critics for trampling on the compact between reader and writer attests to the fact that the compact was there in the first place. You can't recognize blasphemy until you hold something sacred. *Elsie Dinsmore* could only be so very bad because *The Lion, the Witch and the Wardrobe* was so very good.

It was precisely the propaganda aspect of *Elsie Dinsmore* that offended me, the subservience of the story and characters, of the entire book, to the task of instructing me morally. I recognized that the Chronicles also sometimes spoke to me about virtue — in fact, I regarded those parts of the books as among their most thrilling and important moments. The difference was, as I saw it, fundamental. The morality of Elsie Dinsmore was the morality of childhood, where the choice was between obedience and naughtiness. The morality of Narnia was grown-up, a matter of good and evil.

Adult readers, who detect the Christian symbolism of the Chronicles so readily, often can't see the distinction. In her book *Boys and Girls Forever: Children's Classics from Cinderella to Harry Potter*, Alison Lurie complains, "In Narnia, final happiness is the result not of individual initiative and enterprise, but of submission to the wisdom and will of superior beings." Edmund's treachery in betraying the Narnians and his own siblings to the White Witch might seem heinous, but "misbehavior can be forgiven if it is sincerely repented, and Edmund eventually becomes one of the Kings of Narnia." This is really an objection to Christian faith itself, to its emphasis on obedience to the will of God and its promise of redemption to those who repent of their defiance. But it never occurred to me to look for Christianity in Narnia, and so, in the temptation of Edmund Pevensie, I saw another kind of drama entirely.

To me, the best children's books gave their child characters (and by extension, myself) the chance to be taken seriously. In Narnia, the boundary between childhood and adulthood — a vast tundra of tedious years — could be elided. The Pevensies not only get to topple the White Witch, fight in battles, participate in an earthshaking mystical event, and be crowned kings and queens; they do it all without having to grow up. Yet they become more than children, too. Above all, their decisions have moral gravity. In contrast to how most children experience their role in an adult world, what the child characters in these stories do, for better or worse, really *matters,* and nowhere more so than in Edmund's betrayal. His envy and vanity bring about a cataclysm, the death of God.

I remember feeling that the Chronicles were full of perilous decisions in which it was all too apparent how easily you could drift onto the wrong path. The White Witch entices Edmund with delicious hot drinks and enchanted Turkish delight, but primarily by flattering his laziness, his conceit, and his rivalrous sentiments toward his older brother, Peter—all very human weaknesses I recognized in myself. I wasn't alone. One of the people who wrote to me after reading my essay about *The Lion, the Witch and the Wardrobe* was a musician, writer, and artist I knew slightly named Tiffany Lee Brown. When we met to talk about the books, she described how different Narnia felt from other children's fantasies.

"The first novel I ever read was *The Magic of Oz* in the school library," she told me. "I loved it, and believed every word of it. So I read all the Oz books. I moved on to the Narnia books after that, when I was about seven or eight."

"And how did you think they compared to Oz?"

"Well, I didn't spend too much time in Oz. It was kind of wacky and had a lot of things going on, but there was a certain weightiness to Narnia which really appealed to me."

"What do you mean by 'weightiness'?"

"The fact that people were really being tested. It wasn't just 'Are we coming to the end of the adventure? Will we get back to Kansas?' but, 'Will we get back to Kansas with our souls intact?'"

To the adult skeptic, the evident Christianity of the Chronicles makes their morality seem pat, the all-too-familiar stuff of tiresome, didactic tales like *Elsie Dinsmore*. "The world of Narnia is simple and eternal," Alison Lurie writes, a place where good and evil are too "clearly distinguishable" compared to the "complex and ambiguous and fluid" world inhabited by Harry Potter. But that's an illusion, fostered by an adult's resistance to what appears to be religious proselytizing. True, Lewis does populate Narnia with semiallegorical figures who represent eternal aspects of human nature in addition to more realistic characters like the Pevensies. The White Witch is bad through and through, almost as uncomplicated as a fairy-tale villain. But she's not the ground on which the story's moral battle is fought. Edmund is.

For the novelist Jonathan Franzen, the plausibility of Edmund's corruption is an example of the ethical gravity that gives the Chronicles much of their power. "What I so admire about them as an adult and I think may very well have been a big part of their appeal to me as a child," he told me, "was how well Lewis understands how *real* evil is to children. How real a sense of guilt and having done something very, very bad is. And how vital to having a story with real meaning that possibility is. All of the books I liked best, that really made an impression on me from childhood, had main characters who were not all good, who were not victims of bad things but were actually agents in creating bad things."

Victims, it's true, have an appeal of their own. Frances Hodgson Burnett's *A Little Princess,* like *Elsie Dinsmore,* was one of those stories in which a child is bullied and deprived by nasty authority figures and her peers, only to achieve a satisfying triumph at the book's end. Even with a heroine like Elsie, who bore little resemblance to an actual human being, this kind of narrative can be weirdly enthralling. Vindication, however diluted, is intoxicating to the powerless, and all children feel powerless much of the time. There's something a little unwholesome about even a good children's novel in this particular vein — *A Little Princess* being a fine example. Young as I was, I recognized that my fascination with the injustices suffered by Burnett's heroine, a former rich girl reduced to working as a servant at her boarding school when her father dies, and my hot anticipation of the comeuppance I knew lay in store for her enemies, had an ugly side.

There is even some of this self-pitying thirst for revenge in the Harry Potter books. The long-suffering Harry, forced to sleep in a cupboard under the stairs by his dreadful foster family, the Dursleys, and often unfairly suspected of mischief at school, is always proven to be a blameless hero by the conclusion of each installment. Only at the very end of the series, in the seventh book, do we get a hint (and then only a hint) that Harry's cousin, Dudley Dursley, might not be awful to the core, although in the first few installments he is not much worse than Eustace Scrubb at the beginning of *The Voyage of the Dawn Treader,* and Eustace is permitted to reform. More important, although neither the little princess Sara Crewe nor Harry Potter behaves as badly as Edmund does in *The Lion, the Witch and the Wardrobe,* they are in fact what Edmund only believes himself to be: wronged, aggrieved, undervalued, and due a little payback.

Much of the evil done in the world is committed by people who regard themselves in exactly this light. It's a worthy thing, as Lurie observes, to encourage children to stand up for what they believe is right, even when that means defying authority. Still, this doesn't impress me as a lesson of tremendous complexity or ambiguity. By comparison, I see great moral wisdom in suggesting that children ought to examine their own motives at the times they feel most injured and self-righteous. (Many grown-ups would benefit from the same exercise.)

You can, incidentally, absorb this aspect of Lewis's morality without also subscribing to the Christianity that inspired it (just as professing Christianity is certainly no protection against the excesses of self-righteousness). Lewis himself believed in something he called "the Tao," a term he appropriated from the Chinese to refer to what others have called natural law, a set of core values common to "the traditional moralities of East and West, the Christian, the Pagan and the Jew." Some of those values include the keeping of promises, loyalty to clan or country, and the defense of justice. It is the role of an educator to cultivate these principles in his students.

Lewis didn't, however, think that literature was particularly well suited to this job. It did not escape his notice that people who read a lot of good books aren't necessarily the more virtuous for it. In *An Experiment in Criticism,* he wrote that as far as he could tell, the ranks of nonreaders included many individuals who were superior "in psychological health, in moral virtue, practical prudence, good manners, and general adaptability. And we all know very well that we, the literary, include no small percentage of the ignorant, the caddish, the stunted, the warped, and the truculent." What literature could accomplish by way of moral education was less instruction than an expansion of our capacity for empathy: "it admits us to experiences other than our own."

Late in life, speaking on the subject of writing for children, Lewis remarked that asking yourself "What do modern children need?" can never produce a good story. "If we ask that question," he went on, "we are assuming too superior an attitude. It would be better to ask 'What moral do I need?' for I think we can be sure that what does not concern us deeply will not deeply interest our readers, whatever their age. But it is better not to ask the question at all." As the elements of the story emerge from the imagination, "the moral inherent in them will rise from whatever spiritual roots you have succeeded in striking during the whole course of your life."

The moral dilemmas that Edmund and the rest of Lewis's child characters faced were his own. In his early thirties, he wrote to Arthur Greeves, admitting that his great weakness was pride and the rage that possessed him when his ego had been wounded. "The pleasure of anger," he explained, "the gnawing attraction which makes one return again and again to its theme — lives, I believe, in the fact that one feels entirely righteous oneself only when one is angry." It's tempting, once you're in control of a fictional universe of your very own, to "put absolutely all right, with no snags or reservations, on the side of the hero (with whom you identify yourself) and all the wrong on the side of the villain. You thus revel in unearned self-righteousness, which would be vicious even if it were earned." Instead, Lewis wrote a character like Edmund, who when caught playing a nasty trick, indignantly thinks to himself, "I'll pay you all out for this, you pack of stuck-up, self-satisfied prigs."

I didn't for a moment feel lectured to or patronized by the Chronicles as a child. An adult reader, observing a dose of theology being dispensed, might well experience the irritation that most nonbelievers feel toward someone trying to convert them; it's almost impossible to proselytize without condescension. However, what I saw in Edmund was not a representation of original sin but a boy whose one great, terrible mistake had been made up of many littler, unchecked moments of spite and ire that I could easily have indulged in myself. Because I wasn't yet entirely willing to think of Edmund, and everything else in the Chronicles, as merely the invention of one man, I wouldn't have asked myself if he was psychologically convincing; as far as I was concerned, he was *real*. I would not have believed in him so completely, however, if his creator hadn't as well. His flaws were Lewis's flaws; as a moral illustration, he's a confession, not a lecture. We both hoped to be better than Edmund, and sometimes, no doubt, feared we were worse. In that, we were equals.

CHAPTER SIX

Little House in the Big Woods

A decade before he started writing *The Lion, the Witch and the Wardrobe* in earnest, Lewis jotted down the following paragraph on the back of another manuscript:

> This book is about four children whose names were Ann, Martin, Rose and Peter. But it is mostly about Peter who was the youngest. They all had to go away from London suddenly because of the Air Raids, and because Father, who was in the army, had gone off to the war and Mother was doing some kind of war work. They were being sent to stay with a relation of Mother's who was a very old Professor who lived by himself in the country.

By the time this passage blossomed into a real book, Mother and Father had been erased from the opener (the vagueness of "some kind of war work" suggests just how uninteresting Lewis found them both) and the main character among the children, the youngest, had become a girl. This looks like an odd choice for Lewis, an Oxford bachelor who could at least claim that he remembered what it was like to be a little boy, but who knew next to nothing about little girls. (A small group of refugee London children did come to stay at his

Oxford cottage in 1939, but he doesn't seem to have had much to do with them.) Lewis would later give the name Peter to the eldest child among the Pevensie siblings, suggesting that he still felt a connection to that early false start, but the Peter of *The Lion, the Witch and the Wardrobe* is a far more conventional figure than Lucy. And he is not the child the story is "mostly about." Lucy is.

I identified with Lucy, of course, although, when called to, I could also identify with Edmund and Peter. One of the privileges of the girl reader is this flexibility in performing one of the elementary imaginative leaps of reading fiction. Boys, it is said, have difficulty with — or at least are resistant to — stories in which the protagonist is a girl. For the men I know who read the Chronicles when young, Peter and Edmund seem to loom larger in memory than they do for me, just as Aslan seems to be the brightest point for Christians. Nevertheless, it is Lucy who first gets into Narnia, and it is mostly through her eyes that we see the events of the first three books.

Lewis was a younger sibling himself, but only of two, and in spite of the three-year age difference between Warnie and himself, he was the leader of the pair; A. N. Wilson detects a "real forceful bossiness" in the letters Jack wrote to his brother, detailing plans for what the two of them would do during Warnie's holidays from boarding school. That's quite an accomplishment, pulling off a coup against the seniority system that usually prevails in sibling relationships. Perhaps some memory of this feat went into the character of Lucy, who, in the first two Chronicles, is often charged by Aslan with the task of persuading her skeptical brothers and sister to follow her lead. Lucy has a harder time of it than Lewis did, however, and in *Prince Caspian* she has to resort to threatening to strike off into the woods by herself if they won't come with her. "I was closest to Lucy, because she was the youngest," Jonathan Franzen told me. "I was the youngest kid. And nobody listened to her."

Yet Lewis's own biography can never entirely explain why he wound up switching to a girl protagonist after his initial stab at the story. The Chronicles may reflect some fragments of their author's past, but they are substantially fashioned from bits and pieces of other books. The narrator's voice, for example, owes much to the fiction of E. Nesbit, which Lewis loved as a boy. It is in books, as much as in Lewis's own experiences, that the answer to the puzzle of Lucy lies. She is a believable little girl, as all the girl readers who have loved her can attest, but I suspect she began as a strategic solution to a literary problem. And that problem had its roots not in Lewis's sympathy for little girls per se, but in the shortcomings and limitations of his ideas about boys.

Lewis preferred to conduct his intellectual and social life in a world of men, an old-fashioned but not uncommon attitude in a man of his background. Asked to write a short autobiographical paragraph for the American editions of his popular Christian works in 1944, one of the tidbits Lewis chose to offer was this: "There's no sound I like better than adult male laughter." "Masculine" was a word he often used approvingly in his literary criticism; in *The Allegory of Love,* he praised a group of poets for their "clear and masculine thought." Although he had female students and by all accounts treated them kindly, he didn't take them as seriously as the male ones, or at least didn't place them among the first ranks. When, in the late 1920s, he decided to take an English degree at Oxford (in addition to his degree in Greats—which corresponds with what we would call Classics), he wrote sniffily in his diary, "The atmosphere of the English school is very different from that of Greats. Women, Indians, and Americans predominate and—I can't say how—one feels a certain amateurishness in the talk and look of the people."

Women certainly weren't included in Lewis's annual "English binges," at which his male pupils were invited (or, when reluctant, pressured) to get drunk on beer and bellow out "bawdy"—off-color jokes and songs culled from hoary ballads and Old English sources. (Lewis specified that the bawdy be "outrageous and extravagant," although one younger friend characterized the typical example Lewis offered as "very mild.") Lewis Carroll was a meek, socially maladroit don who told stories about a little girl because he found little girls more appealing (and less terrifying) than adults, but C. S. Lewis was the epitome of hearty British masculinity at the time he wrote *The Lion, the Witch and the Wardrobe.* His manner, according to Wilson, got "bluffer and beerier and louder" as the years went on, but this, the biographer insists, was really a "persona," a kind of act Lewis slipped into during middle age. Lewis's bluffness was a mask perfectly adapted to the compartmentalization he had practiced since boyhood, a wall erected against those aspects of life and himself that he preferred to conceal.

Such a man, when writing a children's book, would naturally begin with a boy hero, and that's just what Lewis did. But the boy characters in the Edwardian children's fiction Lewis grew up with didn't have much emotional range. In *The Lion, the Witch and the Wardrobe,* Peter—fair, brave, ethical, judicious, and decisive but not domineering—is an ideal eldest brother in every way, but as a human being he's badly constrained by his role. Writing about Narnia released something free, lyrical, and tender in Lewis, and none of those qualities fit within the limitations of what he would have viewed as an acceptable boy character.

Practically the first thing we learn about Lucy in *The Lion, the Witch and the Wardrobe* is that she is "a little afraid" of the strange-looking professor and easily creeped out by the huge old house with its empty rooms and corridors. This is perfectly understandable in a small girl, but Peter, unless he were very little indeed, would seem a coward if he expressed the same apprehension. Edmund can be afraid—of the White Witch, to give one example—but only when he is playing the quisling. After his reconciliation with Aslan and his siblings, he has to reclaim our admiration; accordingly, he becomes the most valiant warrior at the Battle of Beruna. Lucy, by comparison, can be vulnerable, can even waver at times, without ever coming across as weak; if anything, her courage, when she exhibits it, is all the more commendable because no one expects it of her. She can plead with Mr. Tumnus not to betray her to the witch and comfort him when he bursts into tears at the thought of his own perfidy — all without appearing "soft."

Lewis is not the only storyteller to find that his own investment in conventional masculinity makes a female protagonist the most appealing choice. In her book *Men, Women, and Chainsaws: Gender in the Modern Horror Film,* Carol J. Clover, a professor of Scandinavian and Comparative Literature at the University of California at Berkeley, considers the curious case of the low-budget slasher films of the late twentieth century. These movies, despite their reputation for catering to the misogyny of their predominantly young male audience, almost always featured a particular kind of young woman as the hero. Clover came up with a name for this recurring figure, usually the only member of a group of teenagers to survive the film's ordeals and defeat a supernaturally monstrous antagonist: she is the "Final Girl." Clover writes, "The Final Girl is…a congenial double for the adolescent male." Providing an "identificatory buffer," the Final Girl allows the men in the audience to experience vicariously "taboo" sensations like fear and vulnerability without shame.

Lucy has many of the traits of Clover's Final Girl: innocence, kindness, modesty, unsuspected reserves of strength. Of course, the Chronicles move through a much broader emotional spectrum than a horror film, and at the positive end as well as the negative Lucy can do and feel much more than a traditional boy character. After Edmund has also been through the wardrobe, and Lucy asks him to confirm Narnia's existence to the other two, he spitefully refuses. Lucy runs off in tears. Her brothers and sister pretend not to notice she's been crying (all of Lewis's child characters aspire to a stiff upper lip), but there's no serious humiliation in this, as there would be for a boy who wept, however hurt or angry. It's impossible, too, to imagine Peter or Edmund in the place of Lucy or Susan on the eve of Aslan's death or the morning after, calling him "dear Aslan" and covering him with kisses. Lucy, then, became the vehicle of Lewis's inner life.

The first person Lucy meets once she arrives in Narnia is, despite his goat's legs and horns, essentially a learned bachelor. Mr. Tumnus has always been my favorite Narnian, partly because he was the first Narnian I met, but mostly because of his hospitality. He may be part animal and live in a cave, but his is the coziest home imaginable, with two comfortable chairs ("one for me and one for a friend"), a roaring fire, and a bountifully stocked tea table. Lewis once met a man who suggested that meals in the Chronicles play the same role that sex does in adult fiction — as a kind of titillation cannily used to beguile the child reader. Affronted, Lewis replied that he put a lot of food in the books not to pander to the kiddies but because *he* liked it. He didn't bother to add that at the time he wrote *The Lion, the Witch and the Wardrobe,* postwar rationing and shortages made good meals a rare occurrence in Britain. The Lewis brothers' letters from those years include countless notes sent to Jack's American admirers, fervently thanking them for gifts of ham and sugar.

As soon as they've eaten, Mr. Tumnus begins to tell Lucy stories:

He had wonderful tales to tell of life in the forest. He told about the midnight dances and how the Nymphs who lived in the wells and the Dryads who lived in the trees came out to dance with the Fauns; about long hunting parties after the milk white stag who could give you wishes if you caught him; about feasting and treasure-seeking with the wild Red Dwarfs in deep mines and caverns far beneath the forest floor; and then about summer when the woods were green and old Silenus on his fat donkey would come to visit them, and sometimes Bacchus himself, and then the streams would run with wine instead of water and the whole forest would give itself up to jollification for weeks on end.

People from our world visit Narnia only when something's gone wrong and needs to be fixed: the White Witch has to be overthrown, the Telmarines ejected, the lost prince retrieved from the northern wastes. Rereading the Chronicles as an adult, I realized that my notion of everyday Narnian life as a merry round of festivals and games comes almost entirely from fireside tales like Tumnus's. Even when you're *in* Narnia, the place can be elusive, constructed out of stories about times that are not quite this one. The titles of Tumnus's books — *The Life and Letters of Silenus, Nymphs and Their Ways,* and especially *Men, Monks and Gamekeepers: A Study in Popular Legend*—peg him as a scholar of sorts, but it is his storytelling that makes him the most likely avatar for Lewis in all of the Chronicles.

Hospitality codes, as anyone as conversant with ancient literature as Lewis would have known, are among humanity's oldest and most sacrosanct taboos. There's no possibility that Mr. Tumnus, having invited Lucy into his home and buttered toast with her, could ever have carried out his initial plan to hand her over to the White Witch. But above and beyond that consideration, he does not do it because they have become friends — that theme again. Lewis considered it lamentable that friendship, in the contemporary view, had been almost entirely overshadowed by filial and romantic love: "Very few modern people," he wrote in *The Four Loves,* "think Friendship a love of comparable value or even a love at all."

Perhaps there's no better illustration of this than the 2005 film adaptation of *The Lion, the Witch and the Wardrobe.* Although a large budget and new special effects technologies have finally made it possible to visually approximate Lewis's Narnia, the emotional mechanics of the book had to be fundamentally changed for modern audiences. It's easy to picture the filmmakers puzzling over the adaptation, realizing that, despite Lewis's reputation as a Christian proselytizer, his values don't necessarily mesh well with the American-style piety of Walden Media, the company that produced the film.

Above all, assertions about the preeminence of family feeling had to be inserted. The book dispenses with the "air-raids" in a sentence or two, while the movie lingers over scenes of the Blitz and the siblings' tearful good-byes with the hitherto faceless Mrs. Pevensie. The movie children talk mournfully about being separated from their parents, and Edmund's nasty behavior is made to seem a symptom of his distress at his father's absence. (He almost gets himself killed when he leaves the air-raid shelter to retrieve a photo of Mr. Pevensie in his soldier's uniform.) Instead of lecturing Peter and Susan about Plato when they come to him with their worries about Lucy, Professor Kirk scolds (nonsensically), "You're a family. You might just start acting like one." By my count, the film uses the word "family" in this charged, almost fetishistic fashion over a half-dozen times. In the book, it appears just once, and then only in reference to the lineage of the giant Rumblebuffin, who, Mr. Tumnus informs Lucy, comes from "an old family. With traditions you know."

I noticed this shift in emphasis most in the scene where Lucy leads her brothers and sisters to Tumnus's cave, eager to introduce them to her new friend, only to find his house ransacked and a notice announcing that the faun has been arrested by the White Witch. In Lewis's book, this discovery precipitates a discussion. Susan immediately suggests that they flee back through the wardrobe, and Lucy cries, "Don't you see? We can't just go home, not after this. It is all on my account that the poor Faun has gotten into this trouble. He hid me from the Witch and showed me the way back.... We simply must try to rescue him." After a debate (with Edmund grumbling), the children agree, and even Susan, the most domesticated of the bunch, admits, "I don't want to go a step further and I wish we'd never come. But I think we must try to do something for Mr. Whatever-his-name-is—I mean the Faun." This conversation never happens in the film.

In Lewis's book, what draws the Pevensie siblings further into Narnia is a sense of obligation having everything to do with honor and friendship (and perhaps even that most neglected of Christian virtues, charity), but little to do with "family values." The difference between movie and book becomes even more marked later in the story, when the film tries to portray the children's involvement in the revolt against the White Witch as largely motivated by their desire to rescue Edmund and get back "home." In the book, it never seems to occur to the Pevensies not to do all they can to help Narnia and the Narnians, even if that means fighting in a war. They are in no particularly hurry to get back to England or their parents.

It's not that Lewis didn't cherish family; he would spend much of his adult life living with his brother, after all. However, the Chronicles show his recognition that children hear a powerful call from the outside world, where their destiny ultimately lies. Relationships with friends and the ethics of those relationships are one of childhood's great preoccupations. It was in friendships with Arthur Greeves, Tolkien, and other men that Lewis finally found the kind of community that suited him best. He had a great talent for friendship. In the 1930s, '40s, and '50s, that talent would make him the gravitational center of the Inklings, a group of like-minded men, including Tolkien, who met regularly to talk about literature and to read their own writings aloud.

Although the Eagle and Child pub in Oxford, one of the Inklings' regular hangouts, has become a pilgrimage site for their fans, most of the group's weekly readings (including the first readings of *The Lord of the Rings*) were held in Lewis's rooms at Magdalen College. The rooms, supplied as part of his fellowship at Magdalen, were shabbily but comfortably furnished, and warmed by a coal fireplace. Bookshelves stood against the walls, and on a long, battered table, the Lewis brothers served tea, beer (when they could get it), and delicacies sent by Lewis's readers via the transatlantic post. The snug picture of these friends gathered by the fire, sharing stories that would later captivate readers all over the world, is a key element in the ongoing popular fascination with the Inklings. Humphrey Carpenter, in his eponymous history of the group, devotes an entire chapter to imagining a typical Thursday evening in Lewis's rooms, complete with the lighting of pipes and the chiming of Magdalen's clock tower.

One thing that makes this image so charming to so many readers is its resemblance to that scene by the fire in Mr. Tumnus's nice little cave. The fans would surely be disappointed, then, to learn that none of the Narnia stories were ever read aloud to the Inklings, mostly because Tolkien disliked them. Lewis showed the manuscripts of the books to Roger Lancelyn Green, an expert on children's fiction who would later become one of his biographers, but others among his friends were astonished to learn of the Chronicles' existence. Dom Bede Griffiths, a former pupil at Magdalen who became a Catholic monk and one of Lewis's regular correspondents, told Wilson that he discovered the books only after Lewis's death and marveled to find in them "a power of imaginative invention and insight of which I had no conception before." Griffiths's Lewis had always presented himself as "a plain, honest man with no nonsense about him." So perhaps Tolkien's disapproval is not entirely to blame for the fact that, with respect to the Inklings, Narnia remained Lewis's private concern.

Once again, his life was divided. It could recover its unity only between the covers of a book. The part of Lewis that produced the Chronicles of Narnia was not especially welcome among the Inklings, and while this strikes me as a little sad, it is also not surprising. The Inklings smoked, drank beer, argued philosophy, and subjected one another's work to ungentle criticism. ("Not another fucking elf!" Hugo Dyson famously moaned at the start of one of Tolkien's readings.) There was no place for the likes of Lucy, really, in the bluff, masculine social world Lewis had created for himself. She was, however, more than welcome in Mr. Tumnus's sitting room, and perhaps that's why the picture of them whiling away an afternoon over sardines and sugared cakes feels so extraordinarily gratifying, less like a first meeting than a longed-for reunion. In Narnia, if nowhere else, the little girl and the learned bachelor can sit down together at last.

CHAPTER SEVEN

Through the Looking-Glass

Not long ago, I read a picture book entitled *Andy and the Lion* to my three-year-old friend Desmond. The book, by James Daugherty, retells Aesop's fable of Androcles, a runaway slave who removes a thorn from a wild lion's paw; when Androcles is later captured and condemned to be thrown to the lions, the same beast saves him, and the emperor spares them both as exemplars of friendship. Daugherty recasts the tale as the story of a barefoot American farm boy who helps an escaped circus lion he meets on the way to school. When I got to the part where a whistling Andy nears a turn in the road and notices just the tip of the runaway lion's tail peeping around the corner, Desmond scrambled anxiously to the other end of the sofa and hid behind a cushion. Next, we read Chris Van Allsburg's *The Polar Express,* and at the moment when Santa put his arm around the book's narrator and called for a cheer from the crowd of onlooking children, Desmond sat up straight, radiating pride.

The twins are always reminding me that identification is a primal experience. (Corinne has been known to run right out of the room if a giant or a big bad wolf appears in a story.) What happens to the main character in any book might as well be happening to them, right now, and that makes stories volatile, potent objects that have to be handled carefully when small children are around. What's primal, however, is also primitive. Many writers and critics get annoyed when readers talk about their need to identify with a novel's characters; to them, this seems naive, a crude and reductive way to evaluate art. When a three-year-old identifies so automatically, can we really call it a literary experience?

It's true that for some readers, identification can be a form of narcissism; they want only books in which the characters are slightly improved versions of themselves. They might read nothing but novels about single women looking for mates in the big city, or tales of angry, disaffected young men who refuse to kowtow to the Man. But there's a difference between wanting all stories you read to be about *you* in the most literal sense, and reading with the hope that you can find a bit of yourself in all stories, however alien they may seem on the surface. When our capacity to identify withers, so does a portion of our humanity. What Androcles (or Andy) sees when he comes across the wounded lion is not a dangerous beast, but a fellow creature in pain. Knowing how the thorn must hurt, he pulls it out and bandages the paw. Identification, or sympathy, is the birth of friendship.

To me, Lucy Pevensie was both an alter ego and a clear glass. Through her I could see the action of the first three Chronicles undistorted; her response to everything felt as fresh and natural as a breeze, because it was so close to my own. She is that rare creation, a character who is good without being a prig or a bore. Her virtues are a kind of reflex or second nature, and her spirit—sincere, blithe, playful, trusty, warm—is so in tune with Narnia itself, that she is almost instantly at home there.

Even today I find it hard to secure any perspective on her. "Lucy goes straight to your heart," Neil Gaiman observes, and once she is ensconced there, it's impossible to step far enough away from her to take her in. Upon first hearing the name of Aslan in the Beavers' house, each of the four children has a distinct reaction. Edmund, naturally, feels horribly guilty, Peter feels brave, and Susan experiences an almost sensuous pleasure, "as if a delicious smell or some delightful strain of music had just floated by." Lucy gets "the feeling you have when you wake up in the morning and realize that it is the beginning of the holidays or the beginning of summer." Hers is a child's excitement, "your" excitement, as the passage explicitly puts it. And the sensation Lewis describes, that flush of freedom on the first day of summer vacation: Is there any child who doesn't know exactly how that feels? Or any adult who doesn't try to recreate it during the pitifully brief holidays we get from our working lives?

As much as I wanted to be Lucy Pevensie, I also wanted to be her friend. I thought I'd do a much better job of it than Marjorie Preston, who makes a cameo appearance in *The Voyage of the Dawn Treader.* Alone in the magician's house, reading her way through his big book of spells, Lucy finds herself tempted to use a charm that will "maketh beautiful her that uttereth it beyond the lot of mortals." (This is a particularly appealing prospect given that in this depart-ment she feels overshadowed by Susan.) Although the illustrations accompanying the spell suggest that its results will be destructive, and Lucy's own better judgment warns her against it, the only thing that really stops her is the sudden apparition of Aslan's disapprov-ing face. Turning the page, Lucy comes upon a charm that allows you to know what your friends think of you, and she resolves that this magic, at least, she ought to be able to try. After she recites the spell, the pictures on the page begin to move, showing her Marjo-rie, a friend from last term at school, bad-mouthing Lucy to a more popular girl.

Lucy has been sent into the magician's house to search his book for an anti-invisibility spell; after she recites it, Aslan appears. He re-proaches Lucy for spying on Marjorie, and tells her that her friend didn't really mean what she said: "She is weak, but she loves you." In spite of this, they both agree that Lucy will never be able to forget what she heard the girl say, and something precious has been lost. "Have I spoiled everything?" Lucy asks Aslan. "Do you mean we would have gone on being friends if it hadn't been for this—and been really great friends—all our lives perhaps—and now we never shall."

I thought of this scene decades after I first read it, during a screening of Ingmar Bergman's *Persona*. One of the film's characters, a nurse who has befriended the actress she has been tending, surreptitiously reads one of the actress's letters to her doctor. In the letter, she finds a patronizing description of herself. Enraged, the nurse confronts her charge, accusing the actress of an inability to love anyone, even her own son, and thus precipitates a wrenching dislocation, signaled by one of the great montages of experimental cinema. For Bergman, the reading of the letter (a variety of eavesdropping that also turns up in his film *Through a Glass Darkly*) flushes the truth about the actress's inner life out into the open; it's assumed—naively, really—that she wouldn't misrepresent her feelings in a letter to her doctor. In *The Voyage of the Dawn Treader,* the result is a little more complicated.

Persona is a film about permeable, fluid identities (at one point, images of the faces of the two women fuse), overflowing the barriers between individuals. Lewis's vignette implies that true friendship depends on the maintenance of those boundaries. That Lewis would champion privacy is no surprise, but there's more to the Marjorie Preston incident than a simple admonishment against eavesdropping. Aslan's remarks about Marjorie's love for Lucy serve as a reminder that people employ personas in all sorts of situations; we shouldn't necessarily assume that what our friends say when we're not around is more truthful than what they say to our faces. This is a particularly valuable bit of wisdom for schoolgirls (though how Lewis could have known this, I can't imagine), who are all too prone to the conviction that they've merged with their best friends—and therefore all too susceptible to feeling betrayed when this belief turns out to be an illusion.

The Voyage of the Dawn Treader includes another passage about friendship, one of my favorites in all of the Chronicles. It comes late in the journey, as the ship sails through waters of preternatural clarity near the edge of the world. Lucy has been leaning over the side, puzzled by "a little black object, about the size of a shoe" racing along after the ship, getting bigger or smaller in the wink of an eye; this she soon realizes is the shadow the ship casts on the bottom of the sea. Then she watches as the *Dawn Treader* and its shadow pass over a city of merpeople and a hunting party led by a warlike king who shakes his spear at them. As the ship glides past the outskirts of this submarine nation, Lucy spots one last sea person, "a quiet, lonely-looking girl with a sort of crook in her hand," who seems to be a "fish-herdess."

> The girl looked up and stared straight into Lucy's face. Neither could speak to the other and in a moment the Sea Girl dropped astern. But Lucy will never forget her face. It did not look frightened or angry like those of the other Sea People. Lucy had liked that girl and she felt certain the girl had liked her. In that one moment they had somehow become friends. There does not seem to be much chance of their meeting again in that world or any other. But if ever they do they will rush together with their hands held out.

Here is the bookend to the sad story of Lucy Pevensie and Marjorie Preston, one friendship lost to the desire for too much knowledge contrasted with another friendship cemented in the absence of any knowledge at all. Lucy's encounter with the sea girl is romantic, an emotional flourish set off by passages of radiant description, but that doesn't make it untrue. If we believe in love at first sight, and friendship is a form of love, why shouldn't we be able to recognize a friend at first sight, too? Aren't some of the most enduring childhood bonds formed in just a few moments on a sidewalk or a playground? Needless to say, at eight I was convinced that I, too, would have befriended that sea girl in a single glance.

Lucy's connection with the sea girl is a matter of faith—the earthly, humanist kind—and faith is precisely what she lacks when she listens in on Marjorie's conversation. What motivates her to recite the spell is not curiosity about Marjorie, but the egotism of insecurity. Lucy eavesdrops on her friend for the same reason that the nurse reads the actress's letter in *Persona*: because she's seeking her own reflection. She's dying to know what other people think of her and hoping that what they say will be flattering. (A lot of snooping comes down to not much more than that.) *Persona* is an indictment of the actress's narcissism, but I've always been a little disappointed that the nurse doesn't come in for the same degree of stern scrutiny.

If Lucy was anything like me (and I was sure she was), then she wanted to know everything about that lonely-looking sea girl: where she lived, what her parents were like, how she kept her fish herd in tow, and what she wanted to be when she grew up. This is an entirely different sort of curiosity from the kind that craves assurances of other people's good opinion. Lucy's faith in her friendship with the sea girl is a leap of the imagination, a belief that however different they might seem, she and the sea girl must have something important to share.

It is also a reader's faith, and it is omnivorous. As Lewis wrote in *An Experiment in Criticism*:

The man who is contented to be only himself, and therefore less a self, is in prison. My own eyes are not enough for me, I will see through those of others. Reality, even seen through the eyes of many, is not enough. I will see what others have invented. Even the eyes of all humanity are not enough. I regret that the brutes cannot write books. Very gladly would I learn what face things present to a mouse or a bee; more gladly still would I perceive the olfactory world charged with all the information and emotion it carries for a dog. Literary experience heals the wound, without undermining the privilege, of individuality... in reading great literature I become a thousand men and yet remain myself. Like the night sky in the Greek poem, I see with a myriad eyes, but it is still I who see. Here, as in worship, in love, in moral action, and in knowing, I transcend myself; and am never more myself than when I do.

The characters in books can never really be our friends because as much as we might learn about them, they can never know anything about us. Still, they exercise our capacity for empathy, extending it beyond the boundaries of race, gender, species, even virtue. Readers will sometimes blame a morally objectionable main character for a novel's failure to engage them; really, the fault lies with the author's inability to make us stop quibbling about such things. If characters had to be admirable or even likeable to captivate us, then Humbert Humbert and Scarlett O'Hara would not be people you recognize without my having to explain which novels they come from.

Lewis, for example, makes us feel sorry for Eustace Scrubb, who is just about the most insufferable boy in the world before his transformation on Dragon Island in *The Voyage of the Dawn Treader*. Even the slave traders on the island of Doorn are reduced to offering him as a free gift with purchase, and still they get no takers. Eustace's penchant for the wrong kind of books is once again part of his problem. His habit of reading practical nonfiction renders him blind to his companions and even to his surroundings. One of the funniest bits in the Chronicles is Eustace's preconversion shipboard diary, a crafty litany of excuses, rationalizations, self-justifications, and outright whining that makes it abundantly clear just how miserable it is not only to be around him, but to *be* him. Eustace simply can't see the *Dawn Treader* as Lucy does—"a beauty of her kind, a 'lady' as sailors say, her lines perfect, her colors pure and every spar and rope and pin lovingly made." In his eyes, the ship is "a rotten little tub," bereft of both wireless and stateroom.

Nevertheless, Eustace's diary does succeed at slipping us into this unfortunate boy's head. Somewhere along the way, as Eustace sneaks off to avoid doing his share of the work on Dragon Island, then finds himself hideously transformed, he snags our sympathy. Rendered enormous, scaly, and fire-breathing, he enjoys a few moments of reveling in his terrible new power before realizing that he'd much rather "get back among humans and talk and laugh and share things." His reform begins only when he resembles on the outside the monster that he's long been on the inside, and realizes what an "unmitigated nuisance" he's been to the others from the start.

Fixing Eustace requires divine intervention, so severe is his inability to put himself in anyone else's place. My condition was not so remedial; after all, like Lucy, I had read the right books and instantly appreciated the *Dawn Treader* for the marvel she was. Simply reading about Lucy—her compassion, modesty, and generosity—probably improved me, a child not richly endowed with any of those qualities. It wasn't that I wanted to be good for the sake of being good, or even to please Aslan; it was that I could see how Lucy's way of being good was the opposite of Eustace's awfulness. It made her happier, and drew her closer to other people. I hoped that I was already a lot like Lucy, but I was inclined to try to be more so mostly because I loved her. Like the sea girl, she inhabited another, unreachable world, but we would have been the best of friends if we ever met, I was sure of it.

Part Two

Trouble in Paradise

CHAPTER EIGHT

Forests and Trees

Mrs. Belden may not have been able to get much out of me about my revelatory first encounter with *The Lion, the Witch and the Wardrobe,* but she learned enough to assure her that I'd missed the book's religious symbolism. Adults marvel that this subtext, so glaringly obvious to us, is invisible to children. Children, after all, are usually adept at discovering most of the things we try to hide from them: profanity, sharp objects, Christmas presents, preferences for one child over another.

But children are literalists: they lack not only the cognitive skills but also the sheer bulk of information it takes to formulate abstractions and recognize general patterns. They think in specifics, of the concrete, tactile reality they encounter every day. As Philip Pullman, the author of His Dark Materials, an epic and intellectually demanding fantasy trilogy for children, is wont to say, "Children are not less intelligent than adults; what they are is less informed." Sometimes they do not see the forest because they're still getting acquainted with the trees. Once, when my three-year-old friend Corinne and I were reading a book about the ocean, we came upon a painting of a blue whale.

"This is very high up," she informed me, pointing at the whale.
"It is?" I replied.

"It's very, very high," she explained patiently. "Sadie really likes it."

Sadie is her babysitter, and like many people caring for little children in Manhattan, she has only a few places to take Corinne and her brother on rainy days. One of those places is the American Museum of Natural History on West 79th Street, and in the vast Milstein Hall of Ocean Life, where toddlers are allowed to run around loose, there is a life-size model of a blue whale hanging from the ceiling. When I looked at the picture in the book, I thought "blue whale," summoning up a generalization, a typical blue whale distilled from everything I know about the creatures, including the fact that they live in the ocean, which is "down." When Corinne looked at the picture she had one memory to call upon, the only representation of a blue whale that she had ever seen before. She thought not of blue whales in general, but of one whale in particular. And that whale is very high up.

Corinne and I were both correct; we simply read the image in the book differently. I saw a reference to a concept, and she saw a depiction of a familiar thing. Soon, as she gathers more data, Corinne will learn to look at the museum's whale model and see it as a representation of an animal that lives down in the sea, even if this particular representation is suspended from the ceiling in a room full of dioramas. She'll recognize that the high-up-ness of the model is an irrelevant (if cool) detail, while its color and size are telling her something meaningful about the animal it stands for. Eventually, though not for many years, she'll learn to apply the same sort of understanding to more sophisticated artifacts, like stories.

To someone who has heard and read many stories about the self-sacrifice of god-kings or other saintly heroes who suffer for the salvation of others, Aslan is obviously an analog of Christ. But to someone who is still encountering instances of the great themes of Western culture for the first time, Aslan cannot be Jesus because Jesus is a bearded man in sandals and robe, while Aslan is a lion. We shouldn't, however, mistake the less-experienced reader's interpretation as simply wrong; *Corinne's* whale was in fact very high up, and Jesus *was* a bearded man in sandals. If not being able to see the forest for the trees is one kind of blindness, so is not being able to see the trees for the forest. When Corinne was even younger, sitting in her stroller in a parking lot, she began to repeat the word "bubbles" to her mystified parents. Nowhere around them could they see any bubbles, and besides, the baby was pointing to a car. Then they noticed that it had rained while they were inside the store, and that the drops of rainwater that beaded up on the smooth surfaces of the car looked just like bubbles. Once we learn to see things with the idea that they belong to a particular category, we're in danger of missing all the qualities they share with things in other categories, not to mention all the qualities that are theirs alone. What's in front of our noses can become invisible to us if we can't fit it into one of the frameworks we have set up for understanding the world and ourselves. Sometimes the "irrelevant" facts we screen out are poetic as well as physical (like the similarity between drops of rainwater and bubbles) and occasionally they're crucial. There's an Agatha Christie novel, *Hercule Poirot's Christmas,* in which the solution hinges on the fact that what several characters have described as a "bit of red rubber" is actually two different things; the murderer has substituted an innocuous rubber object for the deflated balloon that was evidence of his crime. Both ways of thinking—the generalized and the concrete, the deep and the broad—can be powerful, and both are limited. If we want to understand the world around us more completely, we need to keep both methods in play.

All this is by way of saying that the child readers of *The Lion, the Witch and the Wardrobe* who do not recognize its parallels to the biblical story of the Crucifixion and the Resurrection are not necessarily mistaken. Our particular, immediate experience of something is as true as the conclusions we reach after we have sorted all the details, figured out which ones match a pattern we've observed before, and discarded the rest. To me, the fact that Aslan was a real, material, warm, and furry lion was as important as the fact that he died and was brought back to life. It was even more important, really, since death wasn't especially interesting to me, and animals were.

In his youth, Lewis lost what faith he had had as a small boy. Explaining this estrangement in later years, he wrote, "The externals of Christianity made no appeal to my sense of beauty. Oriental imagery and style largely repelled me; and for the rest, Christianity was mainly associated for me with ugly architecture, ugly music, and bad poetry." When, as an adult, he decided to embed a Christian message in *The Lion, the Witch and the Wardrobe,* his plan was to strip the theme of Christianity's unattractive "externals," its "stained-glass and Sunday School associations," in hope that his young readers would then perceive these themes "in their real potency."

Lewis didn't intend his audience to recognize what he was doing, or at least not right away. In an essay titled "Sometimes Fairy Stories May Say Best What's to Be Said," he described this plan as an attempt to elude the defenses readers set up against authors and stories that aim to teach them something for their own good. He wanted, as he memorably phrased it, to "steal past those watchful dragons."

Yet it's worth asking whether the stained-glass and Sunday school associations aren't as much a part of Christianity as the mystical Resurrection of Christ, even if they aren't supposed to be as important a part. Is a religion a great story about the meaning of life or a daily practice, or is it perhaps something else — a collection of icons? Although, doctrinally speaking, accepting Jesus Christ as one's lord and savior is the key act of Christian conversion, many Christians seem to believe that going to church and abiding by a list of detailed restrictions are just as important.

For Lewis's friend J. R. R. Tolkien, a Roman Catholic, such practices as taking Communion and making confession were as central to his religion as its core metaphysical beliefs, if not more so. Lewis participated in similar rites, but primarily regarded his faith as an object of contemplation and analysis. Religions are forever being pulled in one direction or the other. Islam was originally intended to be a streamlined faith, asking only five simple, practical duties from believers: acknowledgment of Allah as God, prayer five times daily, charity, pilgrimage to Mecca, and fasting through Ramadan—the "five pillars of Islam." Over time, this minimalist architecture was embellished. Visionaries and clerics developed variations, such as the mystical philosophical tradition of Sufism or those elaborate lists of rules about veils, dancing, and kite flying, rules that some believers now consider essential enough to kill or die for.

In her book *The Battle for God,* the scholar Karen Armstrong writes of the indivisibility of belief and rite in ancient religions: "Myth only became a reality when it was embodied in cult, rituals, and ceremonies, which worked aesthetically upon worshipers, evoking within them a sense of sacred significance and enabling them to apprehend the deeper currents of existence." The sacrament of the Eucharist is one such rite. Holy Communion allows worshippers to act out and mystically embody the story of Jesus feeding transubstantiated bread and wine to his followers. The ritual is essential; religion is as much something you *do* as something you *believe.* It's also something you paint and carve; the "externals" of a faith include everything from the bowls of holy water and statues in a church to the hymns sung and the devotional art and shrines that believers keep in their homes. How can these be separated from the "real potency" of a faith's myths, any more than the ritual service of bread and wine to communicants can be separated from the metaphysical import of the Last Supper?

So when Lewis's child readers don't see Christianity in the Chronicles, they are in fact perceiving a truth about Narnia that adults usually miss. The Christianity in Narnia has been substantially, rather than just superficially, transformed—to the point of being much less Christian, perhaps, than Lewis intended. In his essay "On Stories," Lewis describes a conversation he once had with "an intelligent American pupil," who remembered being thrilled by a scene in a Fenimore Cooper story in which the sleeping hero is stalked by an Indian brave. To Lewis's surprise, the student remarked that he would have been just as excited if the villain were "a crook with a revolver," sneaking up on a twentieth-century version of Natty Bumppo. Not so Lewis: "Take away the feathers, the high cheek-bones, the whiskered trousers, substitute a pistol for a tomahawk, and what would be left? For I wanted not the momentary suspense but that whole world to which it belonged—the snow and the snow-shoes, beavers and canoes, war-paths and wigwams, and Hiawatha names." Without those trappings, it was not the same story at all.

It would never have occurred to me to liken Narnia to the Roman Catholicism in which I was raised. They were as different as cheese and chalk. And despite Lewis's own lifelong uneasiness with Catholicism, his High Church Anglicanism was not so very different from it, a fact which struck me when I stood in the chapel at Magdalen College in Oxford, a place where Lewis prayed almost every day after his conversion in 1931. In that room, I felt almost materially transported back to the church where I took my first Communion. My church called its weekly classes "catechism," instead of "Sunday School," and we attended it on Tuesdays, but we had the very same stained-glass windows and candles flickering in little wells of red and blue glass.

Ours was a mild form of Catholicism—so mild, in fact, that you could say it was almost Anglican. These were the years during and just after Vatican II; if I dig deeply enough, I have very dim memories of hearing Mass conducted in Latin. When I was still small, however, we switched to a progressively minded parish more in line with the leanings of my Kennedy Democrat parents. In our new church, Sacred Heart, youthful nuns played guitars during folk mass and no one talked about martyred saints. No crucifixes hung on our walls at home and I barely knew who the pope was. I knew the name of our parish priest (all I can remember about him now is that he had a glass eye), but we didn't socialize with him and he certainly never came to our house. The first time I encountered a truly gruesome image of the bloodied, tortured Christ was at the local art museum, where a Spanish painting of Jesus with rolling eyes, crown of thorns, and gore dripping down his face so terrified me I was afraid to venture back into the building for years. (Even today I experience a twinge of dread whenever I pass it.)

Nevertheless, I was raised in the Catholic Church and confirmed in the faith at the age of thirteen. In catechism classes we learned about sin, about obedience to authority, and about the necessity of the sacraments to the salvation of our eternal souls. My family's strain of vaguely Scottish Catholicism put a particular emphasis on self-denial. I can remember a conversation with my grandmother before church about the possibility of my putting part of my allowance into the collection plate; it wouldn't really count, she informed me, unless I gave all of it. Otherwise, it wouldn't be a sacrifice. Most of the things required of me by my religion—church attendance and participation in other dull ceremonies, fasting before taking Communion, giving up various pleasures for Lent—persuaded me that unhappiness was next to godliness and that virtue was consolidated by suffering.

Traditionally, the Catholic Church doesn't encourage independent study of the Bible, but we did read the New Testament in catechism. (The Old Testament I wouldn't read until I got to college.) Children believe what adults tell them as a matter of course, and so I suppose I considered the stories in the Gospels to be "true." But did I ever really believe in the Christian God? When I consider the profound, passionate faith of Lewis and other real Christians, I can't honestly say that I did. Certainly, I never believed in Christianity as fully as I believed in Narnia, and this was largely because Christianity as I knew it offered such a drab, grinding, joyless view of life. Perhaps this was a failing of my teachers, but I saw our religion primarily as a body of onerous rules and red tape, like a secular code of law, or interstate commerce regulations. And so, with the determination of a corporate tax attorney, I set about discovering how those rules could be gotten around.

At first, I searched for loopholes, but the Catholic Church had had almost two thousand years to anticipate this very tactic, and my eight-year-old's ingenuity was overmatched. I was impressed to learn that the Church had already worked out a policy on sins that were interrupted by forces beyond the sinner's control (guilty!). Doctrine, surprisingly enough, turned out to be much more vulnerable to full-frontal attacks on its moral legitimacy. The fate allotted to newborn babies and other blameless people who die without the chance to be baptized turned out to be the ideal test case for my personal campaign to invalidate the authority of the Church. Why, I demanded of the nun teaching our catechism class, should innocents be condemned to Limbo simply because of an accident of birth or misfortune?

On the day we discussed the exclusion of unbaptized babies from heaven, I was only one among several children who protested. The nun replied with a boilerplate defense of the sacraments; these were the rituals that God required, administered by the one true Church, for the eternal salvation of our souls. But, we replied, he was God, wasn't he, and if he couldn't be expected to make exceptions to his own laws, couldn't he have come up with a system that wasn't so manifestly unfair?

There was a whiff of desperate improvisation in the whole idea of Limbo, I remember thinking. It had so obviously been cooked up as an afterthought because someone hadn't properly worked through the baptism rule. Limbo was a quick and dirty fix, and if God really were responsible for this mess, he could hardly be as wise or as loving as the Church made him out to be. On the other hand, if (as seemed likely) it was really human beings who'd come up with the sacrament system, then who was to say that human beings hadn't invented all of Catholic doctrine?

Skepticism, like faith, is more a matter of temperament than indoctrination. Any one of a half-dozen serious flaws in any theological worldview can undermine the beliefs of someone who doesn't much want to believe in the first place. (One man I know says his moment of disillusionment came when he looked at a map depicting the distribution of all the world's religions and realized that which one you belonged to depends more on where you were born than on the irresistibility of divine revelation.) On the day we discussed Limbo in catechism, I was already looking for an out. The sacrifice of Jesus had not impressed me as especially meaningful or moving. The tedium of Sunday Mass had not become any more endurable with age and an English liturgy. I hated church. I bridled at the ritual of confession and was suspicious of the idea of original sin. Above all, I was bored by all the stories of men in beards and sandals endlessly gabbing on about mustard seeds, fishes, and vineyards.

In short, I was a lot like Lewis as a child, and in more ways than one. He disliked the trappings of his father's faith, but he also resisted it out of what he later called "my deep-seated hatred of authority, my monstrous individualism, my lawlessness." We are each the product of different nations and historical moments, however. The individualism Lewis calls "monstrous" is a quality Americans admire, and no more so than in the 1960s and '70s, when I was a kid. I grew up with a lot of ambient encouragement to rebel against authority, and with few incentives to reconcile myself to a hidebound institution like the Catholic Church.

While the Narnians' obedience to Aslan irks some adult readers, for me it was essentially different from the docility demanded by the Church. First and foremost it wasn't founded on self-denial. The Narnians did as Aslan asked because he was strong, kind, warm, and lovable, and because his requests always led to that most desirable of ends: the continuation of Narnia as it should be, the most wonderful country imaginable. Christianity instructed me to comply with a list of dreary, legalistic demands because Jesus, whom I had never met, reportedly loved me and had redeemed me from the guilt of a sin I had never committed by dying before I was even born. The proof of his love was his suffering; I owed him, and he expected to be paid in kind. Narnia and Aslan made me happy. Jesus wanted me to be miserable.

Perhaps most important, however, I shared with Lewis the book-ish child's stubborn insistence on retaining some ultimate privacy. I did not take kindly to being told how to think and feel in my deep-est self; the order to love God whether I liked him or not made me dig in my heels. Wrote Lewis, "I wanted some area, however small, of which I could say to all other beings, 'This is my business and mine only.'" For me that sanctum was Narnia, and Narnia was so incompatible with my understanding of Christianity that it never would have occurred to me to connect the two.

Narnia was the transport Lucy experiences when Mr. Beaver first mentions Aslan's name, "the feeling you have when you wake up in the morning and realize that it is the beginning of the holidays or the beginning of summer." Narnia was liberation and delight. Chris-tianity was boredom, subjugation, and reproach. For all the simi-larities between *The Lion, the Witch and the Wardrobe* and the New Testament, and for all Lewis's evangelical intentions, I don't think I was that grievously mistaken. The Christianity that I knew — the only Christianity I was aware of — was the opposite of Narnia in both aesthetics and spirit. More than just opposite, really, since the Church was a major part of the lackluster world I sought refuge from in Lewis's books. For me, Narnia was Christianity's antidote.

CHAPTER NINE

The Awful Truth

B y the time I turned thirteen, I'd become pretty adept at searching out my kind of book — the ones "with magic" — at the
local branch library. An enormous, musty-smelling used bookstore
downtown, the shrine at the end of an hour-long pilgrimage by bus,
had a more promising selection, but it was less organized and more
difficult to plumb. I was always on the lookout for clues that might
lead me to further treasure.

On my own, I'd discovered Ursula K. Le Guin's Earthsea Trilogy
and Lloyd Alexander's Chronicles of Prydain. Cheap paperbacks with
dragons and unicorns printed on their covers began to appear on the
racks at our neighborhood newsstand. Among them I found a book
with a strange cover illustration. Against a background of leaves and
flowers was an opening shaped like a woman's head and neck, revealing a vista with a castle, a knight in armor crossing a bridge, and a
unicorn. The unicorn and the arch of the bridge formed the woman's
eyes, a butterfly was her nose, and for a mouth she had...a mouth,
floating in midair. The picture was both pretty and creepy, evocative
of the alarming hallucinatory art of the hippies who had settled in our
beachside neighborhood. The book was called *Imaginary Worlds*.

Lin Carter, author of *Imaginary Worlds,* was a novelist who served
as editorial consultant for the Ballantine Adult Fantasy series, the

publishing imprint responsible for most of the dragon- and unicorn-bedecked paperbacks I'd seen at the local newsstand. But *Imaginary Worlds* was not itself a novel; it was a history of fantasy, a genre that had only just been so identified, on the heels of the success of *The Lord of the Rings*. Carter, one of those inexhaustible autodidacts who flourish at the margins of American culture, wanted to inform all the bright-eyed, Johnny-come-lately Tolkien buffs that a long tradition of "imaginary-world romance" had preceded the Oxford professor's trilogy; Ballantine hoped to capitalize on their hunger for more.

Imaginary Worlds was the first literary criticism I ever read. It was exciting to learn that a label had been devised for the sort of stories I liked, but *Imaginary Worlds* left me unsatisfied for a couple of reasons. Carter was not himself a particularly good writer, and he enthused over books that even I could tell were mediocre, notably the sword-and-sorcery pulp genre founded by Robert E. Howard, who created Conan the barbarian. Strangest of all, I had never before had the experience of reading someone else's calm, equable opinions of stories that felt as though they were written on my own heart.

People read criticism of works they already know well because they hope to expand their understanding, perhaps even to relive the experience through someone else. Great critics show us new dimensions of a book or a film, but they also articulate what it feels like to encounter the work, a sensation many of us can't adequately capture on our own. *Imaginary Worlds* didn't do much of either for me. On a less exalted level, however, there's always the juvenile gratification of seeing a book you love (or hate) being praised (or denounced) by a writer who is swathed in the authority of print, a pleasure I've never managed to outgrow even though by now I really ought to know better. I kept reading *Imaginary Worlds* partly for leads to other books, but also because I wanted to see Lewis and the Chronicles celebrated by someone, a *real author,* more important than myself.

What I discovered instead was that Aslan's death in *The Lion, the Witch and the Wardrobe* was really a "blatantly symbolic Crucifixion-

and-Resurrection scene," which Carter deemed "beautifully and simply written" but "very out of place on these pages." His criticism troubled me less than the revelation itself. Lewis, Carter explained, was famously Christian, a fact I'd somehow managed to miss. I was shocked, almost nauseated. I'd been tricked, cheated, betrayed. I went over the rest of the Chronicles, and in almost every one found some element that lined up with this unwelcome and, to me, ulterior meaning. I felt like a character in one of those surreal, existential 1960s TV dramas, like *The Prisoner* or *The Twilight Zone,* a captive who pulls off a daring escape from his cell only to find himself inside another, larger cell identical to the first.

Here was a moment of truth. If the Chronicles had worked according to Lewis's plans, and in the way many of his Christian admirers believe them to, I would have reassessed my attitude toward my religion. I would have realized that Narnia and Aslan represented another face of Christianity, a better one than the Church had ever shown me, and that in turn would lead me back to the faith. "This was the very reason why you were brought to Narnia," Aslan explains to Edmund and Lucy at the end of *The Voyage of the Dawn Treader,* in a scene whose heavy-handed imagery (a lamb, a meal of fish) had gone utterly over my head, "that by knowing me here for a little, you may know me better there."

Can a book win over a soul who is fundamentally disinclined to believe? If any books could have persuaded me, it would have been these, yet I didn't budge. Lewis makes a great deal, in *Surprised by Joy,* of having been "the most dejected and reluctant convert in all England" when, in his rooms at Magdalen in 1929, he realized that he really *did* believe in God, after all. He was, he insists, dragged through that portal "kicking, struggling, resentful, and darting [my] eyes in every direction for a chance of escape."

This strikes me as a case of protesting too much, for as A. N. Wilson has pointed out, myriad factors in Lewis's life and environment had long been pushing him back to the Church. Lewis himself half admits as much when he writes, also in *Surprised by Joy,* that "everything and everyone had joined the other side." His closest friends were all Christians; the writers he admired were Christians; the medievalism he found so appealing was saturated with the stuff.

Why the Chronicles didn't "work" as intended on me is a tricky question. I was, of course, young and on the verge of the most rebellious and discontented stage of life, rather than just settling into a life well suited to me, as Lewis was when he converted. But there is, I believe, more to it than that. I lacked—and still lack—the disposition to believe. Like Lewis, I hankered after the ineffable and the sublime, but the story of Jesus had never spoken to that part of my imagination. Christianity was too monolithic, comprehensive, and established. Temperamentally, I preferred uncertainty, slippery boundaries, little neglected corners of the world where magic lurked unnoticed, and strangeness.

To me, the universe didn't require much explaining. Although I wouldn't read Keats until much later, I was already inclined toward what he called "Negative Capability…capable of being in uncertainties, Mysteries, doubts without any irritable reaching after fact & reason." Unlike Lewis, I hadn't lost my mother as a child, and I wasn't left hungering for an enfolding, benevolent protector and redeemer. I didn't know death and loss well enough to need the reassurance of an afterlife. For these and no doubt other reasons I was and am very different from Lewis; I've never found a good reason to believe, while he was a man who ran out of reasons not to.

If the Chronicles were not going to save Christianity for me, Lewis's duplicity (as I saw it) was certainly capable of contaminating Narnia. He had hoped that his child readers, as they got older, would eventually come to see Narnia as filled with Christian meaning; perhaps he even hoped that Christianity might be enriched by Narnia's magic (though he would never have permitted himself the vanity of suggesting as much). Possibly, if my early experiences of the religion had been better, I would have reacted to my discovery of the books' "secret" significance with no more than a shrug. But for me, Christianity worked like a black hole, sucking all the beauty and wonder out of Narnia the moment the two came into imaginative contact. I was furious, but I was also bereft; I'd lost something infinitely precious to me.

Lewis was fond of repeating a conversation that he'd once had with Tolkien, on an occasion when they were grumbling about having their literary interests labeled as escapist. "What class of men," Tolkien asked, "would you expect to be most preoccupied with, and most hostile to, the idea of escape?" The response, also provided by Tolkien, was "jailers." Tolkien, even more than Lewis, thought it was only natural to want to flee a world increasingly dominated by industry, science, capitalism, modernism, and secularism. Religion, for these men, meant hewing to the good old ways.

I, too, longed for escape, but as I saw it, Christianity was one of the jailers. *The Lion, the Witch and the Wardrobe* seemed to promise another, better world, one that was wild, merry, enchanted, boundless. And when I could no longer kid myself that Narnia actually existed, it remained the province of my imagination where I felt the most free. What Lin Carter told me about Aslan and Jesus ruined even that.

I recently ordered a used copy of *Imaginary Worlds* online, and when the book arrived, I had to look twice at its publication date. There's no possibility that I could have read the book before my thirteenth birthday. Had it really taken me so long to learn the truth? This got me wondering about the readers who'd responded to my *Salon* essay on *The Lion, the Witch and the Wardrobe*, and about the writers I'd met over the years who'd mentioned the Chronicles as an early influence. When had *they* found out about the Christian symbolism in Narnia, and how did they react?

One correspondent I'd never forgotten was Pam Marks, who'd written to tell me how much she'd loved the Chronicles when she was growing up in one of the few Jewish families in a small English village in the 1950s. I decided to telephone her to ask how she'd responded to the Christian element in Narnia.

Pam's family wasn't religious, so for her being Jewish meant little more than occasionally feeling like an outsider. "In England," she told me, "you had to sing Christian songs in school: 'Away in the manger no crib for his bed, the little Lord Jesus lay down his sweet head.' I wasn't too sure about *that,* so I asked my mother, and she said, 'Well, when you come to that part, just don't say the word "Jesus." ' "

As Pam saw it, her real problem was not Christians, but her father, "a harsh disciplinarian, very. He believed in obedience. He thought that I had way too much spirit and that he could beat it out of me." When they were alone together, her mother would tell Pam that she thought the punishments were unjustified, but she never spoke up against them when her husband was around. For Pam, the moment in *The Lion, the Witch and the Wardrobe* when Edmund betrays Lucy by telling Peter and Susan that he hasn't been to Narnia after all was particularly piercing.

"I wanted a place where there was fairness and understanding," she said. "There wasn't that in my life. It's not like I had an adult I could go to, getting through that childhood. When a child is mistreated and told that it's because they're bad, they're left to either think that they're bad or that their parents are extremely cruel and they're victims. That becomes such a conflict that there becomes a great need to understand the nature of right and wrong, more so than with other children. And those books really talked about that."

"When did you realize that there was a Christian subtext to the books?"

"When I read *The Last Battle,* once I understood that line about the stable that was bigger inside than outside. [Lucy makes a remark about a stable "that once had something inside it that was bigger than our whole world."] That line really upset me."

"Did you go back and read the earlier books after that? And did the lightbulb light up then?"

"I'd already reread them many times, but yes, I did go back, and I saw it completely."

"How did you feel about it?"

"I felt betrayed. But then, not too long after that, I decided, Well, I don't really care what he was trying to do there, this is what I get out of it. Those books communicated really deep, why-we-are-here, life-and-death concepts to me. And I think I perceived even then that they were universal symbols. I had a feeling about the characters and about the writing. Even though I'd never read any of it before, it was as if I knew it. The rhythms of the language and the characters, it was as if I knew them all before I read them."

"So you felt that there were currents in the books that transcended any particular religion?"

"Absolutely. I still do."

For Pam, then, it was indeed possible to see past "stained-glass and Sunday School associations" to the "real potency" of the Chronicle's themes. However, in the process, she also saw right past the books' *Christianity,* as well, something that Lewis apparently never anticipated. But if the wine and robes and cross of Christianity are, if not dispensable, then at least interchangeable with other motifs, as Lewis seemed to suggest, then so, perhaps, are the sacraments and even the Savior himself. Pam describes herself as a person with strong spiritual feelings, but says she has never developed an interest in any organized religion. She still occasionally revisits the Chronicles, and there she finds much that, as she puts it, "is almost subversive of Christianity. It may have some of the symbols in it, but there are concepts of relativity and alternative worlds that go past Christianity."

It occurred to me that the vehemence of my own reaction to the Christian subtext in the Chronicles had to do with the fact that someone else had told me about them; would I have felt less duped and misused if I'd figured it out for myself, the way Pam had? Perhaps, but although I shared Pam's longing for imaginative freedom in another, better place, we sought refuge from different things. For

Narnia to be Christian was, in my eyes, a little like what philosophers call a "category error." As far as I was concerned, one of the essential, constitutive qualities of Narnia was that it was *not* Christian. I was a fierce little dualist on this count. When I realized how wrong I'd been, I felt that I had to make a choice. If I wanted to keep Narnia, I'd have to submit to Christianity, and that I was not willing to do.

For other children who didn't harbor the same insurrectionary urges as Pam and I, enlightenment came as less of a jolt. Jonathan Franzen recognized the Christian aspect of Narnia when he reread the books in high school. "I thought it was kind of cool," he told me. "I wasn't afraid of Christianity at all because I had this very benign experience with liberal, suburban Christianity in junior high and high school, so I was predisposed to find those metaphors." He thinks his Christian education primed him to like the books: "the gestalt of the world, of Narnia, made sense to me because of going to Christian Sunday school."

Of all the people I talked to, Tiffany Brown had the most remarkable history with Narnia and Christianity. She was the kind of child for whom the barriers between the inner and outer worlds are highly permeable. For her, the spirituality in Narnia seemed spun from the same fabric as a life spent playing in the woods of rural Oregon and going to church. "I don't actually know when I realized that the Christian message of it was so literal," she told me. At around ten, she had recognized the similarities between Aslan's death in *The Lion, the Witch and the Wardrobe* and the Crucifixion, "and it was fine with me. I just thought, Well, this is what gods do." Her Jesus existed on a continuum with Aslan — if not the same thing exactly, then the same kind of thing:

"Jesus Christ was great. He would talk to me. It wasn't this one-way prayer. What I experienced was an actual being who would come and literally talk to me. He was very sweet and very soothing and comforting, which is a kind of presence that I needed at that time. But [he] was really funny, which I wasn't expecting."

"Your Jesus had a sense of humor? That would have been inconceivable to me."

"Yeah, he liked to laugh, and he was a lot less serious than the Church would have had me think."

When she was six years old, Tiffany was born again. She'd wandered into an after-school program run by what she describes as a "nondenominational group of people with some very sophisticated brainwashing techniques." Nice ladies rolled out a felt board and told the children wonderful stories using little cutouts of characters in the Bible. "The first one that they told us was about Moses, and I thought it just rocked, that baby in the basket." The children sang songs and were taught how to recite simple prayers while an adult held up colored cue cards; when she held up a black card, they repeated, "My heart was black with sin." A red card signaled, "But Jesus's blood...," and a white card, "...turned it white as snow."

Tiffany's newfound religious fervor eventually drew the rest of her "Sunday-go-to-church" family into fundamentalist Christianity. Except for her, they remain born-again Christians to this day. Around the same time, she fell in love with Narnia, which the adults around her saw as perfectly compatible with their faith. Lewis was a famous Christian, and his intentions with the Chronicles were frankly evangelical, so how could the books do any damage to Tiffany's soul? Yet, ironically, Narnia led to Tiffany's estrangement from her church.

There is a much-cited passage in *The Last Battle,* in which Emeth, a noble warrior of the Calormene people, describes meeting Aslan after the end of the world. At first he is terrified, since he knows this god of the Narnians is the enemy of the Calormene god, Tash, and he has worshipped Tash all his life. Then Aslan explains to him, "I take to me the services which thou hast done to him. For I and he are of such different kinds that no service which is vile can be done to me, and none which is not vile can be done to him. Therefore if any man swear by Tash and keep his oath for the oath's sake, it is by me that he has truly sworn. And if any man do a cruelty in my name, then, though he says the name Aslan, it is Tash whom he serves, and by Tash his deed is accepted."

This is one of the few overtly religious passages in the Chronicles, if by religion you mean explicitly pertaining to worship. Aslan may be the god of Narnia, but he has no churches, and requires no rites or sacraments. What he says to Emeth is consistent with how he has always treated the Narnians: if they behave ethically, generously, and kindly, then they are in his flock; he ordains no sacraments. Emeth isn't going to be sent to Limbo because of an accident of birth or for abiding by the nominal faith of his fathers; his honorable life and honest heart have earned him a place in the Narnian version of heaven.

In our world, Christian churches do not agree that righteous thoughts and actions are enough to redeem a soul that hasn't accepted Jesus Christ as its Savior. Some of Lewis's more conservative Christian readers have found the Emeth passage unsettling; David Downing's *Into the Wardrobe: C. S. Lewis and the Narnia Chronicles* is fairly representative. As is often the case in such books, Downing's interpretations of Lewis's fiction are mostly confined to exegesis, detailing how each aspect of the Chronicles illustrates and conforms to a preferred version of Christian doctrine. These writers tend to avoid discussing any aspects of Lewis's work likely to raise doubts or reservations.

Downing is a bit more courageous than most, however, in his willingness to tackle the Emeth passage. He hastens to explain that Lewis is not embracing "universalism" (the belief that even the damned will eventually be reconciled with God) but "inclusivism." Inclusivism, which has the advantage of coming with the endorsement of the evangelical superpreacher Billy Graham, addresses age-old worries about the "righteous heathen." Good men and women born before the coming of Christ and anyone else who behaved virtuously but never had the opportunity to hear the Gospel during life, may also be admitted to heaven. (The new *Catechism of the*

Catholic Church, the authoritative exposition of Catholic doctrine, published in the late 1990s, sanctions a similar concept called "baptism by desire.")

Lewis himself explicitly disavowed universalism, but inclusivism, like Limbo, invites the kind of technical scrutiny that can itself lead to skepticism. Presumably someone who lives and dies in a place where Christianity is entirely unknown would be covered by this dispensation, but what about someone who heard a little bit about it, or who once came across a Bible at some point, but who didn't know any other Christians and never bothered to investigate further? What about someone whose only exposure to Christianity came from people who misrepresented it? What about someone who believed that Jesus Christ was the son of God, but chose to belong to some irregular faith instead of one of the approved churches—a Catholic, say, or a Greek Orthodox communicant? What about someone who believes but refuses to belong to any church at all, and dies unbaptized?

Many Christian churches seem to be torn between their own claims for legitimacy as the one true way and Christianity's general protestations of love for all mankind. These are complicated theological questions. Individual congregants, however, often don't make subtle distinctions between concepts like universalism and inclusivism. The people in Tiffany's church leaned toward exclusion, and this spelled trouble once her Christian education progressed beyond felt-board fairy tales and colored cards.

"If you had such a positive experience with Jesus," I asked, "how did you wind up leaving the Church?"

"We got to the part where they explain that you have to be practicing Christianity in this particular way or you're going to hell," she replied. Tiffany had a Catholic friend. Was she going to hell? Yes. She liked to read her father's copies of *National Geographic,* full of photographs of people who'd never heard of Jesus. Were they going to hell, too? Yes. "Someone in the fundamentalist camp, my mom or somebody at the church, was coming down on the side of, well, tough. If you worship some idol, some false god, you are going to hell. And one of the first things that I thought of was the people who live in Narnia. They couldn't be going to hell. They're in Narnia. And they have Aslan. And it would be evil for them to not believe in Aslan."

"This was the very reason why you were brought to Narnia," Aslan said, "that by knowing me here for a little, you may know me better there." But the inversion of Aslan's statement works, too: knowing him there also enables us to see where he *isn't* in this world. Tiffany wasn't seeing the spirit of Aslan in her church. "That was how I started understanding the idea of other cultures and other religions," she said. "Because [Narnia] was so real to me. And possibly *really* real. I believed [Narnians] existed somewhere out there. And if my religion was going to say that all of those guys are doomed, then I didn't want to have anything to do with it."

Evangelicals have tried to make a patron saint out of Lewis, but the fit is an uneasy one. Fundamentalism is literalism, and Lewis was a profoundly metaphorical novelist. In real-world conversation, and in his theological writings, even he admitted that he could sometimes be dogmatic. Yet dogmatism was not his only, or even his primary trait. "The imaginative man in me," he wrote in 1954, not long after finishing the Chronicles, "is older, more continuously operative, and in that sense more basic than either the religious writer or the critic." The fact that Lewis thought he could retell the story of Jesus with a lion god, talking animals, and semihuman creatures from classical myths set in an imaginary country where the Bible doesn't exist—all this militates against strict interpretation. If the Bible is word-for-word true, as fundamentalists insist, instead of a truth conveyed via poetry and legend, as more liberal-minded Christians view it, then it *can't* be retold in any other way without being corrupted, lessened, defiled.

Introduce metaphor, symbol, and all the other indirect, eloquent tools of art, and you introduce uncertainty, wiggle room, differences of interpretation. Fundamentalism is like an allergic response to a world where what God really said and meant can be argued this way and that, and where the rules aren't absolutely clear. Tiffany had no interest in making that sort of retreat from the world, and it was inevitable that she'd fall away from her church eventually. But what precipitated that departure was the power — and, depending on your point of view, the treachery — of Lewis's art. Novels that were intended to bolster her faith wound up undercutting it. This happened partly because of a mistake — that is, Tiffany's own childish literalism, which insisted on seeing the Narnians' belief in Aslan as different from her fellow congregants' belief in Jesus. Yet Tiffany was also correct, because the Christianity that Lewis seemed to espouse (and he is by no means consistent, even within the Chronicles) told her that what matters is the virtue of someone's thoughts and actions, not the god he or she professes to serve.

I was tempted to see Tiffany's story as a lot like my own; we both objected to the exclusiveness of our churches, and we both eventually left them. But unlike me, Tiffany has always had an affinity for mysticism and an intimate relationship with the spiritual; she is a believer by constitution, even if what she believes in has changed over the years. Her quarrel with her childhood religion was considered and principled (amazingly so, given her youth); mine was reflexive, like a kid thrashing her way out of an itchy sweater. Though we both detected the hypocrisy in churches that professed love on the one hand and on the other responded to any infraction with threats of eternal torment, for Tiffany this led to a lot of painful soul-searching. She would spend her teenage years "bopping in and out of Christianity and hating Christianity and then giving it another chance." For me, the Church's flaws just offered more reasons to get out of something I never really wanted to be part of in the first place.

Perhaps that's why Tiffany—even in her twenties, when she'd come to see the religious symbolism in the Chronicles as "jarringly" obvious—never rejected them as vehemently as I did. Like Pam, she saw deeper, and she could detect the better side of Christian belief, the one that I refused to acknowledge in my determination to detach myself from my church. "I always thought of Narnia as being this benign thing," Tiffany told me after she'd heard my story. "I don't recall ever feeling that sense of betrayal. It was more like, 'Oh, well, thanks for hooking me up with this kind, sweet metaphor for Christianity. Wouldn't it be great if all Christians were like this?'"

CHAPTER TEN

Required Reading

C. S. Lewis lost his own faith sometime during what he calls, in *Surprised by Joy,* the "dark ages" of boyhood, between childhood and adolescence, when all seemed "greedy, cruel, noisy and prosaic." He lists several causes. First, he had somehow gotten hung up on the idea that he had to "really think" about every prayer he said, which made praying a daily ordeal he became increasingly eager to jettison. Then there was what he describes as his "deeply ingrained pessimism." This attitude was not, Lewis insists, a result of his mother's early death, but rather a by-product of his thwarted and frustrating relationship to the physical world. He was hopelessly clumsy and had come to expect every object "to do what you did not want it to do." He was no good at the sports that matter so much at school. And even though he'd learned to regard his father's financial panics as overblown, the often gloomy mood at home completed the picture of a world too miserable and misbegotten to be the work of any respectable god.

At school, a kindly matron introduced him to "Occultism," a hodgepodge of esoteric beliefs comprising Rosicrucianism, Theosophy, and Spiritualism—precursors to today's New Age movement—then all the rage in England and Ireland. There was also a dandified, theater-loving young teacher, worshipped by Lewis and his schoolmates, who contributed to his atheism in some unspecified way; perhaps he made piety seem uncool. Above all, Lewis studied the classics; his schoolwork consisted predominantly of reading and translating Greek and Latin texts. This curriculum, typical for boys of the time, introduced him to the pagan religions of the ancients. However much his teachers revered the classical authors, they made it clear that they regarded Greek and Latin religious beliefs as a "farrago of nonsense." Lewis was not the first nor would he be the last young person to find this scorn disconcerting; no one bothered to satisfactorily explain to him why his own religion should be exempt from the same scrutiny.

Education and skepticism do seem to go hand in hand; "critical thinking" is what most of us say we want schools to teach kids. At the same age that Lewis was wondering why Jehovah got more respect than Jupiter, I was learning that a story is not always what it appears to be. Some books carry messages — not just morals, those pat lessons offered by books like *Elsie Dinsmore,* but a new, submerged level of meaning, accessible only to the initiated.

Finding that level of meaning is a skill most readers have to be taught, and American children of my generation learned how to do it by reading books like *Animal Farm, Lord of the Flies,* and *A Separate Peace* for school. This is a peculiar species of novel, as awkward and uncongenial as early adolescence itself. I wonder: Does any adult ever return with pleasure to the assigned reading of sixth grade? *To Kill a Mockingbird* may be the only exception. (I put *The Catcher in the Rye* in a different category. For years, and for all the obvious reasons, J. D. Salinger's paean to youthful rebellion wasn't included among the "serious" novels officially sanctioned by grammar school teachers. You can date the moment at which reading became officially considered endangered to the year when they got desperate enough to start assigning it.)

Animal Farm, the ur-book of this type, comes closer to a true allegory, really, than *The Lion, the Witch and the Wardrobe;* the fate of the farm animals who rebel against their human oppressors mirrors the rise and moral decay of the Soviet Union more closely than Lewis's book follows the New Testament. Orwell's fable is, like *Lord of the Flies* (another parable of ineradicable violence), deeply sunk in misanthropic gloom. That's part of its allure for the kind of young reader who yearns to demonstrate his or her maturity; any book this depressing has to be very grown-up. At least, that's what I thought.

Our teacher explained to us that *Animal Farm* was really about politics — about communist Russia, no less! — and I and the other bookish students discussed its deeper meanings with the thrilling awareness that we were being initiated into a province of adulthood. Maybe we didn't fully understand what communism was, but anyone could recognize the way that power and hierarchy crept into Orwell's ostensibly egalitarian animal society. By age twelve, almost every child has some experience of "fair" situations that are actually unjust; it's not such a great leap from that to the idea that some animals are more equal than others.

Not long ago, while writing a piece about the fiction routinely assigned to grammar school students, I reread *Animal Farm* and *Lord of the Flies.* The experience was claustrophobic, and at first I blamed this on my foreknowledge that most of the sympathetic characters in each book are doomed. But so, too, are the main characters in *King Lear* and *Tess of the D'Urbervilles,* and rereading either of those has never felt grim or dutiful to me. I decided, finally, that *Animal Farm* and its fictional cousins feel constricted for the same reason that they're useful to teachers; their purposes are simple, and so are their meanings.

If literary writing has any distinguishing characteristic, it's that the more you look at it the more you see, and the more you see the more you want to go on looking. It invites a plurality of interpretation. "A genuine work of art must mean many things," wrote George MacDonald, the Scottish writer whom Lewis regarded as his master. "The truer its art, the more things it will mean." The meaning of *Animal Farm* is fairly obvious, but what's the meaning of *King Lear*? The question doesn't even make sense, really; it's like asking what I mean, or what *you* mean. Works of art, like human beings, are irreducible. This is why contemporary readers dismiss allegory, because it appears to lack the density of significance we associate with art. The closer and more completely you can come to explaining what a work of art means, the less like art it seems.

I don't mean to suggest that *Animal Farm* isn't moving. Even as an adult, I found the novel terribly sad. I pitied poor Boxer the draft horse, who dies serving a regime that he can't even see has betrayed him. I pitied him so much that I almost wept. But pity always contains a seed of superiority and therefore contempt. We pity those we regard as less than ourselves: animals or simpletons. As maddening as Lear and Hamlet can be, I don't pity them. I'm too smart to make Boxer's mistake, but Shakespeare's tragic heroes err in ways that I can all too uncomfortably imagine succumbing to myself (if not in so grand a manner).

Nevertheless, to get to the point of being able to read—really read—*King Lear,* you must first serve an apprenticeship with more manageable books, like *Animal Farm.* So direct and clear-cut are Orwell's intentions that the book can be used as a kind of primer for thematic analysis. A double meaning is far easier to recognize than an infinite one. There are better books for younger readers that couldn't serve this purpose nearly as well. *Where the Wild Things Are* and *Harriet the Spy* are both better than *Animal Farm,* I'd say, and most of us could reread either one of them again and again with a gladness that *Animal Farm* will never invoke. But *Animal Farm* is nevertheless a good enough book, and, more important, it's a fine book on which to cut your critical teeth.

It was with *Animal Farm* that my classmates and I learned to read fiction with a critic's detachment. Up to that point, we experienced stories as truth, if not always as *fact.* It's not that we believed that the events in, say, *The House at Pooh Corner* had actually occurred; rather, our limber imaginations let us occupy a world where made-up stories had the same legitimacy as reality. Like real events and real human beings, the characters and events in those stories didn't stand for something else. They were what they were, and it's only with great effort and fairly late in the game that a child can understand them as *created* rather than simply *existing* the way that the people and objects in the world around us do. If we love a story enough, as I loved *The Lion, the Witch and the Wardrobe,* we might decide that it *has* to be real, that a place like Narnia is so necessary that it must be out there somewhere, as palpable as California or Boston (the fabled city my mother came from).

Novels like *Animal Farm* and *Lord of the Flies* are usually given to children with a specific, if unspoken agenda: *Animal Farm* was meant to inoculate us against communism, and *Lord of the Flies,* I've always been convinced, was intended to warn us off the naive Rousseauian idealism then running rampant in the counterculture. But above all, these books were supposed to teach us how books work, to show us how what seems to be a story can actually be an argument about ideas or beliefs or the best way to run a country. Stories can be enlisted to serve a rational cause, such as a political ideology, and this, we are led to believe, elevates the fiction, making it useful and worthy in a way that a mere pastime or diversion could never be. According to this formula, *Animal Farm,* which takes up the weighty responsibility of critiquing totalitarianism, is naturally a more substantial and worthy book than *Harold and the Purple Crayon,* even if we don't enjoy it as much.

In sixth grade, when I first studied *Animal Farm,* I felt that I had embarked upon a journey of great consequence, and I was right. I was making a momentous transition, and I'm surprised to find that few writers have ever attempted to describe it. Even *Surprised by Joy,* the memoir of a consummate reader, doesn't. What Lewis does write about is a period, during the dark ages of boyhood, when he briefly gave up reading fairy tales and switched to school stories and fat bestsellers in the sword-and-sandals vein — *Quo Vadis* and *Ben-Hur* — "mainly rubbish," as he characterizes them. This change, he felt, marked "a great decline in my imaginative life."

It didn't last, fortunately, and he would return to the old, resplendent inner life when he rediscovered Norse mythology in his early teens. Literature, it seems, was about the only aspect of his life that Lewis didn't second-guess during his adolescence. But then, reading English poetry and prose was for him an almost entirely independent, extracurricular activity, and as a result, his teachers rarely set him to analyzing the kind of books he liked to read for pleasure. Reading remained part of his untouchable private world. "Never in my life had I read a work of fiction, poetry, or criticism in my own language except because, after trying the first few pages, I liked the taste of it," he wrote of the years before he was sent to Malvern College in Worcestershire at the age of fifteen.

At Malvern, the last of the series of boarding schools he attended in England, Lewis was, by his own report, transformed into a "prig." The term as he used it has a meaning more akin to "intellectual snob" than it does today, when it's often regarded as a synonym for "prude." But used either way, it indicates a disdain for other people's pleasures. Lewis learned that he was not the only person who harbored a secret ardor for poetry, but with that knowledge came what he described as "a kind of Fall. The moment good taste knows itself, some of its goodness is lost." His once-pure love for certain books and authors became a justification for looking down on the philistines who didn't share it.

For my part, I never really much liked *Animal Farm,* but that seemed beside the point. Here, for once, my experience of religion and my reading life converged. The Church had instructed me that the holiest activities were necessarily the dreariest ones, and now school was teaching me that the delight I took in a story was not the only—not even the best—criterion for judging how good it was. If anything, the more I enjoyed a story, the less likely it was to be serious, worthwhile literature.

Still, learning has a pleasure all its own; for some people, taking a car apart can be as much fun as driving it. I found that I wanted to figure out how books worked, almost as much as I wanted to feel them work on me. I also wanted, very much, to grow up, and studying books like *Animal Farm* was the sort of thing grown-ups did. And I *was* learning. Through Orwell's novel, I gained a perspective on political power and how easily it can be misused. I also could see the way that good writing draws a collection of vague impressions into a coherent pattern until you both recognize your own experience and see it clearly for the first time. And beyond all this, I had come to recognize stories as made things, rather than as given phenomena of the universe, like the wind, a tree, or my brothers and sisters. If *Animal Farm* had a purpose, it could only be because somebody had created it to achieve that purpose — a writer, the author, George Orwell.

To me, the reality of authorship — the origin of every story in the imagination of a flawed human being — was both liberating and dispossessing. The presents you find under the tree on Christmas morning aren't any less desirable because they've been left there by your parents instead of by a jolly fat man in a red suit who came down the chimney, but some of the thrill has gone out of receiving them all the same. Still, discovering that there is no Santa Claus has its compensations. You have been trusted with secret information that younger, greener children aren't allowed. And you recognize that more of the world is under merely human governance than you had once thought; it's a relief to know that a supernaturally industrious stranger at the North Pole isn't really documenting how well you behave over the course of the year.

Adults remember learning the truth about Santa Claus as a miniature tragedy. Some of us cried. In the years since, most of us have forgotten that we were also gratified to be recognized as grown-up enough to know the truth. (I recall being impressed with how skillfully my parents had created the illusion, and I tried carefully to maintain it for my brothers and sisters — which was, strangely enough, almost as much fun as actually believing in it.) Likewise, when we mourn the way we used to read as children, that effortless absorption and unquestioning faith, we would do well to remind ourselves of the dangers of putting ourselves at the mercy of a book. For every *Animal Farm*, propaganda you probably agree with, there is a *Turner Diaries*, propaganda I hope you don't. If we sometimes place a petty, priggish value on reading critically, we nevertheless learn to do it for excellent reasons.

Graham Greene, in his essay "The Lost Childhood," suggested that reading loses its first, mighty power when books stop telling us what we don't already know about our lives. Once, each volume was a "crystal in which the child dreamed that he saw life moving," but eventually what we read only confirms or contradicts what we already believe: "As in a love affair it is our own features that we see reflected flatteringly back." But Greene was a Catholic who was unfortunate enough not to lapse and this made him morose. Think of it another way: We start out with a simple, even religious, relationship to the written word; its authority is unquestioned. We end up with something more complicated, but also something more our own. And then the time comes to decide a few things for ourselves.

CHAPTER ELEVEN

Garlic and Onions

In *The Horse and His Boy,* the foundling Shasta joins a runaway princess named Aravis and two talking horses in a desperate escape from Calormen, Narnia's large, powerful neighbor to the south. We've met Calormenes before, in *The Voyage of the Dawn Treader,* where they appear at the slave market in the Lone Islands. They have "dark faces and long beards. They wear flowing robes and orange-colored turbans, and they are a wise, wealthy, courteous, cruel and ancient people." In *The Horse and His Boy,* the fugitives' route takes them through Calormen's capital city, Tashbaan, and as they make their way along the streets, they're bombarded with smells. The stench comes from "unwashed people, unwashed dogs, scent, garlic, onions and the piles of refuse which lay everywhere." Although the Calormene capital looks magnificent from a distance, up close it stinks.

The Calormenes are vaguely Turkish, with the exotic clothes and florid manners of characters from the *Arabian Nights,* a book Lewis disliked. Their civilization is grand yet decadent. Great lords and ladies are carried through Tashbaan on litters, and "there is only one traffic regulation, which is that everyone who is less important has to get out of the way for everyone who is more important." So when Shasta catches sight of a fair-skinned delegation from Narnia,

walking on foot with an easygoing swing to their step and looking as though "they were ready to be friends with anyone who was
friendly and didn't give a fig for anyone who wasn't," he understandably decides that he has never before seen anything so "lovely." The
Narnians are, figuratively and literally, a breath of fresh air from the
north, an antidote to the Calormenes' garlic and heavy perfume.

Recognizing the Calormenes for the racial and cultural stereotype they are was an insight I wouldn't acquire until my college years,
but even as a child I was mystified by the role of garlic and onions
in their villainy. Both alliums turn up again in *The Last Battle,* twirl-
ing their figurative mustaches for the end-times. The Calormenes
have formed an alliance with Shift the Ape, who has tricked many
Narnians into following a false "Aslan" (the donkey Puzzle disguised
in a lion's hide). According to Shift, the lion god has ordered the
enslavement of the talking beasts and the harvesting of the talking
trees for timber.

Early in the book, Narnia's monarch, King Tirian, and his companion, the unicorn Jewel, kill some Calormene soldiers, and then,
overwhelmed with guilt, decide to turn themselves in. The king de-
spairs at the thought that "Aslan has come and is not like the Aslan
we have believed in and longed for." It would be better to be dead
at the hands of the Calormenes, Tirian swears, than to live with the
knowledge that this is what Aslan really wants for his chosen people. The young king's surrender is a moment of utter wretchedness,
culminating as "the dark men came round them in a thick crowd,
smelling of garlic and onions, their white eyes flashing dreadfully in
their brown faces."

For Lewis, garlic was an unwelcome exoticism. He liked his meals
mildly seasoned and unsauced; anything livelier he rejected as "messed-
up food." His feelings on this matter were pronounced enough that
his brother devoted a whole paragraph to the subject in his introduction to *The Letters of C. S. Lewis.* "Plain domestic cookery was what
he wanted," stated Warnie, and apparently he shared his brother's pref-

erence—although, unlike Jack, Warnie had seen enough of the world during his military tours of Africa and Asia to know what splendors lay beyond the ken of the average British kitchen. The fancy dishes that the Lewis brothers disdained back in England were probably limited to French cuisine and perhaps the Indian curries brought home to the motherland by more gastronomically adventurous Britons. Both types of food would have been redolent of garlic.

In their culinary conservatism, Jack and Warnie remind me of the characters in Barbara Pym's comic novels of genteel provincial English life. For the staid wives and maiden ladies Pym wrote about, bland cooking symbolized fidelity to all the conventions and proprieties of their class and nationality. When someone in a Pym novel begins to cook with garlic (or oil or saffron), she is running a little wild—often outside the kitchen as well as in it. But for Pym, if not for the Lewises, a certain wistfulness also attaches itself to garlic; it speaks of Latin passions as well as Latin appetites. In *Jane and Prudence,* Jane, a forty-one-year-old vicar's wife, thinks, "I should have liked the kind of life where one ate food flavoured with garlic, but it was not to be."

Garlic, for early- and mid-twentieth-century Britons, was the badge of the foreigner, whose extravagant emotions and behavior matched his excessive cookery. The odor of garlic permeates the houses where it is used, insisting upon the carnal nature of those who live there. For well-bred Britons, being reminded of cooking was almost as repugnant as being reminded of sex and other, even more unmentionable bodily functions. Lewis expected his description of the Calormenes and their reek of onions and garlic to provoke an unthinking disgust in his readers, who he assumed would also regard the smell as alien and offensive. This wasn't an unreasonable conviction in his day; when I mentioned to a bookish friend that I was thinking about the role of garlic in British fiction, he exclaimed (over a plate of spicy Thai noodles), "Oh God! It's *always* the symbol of the dirty foreigner!"

Smell is so visceral a sensation that it's strange to think of it as a *symbol* for anything, especially for a relatively abstract concept like "foreigner." When we walk into a room, we notice the fact that we smell mildew or rotting food before we conclude that the place is filthy. Our response to smell feels primal, and yet it, too, can be shaped by culture and history. Unlike Lewis, I grew up in a house that often smelled of garlic. My mother, an excellent cook, used plenty of it in her famous spaghetti sauce, and my father was known not just as one of the few husbands who cooked but as a pretty decent amateur Chinese chef. He could be found, every other week or so, stirring garlic and fermented black beans in the sizzling oil at the bottom of his wok. So I don't share Lewis's disgust for exotic, strong-smelling foods. To me, the aroma of garlic is appetizing and also welcoming, the smell of dinner at home.

On the other hand, both of the Lewis brothers were very fond of their pipes, and they made a game of stopping up the windows and doors of their ground-floor sitting room, lighting a coal fire, and puffing away until clouds of tobacco and coal smoke filled the room; "fugging up" the place, they called it. My parents were committed nonsmokers—even their friends rarely lit up in our house. The odor of stale tobacco smoke on upholstery or someone's clothes makes me queasy, probably because I associate it with the motion sickness I got while flying as a child, back in the days when people still smoked on planes and left the strange, bitter stench of old cigarettes behind. I think of the Lewis brothers' "fugged up" room with horror, and if, at age ten, I could have met them, chances are I'd have found them much stinkier than the garlicky Calormenes.

Disgust, however elemental it feels, is often just a matter of the company you keep. Some of its objects—human waste, for example—are universally abominated, while others—certain foods or grooming customs—are prized in one society and reviled in another. A sophisticated and open-minded person makes a point of learning to tell the difference between the two, although acquiring that ability is harder for some than for others. Many see no reason to try.

Lewis, who left the British Isles only twice (he went to France in World War I and on a last-chance holiday to Greece in 1960), belonged to the latter group; rejection of the unfamiliar was his default setting. According to one Lewis family legend, Jack, at the age of four, informed his father that he had conceived a prejudice against the French. When Albert asked for his reasons, Jack replied that if he knew the reasons it wouldn't be a prejudice.

Conservatism can be principled. (Note: I'm speaking here of classical conservatism, the variety that Lewis adhered to, not of what Americans usually mean by the term. Confusingly, the American institution of free-market "conservatism" is often referred to as "neoliberalism" in Europe, and Lewis would have rejected its faith in unrestrained capitalism.) It seeks to preserve ways of life that people sometimes don't value until they begin to slip away. Lewis and Tolkien mourned the loss of the Britain of their youth and generations past, a rural Britain of ancient social hierarchies, unspoiled by automobiles and factories. Theirs was a conservatism that led them to rail against a grab bag of phenomena ranging from coed schools to real-estate development. Though neither was politically active (and Lewis boasted of never reading the newspapers), some of their strongest political feelings align with what we would now call environmentalism.

With its focus on halting all change, however, conservatism — especially the unconsidered brand of it that Lewis espoused — can be merely reflexive. It is always in danger of enshrining prejudice in the name of tradition, of treating garlic as an emblem of iniquity simply because your own family never cooked with it. Prejudice, alas, runs through the Chronicles, although not all of it is as blatant as Lewis's descriptions of the odiferous, dark-skinned Calormenes. Some of what I call prejudice wouldn't be so labeled by other Lewis admirers, even today. A member of the New York C. S. Lewis Society, a group that meets right around the corner from my apartment in Greenwich Village, recently explained to a *New York Times* reporter, "Lewis's vision was not that we all are equal, but that we are all different in our natural attitudes and natural creativity. Narnia is not about a hierarchy of power, but each kind of creature joyfully living out their natural attitudes." That's an accurate enough characterization of Lewis's thought ("I do not believe God created an egalitarian world," he once wrote). It doesn't, however, account for the fact that tyrants always talk of the need for their subjects to accept their proper (and often divinely ordained) station in life.

We could deplore the Calormenes for many reasons—they keep slaves, their society is overly hierarchical, they have imperial designs on Narnia, they compel young women to marry men they don't love, their government is despotic—and we would be right to do so. Recoiling from them because they eat garlic and onions, or because they have dark skin, might (if we're brutally honest with ourselves) be our instinctive response, but it is, of course, fundamentally different and fundamentally wrong. This was a distinction Lewis often failed to make, either because he couldn't see it or because he couldn't be bothered to look. For him, the wickedness of the Calormenes was of a piece with their foreignness, which was integral to their wrongness; the dark skin and strange smells were all tangled up with the slaveholding and the tyranny and the devil worship, and just about as bad, too.

Lewis's critics have accused him of many prejudices, but the main ones are racism, misogyny, and elitism. Philip Pullman has complained that in the world of the Chronicles "boys are better than girls; light-colored people are better than dark-colored people; and so on." Lewis's champions frequently respond to the racism charges by pointing out that the Calormenes, in addition to being dark-skinned, have a genuinely wicked society and that some of the most evil figures in the Chronicles—the White Witch most notably—have pale skin. Furthermore, at least two of the Calormenes are sympathetic: Aravis and Emeth, the nobleman who is saved by Aslan at the end of

The Last Battle. (This last and least convincing defense sounds sus-
piciously like "some of my best friends are..." and it doesn't go very
far in counteracting the penny-dreadful phobia evident in lines like
"their white eyes flashing dreadfully in their brown faces.")

The impulse to hero-worship our favorite writers is a leftover of
our starry-eyed adolescence, as much a part of that period as the urge
to rebel against the authority figures closer at hand. We want the artists who have changed our lives to lead exemplary lives of their own. A
college friend of mine was crushed when he learned of the messy and
ignoble intimate relationships of his literary idol, George Orwell, who
cheated on his first wife and later, when he was at death's door, married
a much younger woman. My friend, a romantic soul, expected Orwell
to be, if not faultless, then at least a paragon commensurate with his expressed ideals. One of the things we look for in books, especially when
we're young, is guidance on how to live, and however much we might
admire what a great man has to say on this count, his credo loses some
luster if he turns out to be unable to abide by it himself.

Even more unrealistic, we also like to believe that our literary
sages and mentors had the ability to see through the errors and
prejudices of their day and to prefigure the wisdom of our own.
T. S. Eliot, for example, was a great poet, but also an anti-Semite.
This was not particularly unusual for someone of his background,
but it was not universal, either. Tolkien admired Jews, and when, in
1938, his German publisher wrote to ask about his ethnicity, he testily replied, "If I am to understand that you are enquiring whether
I am of *Jewish* origin, I can only reply that I regret that I appear to
have *no* ancestors of that gifted people." Tolkien's contemporary fans
are fortunate in this; those who adulate Eliot have on occasion felt
obliged to write long and urgent essays for intellectual journals attempting to explain away such slurs as "the jew squats on the window sill" (from "Gerontion") as "parody."

Imagine, then, how much more defensive a writer's acolytes must
be when the very foundations of their lives depend, to a certain

extent, on his work. This is the case with almost everyone who writes about Lewis today. While Lewis's literary criticism has drifted into obscurity (as A. N. Wilson has pointed out, criticism is a literary genre especially prone to obsolescence), his Christian apologetics remain nearly as popular as the Chronicles. Most of the biographers and scholars who currently study him first became interested in his religious works. Through his writing, Lewis has served as an avuncular theological mentor, a kindly guide who eases the anxious into the fold and continues to provide them with justifications for their beliefs. (This, incidentally, is precisely the job of the apologetic as a rhetorical form, according to the *Oxford American Dictionary*; it is "a reasoned argument or writing in justification of something.")

Among these converts is the geneticist Francis S. Collins, who in his book *The Language of God,* describes his own transformation from "obnoxious atheist" to evangelical Christian, precipitated by reading Lewis's *Mere Christianity.* "Within the first three pages," Collins told an interviewer, "I realized that my arguments against faith were those of a schoolboy." Of course, Collins would not have been reading *Mere Christianity* to begin with if he had not been uneasy in his atheism and searching for some alternative. (He was given the book by a Methodist minister who recognized him as ripe for the plucking.) But Collins, like Lewis, portrays himself as a reluctant convert, and not surprisingly he invests great authority in the writer who persuaded him to cross the line.

For many of the people who study Lewis's writings, finding moral fault with any of his versions of Christianity, including the Chronicles, amounts to discovering termites in the joists supporting their own faith; it's not a possibility they're prepared to seriously contemplate. They may know better than to speak of Lewis's theological writings as a form of scripture—that would be blasphemous—but veneration is also part of their temperament; it is, after all, one reason why they are religious. For them, Lewis has become the rough equivalent of the eleventh-century French rabbi Shlomo ben Itzhak (or Rashi), whose commentary on the Torah acquired so much authority that it was included in the first printed version of the Hebrew Bible.

This, not surprisingly, makes Lewis scholars pretty skittish about examining the rare occasions when he seems to address race. The fact that the worst of Lewis's stereotypes turn up in the Chronicles—mere children's fiction—makes the subject easier to shrug off as inconsequential. David Downing, once again among the braver souls who attempt a defense, picks his battles with exquisite care in *Into the Wardrobe: C. S. Lewis and the Narnia Chronicles.* He begins by dismissing charges (made by the British academic Andrew Blake) that the Chronicles contribute to the "demonization of Islam." Islam, Downing observes, is a monotheistic religion while the Calormenes have more than one god. Downing then goes on to explain that Lewis modeled the Calormenes on characters from the *Arabian Nights* and therefore "every objectionable trait" they exhibit originates in "source materials" that "arose among Middle Easterners themselves." The section of *Into the Wardrobe* that presents these evasive and absurdly technical vindications is entitled "Are the Chronicles Politically Incorrect?" rather than "Are the Chronicles Racist?" implying that such questions amount to no more than left-wing pettifoggery.

In *The Narnian,* a biography of Lewis, Alan Jacobs makes the customary (and not negligible) argument that Lewis wrote "in a time less sensitive to cultural differences." Like Downing, he insists that Lewis merely drew upon the "readymade source of 'Oriental' imagery," generated by Christian Europe's long rivalry with the Ottoman Empire. Jacobs feels sure that the continued popularity of the Chronicles proves that "readers... can tell the difference between, on the one hand, an intentionally hostile depiction of some alien culture and, on the other, the use of cultural difference as a mere plot device." Jacobs's confidence that the average reader would instinctively reject stories with truly racist elements is sadly misplaced; such scruples, if they exist, have done nothing to inhibit the popularity of *Gone With the Wind.* But beyond this, he also seems to be suggesting that because Lewis didn't really know—or even want to know—anything about Turks or Arabs, he can't be accused of deliberately maligning them. At worst, he just didn't care whether he was doing them an injustice as long as it served his needs.

The feebleness of this distinction—it's better to insult someone out of ignorant expedience than out of straightforward antipathy—is pitiful. What is prejudice if not the presumption to judge people you know nothing about on the basis of "readymade" imagery? Perhaps if Lewis had lived in Istanbul or enjoyed a few close Turkish friends, he would not have made this mistake. He might have grown accustomed to the scent of garlic. His pronouncements on homosexuality were notably liberal-minded, for example, no doubt because Arthur Greeves, his best friend from boyhood, was homosexual. Lewis's fault lies in never considering the possibility that he might be wrong about those dark-skinned strangers, the ones he never got to meet; he was ignorant of his own ignorance. His beloved imagination may have served him well on many other occasions, but when it came to people who looked or smelled different from himself, it stopped short.

CHAPTER TWELVE

Girl Trouble

Everybody's favorite characters from the Chronicles are re-united at the end of the final book, *The Last Battle*—all but one. King Tirian, Narnia's staunch defender against the Calormene menace, until the moment Aslan brings his world to an end, suddenly and inexplicably finds himself in a beautiful countryside, where he meets seven of the eight children who have visited Narnia from our world. Among them are Peter, Edmund, and Lucy (now young adults), but when Tirian asks after Susan, Peter tersely replies that she's "no longer a friend of Narnia." Jill explains that, back in our world, Susan would rather not hang around with the rest of them reminiscing about their Narnian adventures. Instead, she's "interested in nothing nowadays but nylons and lipstick and invitations." Polly, also among the redeemed, adds, "Her whole idea is to race to the silliest time of one's life as quick as she can and then stop there as long as she can."

Susan's fate—the rest of the visitants from our world have already died in a railway accident, although they don't know it yet—has bothered many readers. It is one of the most debated aspects of the Chronicles. Presumably, Susan is the only Pevensie to escape the accident (the Pevensies' parents are also killed), which prompted Neil Gaiman to write a short story imagining the rest of her life. In "The

Problem of Susan," she is presented as an elderly college professor, the author of a history of children's literature, giving an interview to a young journalist. Susan recalls identifying the mangled bodies of her siblings at the railway station and barely scraping by financially after losing her whole family. She has lived a full life, illustrated by an obituary in the morning paper that reminds her of a man she kissed in a summer house long ago and another man who "took what was left of her virginity on a blanket on a Spanish beach."

Gaiman pointedly fills "The Problem of Susan" with everything Lewis left out of the Chronicles: adulthood, the uglier realities of violence and death, the brutal side of nature, and, especially, sexuality. Although none of these matters are natural topics for children's books (especially in Lewis's day), Gaiman feels that Lewis takes his aversion to maturity too far. He agrees with Philip Pullman that Susan's "nylons and lipstick and invitations" are emblems of her sexuality, and he maintains that sexuality is really what keeps her out of Paradise. "It's only reading it as an adult," he told me, "that you start to wonder: Where are the nice women of childbearing age?...There was a level on which of course [Susan] doesn't get to heaven because she's just like the witches, and they wear dresses and they're pretty."

Gaiman's friend, Susanna Clarke, the author of *Jonathan Strange & Mr. Norrell,* thinks that both men interpret this passage too freely. "Lewis's critics tend to reduce it all down to a question of sex," she said when I had the chance to ask her about it during a visit to England. "I've seen convincing arguments that what Susan was guilty of in the end was not so much growing up as vanity. I think there are strong reasons to think that's probably true."

"I see what you mean," I replied, "but even so, I believe Lewis did think that women are more prone to that sort of trivial vanity than men are." I told Susanna about a story Lewis wrote, "The Shoddy Lands," in which a man's friend becomes engaged and somehow the narrator finds himself briefly transported into the fiancée's mind. Everything in the world becomes blurry and flimsy, except for the clothes and merchandise in shops, which is clearly all this silly woman really cares about.

"I'm still not sure I agree with you," she replied. "It really depends on whether you just look at the books themselves, or whether you look at his character and his other writings as well. I don't see from the books, the Narnia books, that he thought trivial vanity was a female thing."

"What other examples are you thinking of?"

"Well, you've got Uncle Andrew in *The Magician's Nephew,* who goes off and dresses himself up in his best clothes. And there's also the horse Bree in *The Horse and His Boy.* [Lewis] makes it clear that Bree is vain and socially insecure and worried about what will happen to him in Narnia."

Lewis himself wrote to a child fan that Susan had "turned into a rather silly, conceited young woman. But there's plenty of time for her to mend, and perhaps she will get to Aslan's country in the end—in her own way." Alan Jacobs, in *The Narnian,* defends Lewis against charges of sexism by arguing that Susan really misses out on paradise due to her "excessive regard for social acceptance." Although Jacobs is willing to admit that Lewis "could say some extraordinarily silly things about women," he believes that, for those who object to Susan's fate, especially Philip Pullman, this is really a side issue. To atheists like Pullman, Jacobs claims, Lewis's "greater crime" is his conviction that people can be eternally condemned at all; what they can't stand is the fact that "God gives people the freedom to choose Hell rather than choose to dwell in Heaven."

I don't doubt that Pullman objects to the idea of damnation, but in the case of Susan, what he's protesting is the *grounds* for damnation, not damnation itself. Bree's vanity is a minor flaw in an otherwise good character, and Uncle Andrew's pride runs much deeper than just a preoccupation with appearances. Although Susan is not yet damned and still has the chance to "mend," the implication, in both Lewis's novel and the letter to his child reader, is that if she keeps on as she has been, preoccupied with feminine nonsense, this alone will be enough to bring her to a bad end. And that prompts a question: Why does Lewis consider an interest in lipstick, nylons, and invitations such an especially pernicious form of silliness? What makes these amusements so much worse than pipes and beer and "bawdy" with your buddies at the pub? Why is feminine triviality so much worse than its masculine counterpart?

Lipstick-obsessed flibbertigibbets like Susan or the fiancée from "The Shoddy Lands" were not the only sort of female Lewis found untrustworthy. In the Chronicles, two of the most memorable villains are women: the White Witch of *The Lion, the Witch and the Wardrobe* (later revealed in *The Magician's Nephew* to be Jadis, the empress of the lost world of Charn) and the Lady of the Green Kirtle from *The Silver Chair,* who keeps Caspian's son, Rilian, an unwitting prisoner in her underground kingdom. Both of these witches are very beautiful: the White Witch in the frosty tradition of the Snow Queen, the Lady of the Green Kirtle, or the Green Witch, in the merrier spirit of Celtic sorceresses. These two are after more than just party invitations; they want power. Vain, silly women may be annoying distractions for men who have better things to do; the witches are seducers.

Although the tools the White Witch uses to corrupt Edmund are juvenile enough—enchanted candy and the prospect of lording it over his older brother—the scene in which she ensnares him swims with sensuality; there is the witch's pale skin, her fur-lined sleigh, and the hot drink she conjures out of nothing ("sweet and foamy and creamy"). A friend of mine remembers being deeply unsettled by this episode as a boy; the witch, though frightening, was also alluring in some way he didn't entirely understand. Soon the initially resistant Edmund becomes ridiculously pliable to her demands, red-faced and sticky and preoccupied with getting another taste of Turkish delight.

For her part, the less Freudian Green Witch, with her "voice sweeter than the sweetest bird's song" and "the richest, most musical laugh you can imagine" bewitches Rilian into a perverted form of chivalric servitude. She erases all memory of his former life and grooms him to be the figurehead general of a slave army. Like the knights of the romances Lewis wrote about in *The Allegory of Love,* men who proved their virtue by fulfilling the directives of their ladies, Rilian pronounces himself "well content to live by her word."

Lewis objected to the gyneolatry of some chivalric romances at least as far back as *The Allegory of Love,* and with the Green Witch he got the chance to portray it as an outright evil. In writing about Chrétien de Troyes's *Lancelot,* he called the devotion of Lancelot to Guinevere "revolting" for its tendency to "ape religious devotion." The sin, as he sees it, is primarily Guinevere's; his antipathy toward her has an oddly personal tone. True, she does demand impossible feats and perfect obedience from her lover—but that is her role. Guinevere is the taskmaster whose rigor enables Lancelot to demonstrate that he is the ideal knight. In real life, she'd be a monster, but this is the realm of medieval romance, as Lewis is usually so eager to remind us, not the psychological domain of the modern novel.

Nevertheless, Lewis can't resist treating Guinevere as if she *were* a character in a realistic novel; he refers to one of her tall orders as an example of the queen taking yet "another opportunity of exercising her power." He even sets aside his own admonitions to think medievally long enough to compare Guinevere and other chivalric heroines to twentieth-century ladies who drag their men on shopping trips, expecting them "to leap up on errands, to go through heat or cold," whenever they are bidden. If chivalry was not yet dead, Lewis certainly wished it so; abolishing it was one form of modernization he could wholeheartedly endorse. In *The Silver Chair,* Rilian declares that upon his return from the underworld, "I shall do all by the counsel of my Lady, who will then be my Queen, too. Her word shall be my law." Jill retorts, "Where I come from...they don't think much of men who are bossed about by their wives."

This was a persistent theme for Lewis, who wrote in *Surprised by Joy* that "the two things that some of us most dread for our own species" are "the dominance of the female and the dominance of the collective." He so resented the intrusion of his friends' wives into his social life that he once wrote, "A friend dead is to be mourned: a friend married is to be guarded against, both being equally lost."

Not a terribly remarkable attitude in a hidebound bachelor, perhaps. And a repressed professor is just what Lewis was, according to popular opinion, before the most famous event in his personal life: his late, happy marriage to Joy Davidman Gresham. Their romance has been richly idealized, first by Lewis in his memoir of Joy's death from cancer in 1960, *A Grief Observed,* and later in the biographical radio play and film *Shadowlands.* In its pop culture incarnations, theirs is the sentimentally irresistible story of a tweedy, middle-aged don awakened to the bliss of romantic love at a stage in life when most people believe such things are behind them. ("He thought that magic only existed in books, and then he met her" was the movie's tagline.)

Gresham was an American divorcée, a former communist, and a Jew who converted to Episcopalianism, inspired in part by Lewis's apologetics. She wrote him fan letters and brought her two young sons with her to meet him when she visited England in the mid-1950s, most likely with the intention of deepening their epistolary friendship. The role religion played in their relationship makes their love story especially appealing to Lewis's Christian admirers. I heard a lot about it when I visited the Kilns, the cottage in the Oxford suburb of Headington where Lewis lived for the last half of his life. Today the Kilns is maintained by the C. S. Lewis Foundation, an American group dedicated to "enabling a genuine renaissance of Christian scholarship and artistic expression."

As we walked from room to room, the wholesome young woman who gave me the tour was able to tell me what Joy had done in nearly every corner of the house. I meekly interrupted every now and then to remind her that I was really only interested in what the place was like when Lewis wrote the Chronicles, before he met Joy

Gresham. (That was no simple task. The Lewis brothers had allowed
the house to lapse into squalor, and although the C. S. Lewis Foundation has restored it to impeccable condition, it has painted the ceiling
of the sitting room a dirty yellow, in commemoration of the tobacco
smoke residue that once coated it.) As we poked our heads into one
oddly configured downstairs room, I asked what it had been used for
around 1950, when Lewis was in the thick of inventing Narnia. No
one was quite sure...perhaps they could check...but then, oh yes,
that's it: they were pretty sure that room had been Mrs. Moore's.

Lewis's marriage to Joy Gresham lasted four years, but before
they met he had lived with another woman for over three decades.
Lewis's unconventional relationship with Janie "Minto" Moore is
not the stuff that sentimental movies and other dreams are made
of. In particular, Mrs. Moore presents Lewis's most pious admirers
with a dilemma. She was twenty years Lewis's senior and had a teenage daughter named Maureen. She was married to another man,
although permanently estranged from the husband she referred to
only as "the Beast." And she was an atheist, who derided the Masses
that the Lewis brothers attended as "blood feasts."

Lewis had befriended Janie Moore's son, Patrick, in the army during World War I, and the two young men swore that should either
of them fail to survive the war, the other would care for the parent of
the deceased. Paddy Moore was killed in 1918, and Lewis proved as
good as his word. He remained devoted to his friend's mother, living with and helping to support her (although she did have a little
money of her own) for the rest of her life, and Maureen until she
married in 1940. Janie Moore, along with Warnie Lewis, was one
of the three initial co-owners of the Kilns. When he began writing the Chronicles in the 1940s, Lewis had taken to calling her his
"mother," but most of his biographers concur that the relationship
began as a romantic affair. (There is a tiny contingent who, for religious reasons, prefer to think that Lewis remained a virgin until he

married, and an even tinier contingent who like to think he never consummated his love for Joy, whose divorce was not officially recognized by the Church of England.)

By 1943, when Lewis wrote to decline a speaking engagement at an American college, pleading the "difficulties" posed by a "very aged and daily more infirm mother," his relationship to Minto had surely become platonic. His conversion to Christianity in 1931 would have made anything else unacceptable. But exactly what transpired between them during the thirty years they spent together remains a mystery, since Lewis refused to discuss it with anyone, except perhaps Arthur Greeves, and Arthur made a point of destroying letters he regarded as private. Lewis didn't save copies himself and was an indifferent, impersonal diarist who gave up the practice entirely in 1927.

By default, Warren Lewis's diaries and recollections are the source of much of the biographical material on his brother, and Warnie hated Minto. As a result, she doesn't come off well in many accounts of Jack's life, depending on how much credence a writer lends to Warnie's versions of events. Some of Lewis's biographers, A. N. Wilson in particular, have risen to her defense and insisted the relationship was not, as Warnie claimed, an unremitting trial. We can only guess at Lewis's true feelings for Minto and how they evolved over time.

Janie Moore was an imperious woman, obsessed with the minor crises of the household and given to interrupting Lewis while he was at work, demanding that he run errands, make repairs, and take care of various chores on top of his duties as a university fellow and author. In one characteristic incident, described in Lewis's short-lived diary, she asked him to try to exchange an antiquated iron wringer in downtown Oxford, then after he had hauled the unwanted device all the way back home to Headington, sent him out again to inquire after the purse she thought she'd left at the Oxford bus station—all while he was supposed to be working. He started on *The Lion, the Witch and the Wardrobe* when Minto was in her late seventies and by then she had deteriorated badly. She was bedridden and forgetful, insisting that her incontinent dog (whose health had become her obsession) be walked as many as a dozen times a day. Warnie's occasional alcoholic binges made matters worse; during the year Lewis wrote the first Chronicle, he informed a friend that "dog stools and human vomit have made my day to day."

Warnie had liked Mrs. Moore well enough when he first moved in with them in 1932, but he came to see her as a kind of vampire, sapping his brother's time, health, and dignity; he claimed to have once overheard her telling someone that Jack was "as good as an extra maid in the house." The peculiarities of her personality only intensified as she grew old, sick, and cranky. While Lewis was working on the first draft of *The Magician's Nephew* (later put aside for *Prince Caspian*), he collapsed with a streptococcus infection that his doctor attributed to exhaustion. Warnie's diary describes leaving his brother's hospital room in a fury and arriving at the Kilns, where, he wrote in his diary, he "let her ladyship have a blunt statement of the facts" and demanded that Minto permit Jack a vacation. On the day she died in 1951, Warnie devoted several pages of his diary to reviling her, describing her relationship with his brother as "the rape of J's life…I wonder how much of his time she did waste?"

Even if Warnie was exaggerating, why did Lewis—the man who had written, in *Surprised by Joy*, "always and at all ages (where I dared) I hotly demanded not to be interrupted"—submit to such tyranny? He seems to have acquired in Janie Moore both that feminine preoccupation with trivialities he so disliked and his father's aggravating intrusiveness. For someone who claimed to dread "the dominance of the female and the dominance of the collective," he set himself up in a situation where his own cherished autonomy was constantly overthrown by the needs of the household and its mistress. Perhaps there were compensations that Warnie didn't appreciate. Lewis's more recent biographers (those whom the affable Warnie, who survived his brother by ten years, never got the opportunity to charm) tend to think so. Especially in the early years, the relationship offered Jack, as Alan Jacobs puts it, "a depth of affection and tenderness on both sides from which Warnie was excluded and to which he was blind."

Wilson believes that Lewis's loyalty to Minto was cemented in his early twenties, after he was wounded in the war and hospitalized in England. Lewis's father, who had a neurotic phobia about traveling or otherwise disrupting his routine, never came from Ireland to visit his son. This compounded the hurt Jack had felt when Albert hadn't tried to see him before he was sent to the front; it was a time when everyone knew that many of the young men being sent there wouldn't come back. Janie Moore, by contrast, had comforted Lewis on the eve of his deployment and nursed him after his return. Their relationship, then, began in genuine love and a maternal nurturance that the motherless Lewis no doubt found especially sweet.

Somehow, the important relationships in Lewis's life had a tendency to resolve into obligations felt toward needy, importunate people. Take his brother: Warnie believed that his own best years were spent in the "Little End Room" of their boyhood home in Belfast, where the two brothers invented stories for their shared imaginary world. Warnie often talked of his desire to re-create that idyll with Jack and to live in it till the end of their days. When Albert died, in 1931, and the brothers had to empty and sell the Belfast house, Warnie was so upset at the prospect of other children playing with their old toys that the chest containing them had to be buried, unopened, in the backyard. Warnie could be jealous of Jack's time and affection. Just before he came to live with them, Jack felt the need to write to his thirty-five-year-old brother, delicately explaining that the relationships he'd acquired as a grown man would always prevent a completely faithful reproduction of the Little End Room in Oxford.

In addition to tending to Minto and Warnie, Lewis kept up an exhausting correspondence with the strangers who began writing to him after his apologetics gained a wide audience. He seemed to regard all of the inconveniences imposed by others as lessons in humility and submission. In a letter written to Arthur just after Warnie moved in, he complained that he wasn't getting enough solitude and then corrected himself: "what we call *hindrances* are really the raw material of spiritual life." His relationship with Mrs. Moore was the most immediate and pressing of all these interruptions. You would think he'd be more understanding of Chrétien's Lancelot; both knight and don subjected themselves to the command of an exacting lady as a way of serving a greater principle, chivalry in Lancelot's case and Christianity in Lewis's.

Only a saint (or an allegorical knight) could endure this sort of thing without anger, so it's no wonder Lewis wrote waspishly of Guinevere. She provided a safe target for the rage he must have felt toward Janie Moore. It's unlikely he recognized the likeness consciously, or that he would ever have acknowledged it. For one thing, his own sacrifices had the Christian virtue of being entirely selfless; Lancelot enjoyed erotic fulfillment with Guinevere. Lewis once shared this with Minto, but by the time he wrote *The Allegory of Love* their relationship was quasi-filial. It offered no sensual pleasure as compensation for all those hindrances. Still, who knows if he would have shouldered such a burden in the first place if he had not, long ago, fallen in love?

The beauty and desirability of women troubled Lewis even more than their frivolity. Guinevere's beauty, as well as the attractions of the fiancée in "The Shoddy Lands" and of the domineering twentieth-century shoppers he snipes at in *The Allegory of Love,* are sources of illegitimate power. Desire acts as a honey trap to the unwary male, luring him into unworthy and catastrophic enterprises. The beauty of the Narnian witches isn't ancillary to their evil, but integral to it, one of the weapons in their arsenal. Evil must, after all, appear attractive if it's going to be tempting, and from there it's only a small step further to the conclusion that feminine beauty is inherently wicked. It is certainly the cause of endless trouble in Narnia, even when its possessor means well. The spell that Lucy finds in the magician's book, the one promising to "maketh beautiful her that uttereth it beyond the lot of mortals," also foretells the consequences of such beauty: terrible wars among Lucy's princely suitors that leave "nations laid waste."

Those who wish to defend Lewis against charges of misogyny often point to the many heroines in the Chronicles. Besides Lucy, there's Jill Pole, Polly, and Aravis from *The Horse and His Boy*—all sensible, stouthearted girls. But the first three are still children whose sexuality and physical allure have yet to emerge, and Aravis is a tomboy, in full flight from the womanly fate of marriage to a husband chosen by her Calormene father. While Aravis and her friends are attempting to escape the city of Tashbaan, she encounters a childhood friend, the Tarkheena Lasaraleen, who embodies all the feminine foolishness that Aravis has so wisely rejected.

Lasaraleen simply can't fathom why Aravis would reject her prospective groom—a sniveling elderly sycophant, but also a rich and powerful vizier. Nevertheless, finding the whole intrigue "perfectly thrilling," she agrees to help her old friend escape. Getting Lasaraleen to focus on practicalities, however, proves difficult. She takes forever to pick out an outfit and prattles on about court figures when they ought be on the move. The exasperated Aravis remembers how "Lasaraleen had always been like that, interested in clothes and parties and gossip. Aravis had always been more interested in bows and arrows and horses and dogs and swimming."

The menace threatening Narnia in *The Horse and His Boy* is an invasion from Calormen. The story takes place during the reign of the Pevensie siblings, and it's the only Chronicle in which we get to see much of them as adults. A party from Narnia, led by Edmund and Susan, makes a state visit to Tashbaan to consider a marriage proposal Susan has received from Prince Rabadash, the son of the Calormene potentate, the Tisroc. Now grown-up, Susan has become a great beauty, and her judgment has already begun to weaken.

As Rabadash's true character becomes apparent, Edmund marvels that his sister could ever have entertained the idea of marrying him. Susan says that the prince had deceived her by behaving very "meekly and courteously" while in Narnia. (It's hard to imagine that the arrogant, hotheaded Rabadash could have been very convincing at this.) The Narnians, suspecting that Rabadash won't take no for an answer, are then forced to leave the city by stealth. Afterward, the enraged prince urges his father to invade Narnia: "I cannot sleep and my food has no savour and my eyes are darkened because of her beauty," he wails. "I must have the barbarian queen!"

At best, in Lewis's view, a taste for "clothes and parties and gossip" makes a woman useless and annoying; at worst, the snares of sex lead to danger, war, and devastation. We expect a children's book to avoid depictions of sex, but Lewis takes this further by surrounding almost every approach to the subject with contempt or fear—for what are "clothes and parties and gossip" if not tools in the art of meeting and attracting a mate? Grown women are the chief agents and arbiters of this unfortunate business. Without them around, men can concentrate on the adventures that delighted them as boys, albeit on a larger scale—just as Lewis might have spent far more time on reading, writing, and drinking with the Inklings if he hadn't succumbed to the charms of Janie Moore in the waning years of the Great War.

Girls, of course, aren't necessarily excluded from adventures in Narnia, but they must learn to be less girly first. They ought to abandon feminine wiles and concerns. Lucy, in contrast with her sister, is a paragon in this department. When she turns up, armed with bow and arrows, for the climactic battle in *The Horse and His Boy,* a character remarks that she's "as good as a man, or at any rate as good as a boy. Queen Susan is more like an ordinary grown-up lady." Instead of helping to win the war, Susan causes it.

It took me quite a while to recognize the trap in this. I didn't have much use for clothes or parties myself until I reached my twenties, and I'm still no aficionado of gossip. But unlike Lucy, who apparently dies a virgin, I eventually faced the paradox that confronts most heterosexual women: revel in girly stuff and you're viewed as shallow; reject it and you're unattractively mannish. The best you can hope to be is "as good as a boy," and the worst is a man-eater, a time-waster, a "hindrance" or perhaps, as Janie Moore would discover, the occasion for someone else's martyrdom. The only way out is to remain a child forever, as Lucy does, but somehow even this is much easier for men — nostalgic bachelors like Warnie Lewis — to pull off. Besides, I *wanted* to grow up, didn't I? As a child, I'd always believed that Lewis was on my side in that. As a young woman, I realized he'd disappointed me again.

CHAPTER THIRTEEN

Blood Will Out

The *Natural History of Make-Believe* by John Goldthwaite is a little-known "history of the world's imaginative literature for children," a passionate and partisan work, full of fiery tirades against several titles that are usually published with the words "The Beloved Classic" stamped on their covers. It was recommended to me by Philip Pullman, who said that he'd encountered one of the best articulations of his own criticisms of Lewis in the work of Goldthwaite, an American academic. Pullman thought I'd find *The Natural History of Make-Believe* particularly interesting because Goldthwaite is a Christian, and his animus toward Narnia can't be summarily written off as anti-theist prejudice, the way Pullman's often is.

Perhaps the most unconventional argument that Goldthwaite mounts in *The Natural History of Make-Believe* concerns *Alice's Adventures in Wonderland*, which he regards not as a charming flight of fancy but as a risible "bout of rancor." Lewis Carroll's novel, he maintains, is the toxic product of its author's thwarted artistic and social ambitions. I'm not sure I can entirely agree with that, any more than I would argue that children's fiction ought to be devoid of anger, but he has a point; a friend of mine stopped reading the book to his four-year-old daughter because she found the characters upsettingly "mean."

In Goldthwaite's chapter on Middle-earth and Narnia, he raises some familiar objections to the Chronicles—Lewis's evident fear of powerful, sexual women and the occasional sideswipes at such crackpot progressive notions as coed schooling. He also brings up a few others that I hadn't considered before. Goldthwaite (who knows a thing or two about rancor) has a tendency to work up a full head of rhetorical steam and then let it run away with him for pages at a time. Still, he's undeniably intelligent and he makes a troubling case against Lewis's elitism.

Goldthwaite particularly detests a passage from *Prince Caspian* in which Aslan leads a jubilant procession through a Narnia that he has just liberated from another occupation, this time by humans, the Telmarines. The lion's party comes upon a school. Under Aslan's influence, magical ivy grows over and then crushes the school's walls and desks, freeing a classroom of miserable girls dressed in tight collars and "thick tickly stockings." Most of the girls scatter in fear, but one, Gwendolen, hesitates and is invited by Aslan to join his companions. Gwendolen's school is one in a series of dreary, workaday scenarios Aslan's entourage upends along their way. The procession, which includes Bacchus and his Maenads, releases a river god from a bridge, a boy from a man beating him with a stick, and a tired girl teaching arithmetic to "a number of boys who looked very like pigs," (and who will, à la *Alice's Adventures in Wonderland,* eventually turn into pigs).

This scene, with its rambunctious celebrants, enchanted vines, frisking beasts, and general holiday air, has long been one of my favorites. Jonathan Franzen calls it "erotic," and Lewis himself seemed a bit overwhelmed by the wantonness of all the dancing, drinking, and sticky-fingered grape eating. At one point, he has Susan whisper to Lucy, "I wouldn't have felt safe with Bacchus and all his wild girls if we'd met them without Aslan." This is the only point in the Chronicles where we can sense any concern in the author that his readers might get swept up in all the pagan delirium. For myself, I remember thinking that, contra Susan, Bacchus's "wild girls" sounded like one of the few clubs I'd really like to join.

Goldthwaite sees something else again in Aslan's march. The narrator dismisses the rest of the students from Gwendolen's demolished school, the ones who run away from Aslan, as "mostly dumpy, prim little girls with fat legs." The line infuriates Goldthwaite to the degree that he calls it "the vilest passage ever to poison a children's book." Imagine, he suggests, a vulnerable child somewhere, reading this description and recognizing that her own chubby legs must forever relegate her to the ranks of the unchosen; such a slur, Goldthwaite maintains, constitutes nothing less than "sadism." Fat-legged girls are "Lewis's Jews": "The word evil springs to mind," he fulminates, "and, if not evil, then certainly the word shame."

Goldthwaite's outrage may be over the top, but it's not unfounded. Classic fairy tales, like the ones collected in Andrew Lang's nineteenth-century color books (*The Blue Fairy Book, The Red Fairy Book,* and so on), commonly make their virtuous characters beautiful and their wicked characters ugly. But Lewis, a twentieth-century author attempting to model Christian values, ought to have known better. He wasn't writing a traditional fairy tale; those stories feature brutalities that he would never have dreamed of including in Narnia: torture, people thrown into ovens alive, dismemberment, cannibalism, and so on. Besides, Lewis condemned petty vanity and prided himself on not caring much about appearances; his clothes were notoriously shabby and even his house was run-down. To make the primitive error of linking someone's unattractive looks with spiritual unworthiness (or vice versa) is exactly the sort of thing a "silly, conceited," and superficial young woman like the grown-up Susan Pevensie would do.

Goldthwaite views the crack about fat legs as one among many instances of in-group snottiness in the Chronicles. Caspian rejects a potential bride because she "squints and has freckles." Eustace Scrubb, at the beginning of *The Voyage of the Dawn Treader,* is derided not just for reading the wrong kinds of books, but also for having parents who "were vegetarians, non-smokers and teetotallers and wore a special kind of underwear." Such remarks, writes Goldthwaite, work like "keep-out signs on the clubhouse door." (He also reads a great deal into the name Gwendolen, with its posh intimations of the most popular girl at boarding school.) And true enough, a whiff of clubbiness *does* waft through the Chronicles—an unthinking complacency about the superiority of "our kind" (that is, Lewis's kind) of people which goes beyond even the knee-jerk attitudes about race. Nowhere does this seem more apparent to me than in *The Horse and His Boy,* my least favorite among the books (after *The Last Battle,* of course).

The Horse and His Boy has several villains, but in a way its least appealing character is Corin, a boy made more disagreeable by being offered to readers as one of the good guys. Corin is the twin brother of the book's hero, Shasta; both are born princes of Archenland, Narnia's close ally and neighbor. They were separated in infancy when Shasta was kidnapped, lost in a battle, and then raised by a Calormene fisherman as his son. Even a casual observer can tell Shasta doesn't belong in his adoptive father's smelly seaside cottage; a Calormene visitor describes the boy as "fair and white like the accursed but beautiful barbarians who inhabit the remote North." (That the Calormenes invariably find the light-skinned Narnians beautiful is yet another of this book's unsavory motifs.) Furthermore, Shasta harbors an instinctive fascination with the north, a yearning that Bree, the talking horse who escapes with him, believes comes from "the blood that's in you. I'm sure you're true northern stock." Much later, when Shasta finds his way to Archenland, a northern lord remarks, "The boy has a true horseman's seat, Sire. I'll warrant there's noble blood in him."

Blood will out, and some blood is finer than others: these are persistent ideas in *The Horse and His Boy.* Shasta is modest, loyal, and likeable, and despite being raised amid Calormene "slaves and tyrants," he behaves much like the Pevensies and the other children from our world who get to Narnia. He has been reared by the wily and avaricious Arsheesh, yet he has very Pevensian scruples, objecting to a plan that involves "a certain amount of what Shasta called stealing and Bree called 'raiding.'" He even talks like a British schoolboy: "Oh bother breakfast," he says after waking up saddle-sore on the first morning of his flight north. "Bother everything." Shasta sometimes expects other people to act with a Calormene ruthlessness ("He had, you see, no idea how noble and free-born people behave"), but his own natural responses always resemble those of the fair-playing, unpretentious Narnian lords he first sees whistling through the streets of Tashbaan.

Corin, by contrast, is an unadulterated upper-class alpha boy: cocky, insensitive to others, easily riled, and always up for a fight. In Tashbaan, Shasta is mistaken for Corin in the street and winds up spending an afternoon in the Narnians' quarters while the truant Corin is off getting into a brawl with the locals. Later, in Archenland, Corin disobeys orders by sneaking the two of them into the novel's climactic battle at the gates of Anvard, even though Shasta has no experience with a sword or any other kind of fighting. Corin consistently plays a pint-sized Hotspur to Shasta's prepubescent Hal; perhaps Lewis meant him to be a character like the heroes of the school stories he read as a boy, someone he thought his child readers would admire. And perhaps that's why, for me, Corin contributes to the impression that this novel celebrates what Goldthwaite calls "an elitist clique for Top Boys and Girls."

It is Corin who explains to Shasta that Lucy is "as good as a man, or at any rate as good as a boy." For Corin, merit in battle is all that really counts. He is the first to publicly mock Rabadash once the Calormene prince has been mortifyingly defeated and captured in the battle of Anvard. (A hole in Rabadash's hauberk gets caught on a hook as he is leaping down from a mounting block, and he's left hanging from the castle's wall like "a piece of washing.") Corin's father, King Lune, does reproach his son for the taunt, but that is merely Lewis's way of having his cake and eating it, too, of permitting himself to humiliate Rabadash while pretending that his characters are too good to kick a man when he's down. There's more than a touch of the bully in Corin, yet the narrator clearly expects us to like him, to shake our heads fondly at his excesses just as the adults around him do, with the conviction that at heart he is all right, and he is all right because he is one of us.

More than the other Chronicles, *The Horse and His Boy* is preoccupied with social status and inclusion, and the novel's ambivalence is Lewis's own. In a lecture he delivered in 1944, he said, "I believe that in all men's lives at certain periods, and in many men's lives at all periods between infancy and extreme old age, one of the most dominant elements is the desire to be inside the local Ring and the terror of being left outside." Wanting to belong to this "inner ring" can be corrupting — it compromises the spineless protagonist of Lewis's adult science-fiction novel *That Hideous Strength,* for example — although Lewis hastened to clarify that inner rings aren't pernicious per se. You can see why he might stress that last point, why he would warn against the *craving* to be admitted to the in crowd without necessarily condemning in crowds themselves; Lewis belonged to several official and unofficial cliques, from the faculty of Oxford to the Inklings. Yet he also knew how it felt to be shut out.

Lewis's first taste of the bitterness of exclusion came at age fifteen, when he was sent to Malvern College in Worcestershire. Warnie had spent a couple of years at the school before Jack arrived, and had succeeded socially, if not academically; he loved the place. Jack, however, was bad at sports and had no patience for the exacting rituals of British boarding school life. *Surprised by Joy* includes an entire chapter, entitled "Bloodery," devoted to detailing the social structure he found at Malvern, a rigorous hierarchy in which younger boys were obliged to drop everything at a moment's notice to shine shoes and perform other chores for the older students. At the pinnacle of this order stood the "bloods," the "adored athletes and prefects" who functioned as the school's aristocracy.

Every society of children has its pecking order, but at British boarding schools the exalted status of the most popular boys was both highly formalized and endorsed by adult authority. Alumni of this system could be extravagantly sentimental about it and were its fiercest proponents. (Warnie argued with Jack that the practice of "fagging"—forcing younger boys to work as the personal servants of the older ones—provided a necessary lesson in humility.) In Lewis's father's generation, many middle- and upper-class men were convinced that boarding school had prepared them to be exemplary Englishmen and champions of the empire. The Duke of Wellington supposedly asserted that the battle of Waterloo was "won on the playing fields of Eton"—although historians have since pointed out that there were no organized sports at the school during his time there and that the great Wellington, like Lewis, was no athlete.

Lewis's own feelings about the institution were mixed. When *Surprised by Joy* was first published in 1956, it shocked some readers with its matter-of-fact discussion of "tarts"—smaller boys who served as "catamites" to the bloods at Malvern. But some of Lewis's more conservative readers found it nearly as provocative that he dared to question the public school power structure—an "oligarchy," he called it—in general. Still, as much as Lewis hated being forced to play games that bored him and to abandon his studies to dance attendance on some pubescent lout, he could not bring himself to denounce traditional boarding schools entirely.

At Malvern, Lewis encountered an inner ring at its most impenetrable and abusive. On one occasion, an older boy tricked him into "skipping clubs"—that is, into not showing up for the obligatory sporting events that formed the center of student life. For this offense, he was ordered to report to a blood he calls Porridge for a flogging. The messenger who delivered the summons told Lewis, "Who are you? Nobody. Who is Porridge? THE MOST IMPORTANT PERSON THERE IS." It's not hard to see how this sort of thing might have inspired scenes of Calormene muckety-mucks in litters, barreling through the streets of Tashbaan, knocking the peasantry into the dust. So, too, does the haughty Rabadash feel perfectly free to kick the backside of his father's groveling vizier whenever the spirit moves him.

None of this is surprising in the Calormenes, who are, of course, the bad guys. Yet what is Corin if not an idealized version of the British public school blood, a natural athlete who blithely shanghais Shasta into a battle he's utterly unequipped to fight? Like the bookish Lewis, who was compelled to run ineffectually around a cricket field, Shasta soon loses his sword and falls off his horse — sending him into combat is "mere murder," says the wise old hermit observing the scene — and he barely emerges with his life. While Lewis was at Malvern, he wrote a play based on Norse myth, a tragedy he called *Loki Bound,* in which the title character lashes out at the injustice of the gods. The gods' enforcer is Thor, god of thunder, whose "brutal orthodoxy" demands that power be respected simply because it is powerful. "Thor was, in fact, the symbol of the Bloods," Lewis writes in *Surprised by Joy,* and so it's indicative that when Corin grows up to become a famous boxer who pummels a renegade Narnian bear back into line, he earns the nickname Corin Thunder-Fist.

Corin is Thor redeemed, a blood with the thuggishness scrubbed out. Is such a thing really possible, or is the honorable, decent British public school blood a wishful fiction, the sort of fantasy promulgated by books like *Tom Brown's School Days,* the "school stories" that Lewis once accused of being far more deceptive than fairy tales? His own boyhood misery would not lead to, say, the insurrection of George Orwell, who, in a famous autobiographical essay, "Such, Such Were the Joys," described his stint at a preparatory school (a training academy for boys seeking admission to public schools like Eton) as a sojourn in "a world of force and fraud and secrecy." These schools, Orwell wrote, were infused with "contempt for 'braininess,' and worship of games, contempt for foreigners and the working class, an almost neurotic dread of poverty and, above all, the assumption not only that money and privilege are the things that matter, but that it is better to inherit them than to have to work for them.... Life was hierarchical and whatever happened was right."

This early encounter with the cruelties of Britain's class system

helped make Orwell a leftist. Lewis, whose sentimental conserva-
tivism was really a flight from serious political thought, clung instinctively to the old ways in spite of all he had endured and resented
under their dominion. Although he hated Malvern, in later years he
would fret about excessive taxation, worrying that it might prevent
middle-class Britons from sending their boys to similar schools. In the
Chronicles, this makes for a contradictory attitude toward "school,"
which Lewis usually depicts as a character-warping oppression. In *The
Lion, the Witch and the Wardrobe,* Peter and Lucy attribute Edmund's
nastiness to "that horrid school, which was where he had begun to
go wrong," and one of the many good works the Pevensies perform
after they become kings and queens of Narnia is to make sure "young
dwarfs and young satyrs" aren't sent to school. Human beings aren't
so lucky; the downside to the discovery of Shasta's true identity as a
prince of Archenland, he explains to Aravis, is that now "education
and all sort of horrible things are going to happen to me."

This is a strange attitude in a man so devoted to books and learning. Lewis, it seems, had ruled out the possibility that school could
ever be enjoyable, or even agreeable. His mistrust of anything labeled "progress" set him against the notion that schools could be
improved or reformed; do-gooders would only make them worse.
In *The Silver Chair,* Eustace Scrubb and Jill Pole attend a coeduca-
tional academy called Experiment House, derided by the narrator
as "what used to be called a 'mixed' school; some said it was not
nearly so mixed as the minds of the people who ran it." (Nowhere
does Lewis sound more like the crusty, reactionary old colonel in
an Agatha Christie country-house whodunit than he does in that
aside.) At Experiment House, the smaller children are tormented by
a gang of fellow students known only as "Them."

We are informed that "horrid things" in the line of cliques and
bullying are allowed to flourish at Experiment House, abuses that "at
an ordinary school would have been found out and stopped in half
a term." It's hard to imagine what could be worse than the goings-on

permitted at an "ordinary" school like Malvern—de facto slavery in the form of the fag system, catamites, sanctioned beatings. But whatever the horrid things perpetrated at Experiment House, the school's authorities merely indulge the culprits, drawing them out in long chats and treating them as "interesting psychological cases." Further signs of the school's deficiency include the fact that Bibles are "not encouraged" and the "Head" (headmaster, or principal) is a woman.

The swamp of misguided progressivism that is Experiment House can only be drained with the help of Aslan, who at the end of *The Silver Chair* sends Jill, Eustace, and (briefly) Caspian back into our world with orders to thrash some of the worst bullies. Jill beats them with a switch, and Caspian and Eustace with the sides of their swords, raising a ruckus and driving the Head to hysterics. (Later, we're informed with uncharacteristically leaden wit that this individual will rise to a station more commensurate with her incompetence: a seat in Parliament.) The scene appalls Goldthwaite. All Christians, he maintains, are bound to honor the ideal of pacifism, even if they can't always strictly abide by it. "I cannot imagine," he writes, "a betrayal of one's faith more complete than this last picture of Christ at the playground, putting weapons into the hands of children."

Any child who has ever been bullied relishes scenarios in which schoolyard tyrants get their comeuppance; revenge is an ancient and satisfying narrative theme. It's not, however, a particularly Christian one, and the beating delivered in the coda of *The Silver Chair* does seem gratuitous. It traffics in the sort of self-righteousness that Lewis usually makes a point of condemning elsewhere. Couldn't Aslan have simply appeared before the bullies and terrified them into virtue with a single glance—he is God, after all—without asking our heroes to wallop a bunch of unarmed kids? Is hitting people really the best way to reform them? I suspect Lewis himself sensed how dicey the scene is; he becomes euphemistic when describing the thrashing itself, using the word "ply" instead of "beat" or "whip." The whole episode has an air of bad faith and self-indulgence. Lewis gets the satisfaction of imagining his old enemies, the bloods, being scourged, but he excuses the tradition that gave them the power to persecute him in the first place. In this looking-glass world, progress and reform, not the hallowed institution of "bloodery," have enabled sadists to run amok.

Throughout the Chronicles, Lewis will often play an imaginative sorting game, hoarding everything good and admirable on the side of what's familiar while pushing all vices toward what's not. The Calormenes, the foreigners to the south, are given all the shameful excesses of civilization, and the Narnians in the north get to keep all the justice and virtue. Both nations have hereditary monarchies, but Calormen is ruled by tyrants while Narnia's kings are born noble and true. The hierarchy of Calormen is manifestly unfair, permitting spoiled aristocrats to push everyone else around, while the social ladder of Narnia consists of everybody knowing his place and feeling perfectly comfortable in it.

As the German psychologist Bruno Bettelheim pointed out in his most celebrated book, *The Uses of Enchantment: The Meaning and Importance of Fairy Tales,* such dichotomies are typical of traditional fairy tales. Bettelheim argued that the wicked stepmother figures in stories like *Snow-White and the Seven Dwarfs* and *Cinderella* serve as stand-ins for troubling aspects of a child's real mother. "Although Mother is most often the all-giving protector," Bettelheim writes, "she can change into the cruel stepmother if she is so evil as to deny the child something he wants. Far from being a device used only in fairy tales, such a splitting up of one person into two to keep the good image uncontaminated occurs to many children as a solution to a relationship too difficult to manage or comprehend."

When Lewis wrote "Sometimes Fairy Stories May Say Best What's to Be Said" in 1956, he surely didn't have this particular use of enchantment in mind. He would have hated Bettelheim's Freudian analysis of the tales he loved so much. Nevertheless, in light of *The Uses of Enchantment,* it's hard to ignore how well Calormen serves, unconsciously at least, as a way to "manage" all sorts of difficult relationships and situations. The evils of the British class system could be displaced onto a nation of swarthy foreigners while the romance and poetry of its chivalric past could be kept by the Narnians.

Narnia is an idealized reimagining of a society toward which Lewis felt a deep aesthetic and spiritual affinity, the world of medieval Britain. But Narnia's government is feudalism without serfs (Narnia has no discernible agriculture), a place where the epitome of civic virtue is to mind your own business unless Narnia itself is being threatened. By making the hereditary kings of Narnia human beings who rule over animals and semihuman creatures, Lewis could preserve a hierarchy that seems perfectly natural. A mole or a dwarf doesn't mind being relegated at birth to a life of digging the way a human being would, because, of course, they "don't look on it as work. They like digging." When the citizens are different species, it's easier to see caste as merely a matter of "each kind of creature joyfully living out their natural attitudes." This left Lewis free to savor the romance of Arthurian-style aristocracy without countenancing the kind of underclass (the human kind) that makes any aristocracy viable. No wonder, then, that the half-bred dwarf Doctor Cornelius admonishes Caspian that Narnia "is not the land of men."

All this makes it tempting to call Lewis misanthropic, but he liked people well enough—as long as he believed they were a lot like him. He and his circle saw themselves as surrounded by a hostile world intent on destroying everything they valued. Perhaps this kept Lewis from recognizing that even as he condemned the pursuit of the "inner ring," he was often hard at work constructing such rings and determining who would or would not be let in. Membership was based on a presumed uniformity of taste as well as a generally conservative outlook. "Authors whom he did not admire," write Walter Hooper and Roger Lancelyn Green in their biography of Lewis, "such as James and Lawrence, he would dismiss as 'not for us' in conversation with literary friends." There's not much air between "not for us" and "not our kind," the watch phrase of the snob and the bigot.

But why did Lewis, who suffered so much misery under the reign of the Malvern bloods as a boy, wind up defending traditionalism as a man? Like his father, he was a creature of habit who feared change. He had seen his beloved countryside eroded by the modernization that many of his contemporaries regarded as an unalloyed good. He believed that modern art and literature were implacably set against faith and beauty, two qualities he cherished. And finally, in puzzling out this contradiction, it's worth remembering that the most energetic defender of an inner ring is often the member whose own standing is a bit tenuous.

Many of Lewis's casual readers are surprised to learn that he wasn't actually English, so entirely did he embody the role of shabby-genteel British gentleman. Descriptions of him make it sound as if Mole, from *The Wind in the Willows* (a favorite book of Lewis's, one that he felt embodied the best of Britishness), had jumped off the page and taken a job as an Oxford don. When Lewis first arrived at the university, just before the First World War, he surely must have felt himself to be something of an outsider, the son of an undistinguished Belfast solicitor on scholarship among the wealthy and well-born British graduates of schools like Eton and Harrow. If Lewis rarely discussed the inevitable discomfort of this position, perhaps that was because the type of Englishman he sought to emulate put a high premium on a confident indifference.

Nevertheless, whenever Lewis felt unsure of himself, his Irishness would come flooding back. In the two years after he completed his undergraduate education, his future as a professional scholar remained unclear. His domestic situation with Mrs. Moore and her daughter made relocating to another university town untenable, so his choices were limited. He applied unsuccessfully for a couple of fellowships in Philosophy, a subject that (with Classics, or Greats) was one of his original areas of study. When he took a position on the English faculty at Magdalen College, it was the best alternative he could get, and it meant accepting that he'd never become a professional philosopher, as he had once planned. By way of reconciling himself to this new course, he cited his Irish temperament. "I have come to think," he wrote to his father, "that if I have the mind, I have not the brain and nerves for a life of pure philosophy....What is a tonic to the Saxon may be a debauch to us Celts."

To his Celtic blood (which was really more Welsh than Irish), Lewis attributed all the whimsy, mysticism, and gloom conventionally associated with that ethnicity. This he regarded ambivalently, as an inheritance from his moody father, a descendant of Welsh farmers. To his mind, his mother's family, the Hamiltons, represented practicality, common sense, and a cool, ironic view of life; his mother earned a B.A. in mathematics from Queen's College in Belfast, but her son, sometimes to his despair, never inherited her aptitude with numbers. Through his maternal grandmother he claimed descent from a Norman knight interred at Battle Abbey in Sussex — if not an Anglo-Saxon, then at the least a very English forebear. Jack complained that his paternal relatives and Celts in general were "sentimental, passionate, and rhetorical," but when asked to temper his heavy breathing during a radio recording session, he responded, "Did you ever know an Irishman who didn't puff and blow?"

You can listen to a few audio clips of Lewis reading from his apologetics on the Web. No trace of a brogue — if he ever had one — remains in the deep, plummy intonations issuing from the speakers in my laptop as I write this. What I hear is a stately Oxbridge voice that rolls majestically onward, holding its vowels in the pockets at the back of the cheeks like a chipmunk guarding his hoard of nuts. I have no expertise in accents, but to my ears Lewis did a pretty good job of passing for English. Yet everything about himself that didn't quite fit this persona, and many of the traits that would eventually lie closest to his heart, he would label "Irish" — so at the very center

of his embodiment of tweedy, no-nonsense, old-fashioned Englishness lay a crumb of exception.

There were other reasons why Lewis never felt entirely at home
in Oxford. In his early years, he had to hide his relationship with
Mrs. Moore. As recently as the late nineteenth century, the university had required celibacy of its fellows (who were originally required
to be priests), and it remained fairly straitlaced. Until Minto was old
enough to be presented as a plausible "mother," the scandal of getting
caught living with a married woman might have seriously damaged
Lewis's academic career. (Around the same time, the critic William
Empson was famously sent down from Cambridge in disgrace because a servant discovered condoms in his room.)

There was intellectual friction, too. The little crowd that Lewis
gathered around him at Oxford (including Tolkien, also an odd duck
by virtue of his Catholicism) he envisioned as a rearguard defense
against an atheistic, progressive contingent he believed to be unoffi-
cially running things. Many of Lewis's academic adversaries regarded him as the representative of an entrenched old regime, and when
he and Tolkien succeeded in instating a new syllabus for the English
faculty that excluded works published after 1830, they appeared to
have a point. Even though Lewis won that battle, he never seemed
able to settle into an image of himself as an insider.

On top of this, his contempt for administration and politicking
of any sort made Lewis unpopular among the rest of the faculty. Many
of his colleagues considered the popular success of his Christian apologetics in print and on the radio to be vulgar. Others resented both
his proselytizing and his opposition to any sort of modernization.
Still others found his manner objectionable; he could be rude and
overbearing in debate and scornful of college protocol and anyone
who disagreed with him. Students flocked to his lectures, but they
were not the ones who voted dons into professorships, and when
Lewis campaigned to be made Chair of Poetry at Oxford in 1951,

his peers elected someone else. (He would later accept a similar position at Cambridge.)

No wonder, then, that politics was something of a bête noire for Lewis, an imponderable factor that bored and thwarted him and niggled at his secret insecurities. In Narnia, where biology replaces politics, things are much simpler. Only in *The Last Battle* does anyone—the ape Shift, who is in effect the Antichrist—aspire beyond his station. The beginning of politics is, in Narnia, the beginning of the end of the world.

Of course, it's absurd to speak of the "politics" of Narnia. These are children's fantasies, not designed to address such adult concerns as class systems, nationalism, and economics. They take place in a dream world where talking beavers bake marmalade rolls despite having no surplus goods to trade for oranges and sugar, commodities that can only have been imported from a warmer land. Who raises and slaughters the pigs to make the bacon and sausages gobbled up at almost every Narnian meal? Who grows the wheat and grinds the flour for bread, and who imports the tea and coffee? Even Tolkien, who labored for countless hours to make Middle-earth a consistent, coherent alternative world, never made it entirely plausible economically, and he thought Narnia a disgracefully slapdash creation.

But if Narnia, as Lewis often indicated, exists in the same imaginative realm as fairy tales, then like fairy tales it surely speaks of dreams, archetypes, and drives, the timeless leviathans that swim deep inside our psyches. Here, too, the material that Lewis brought to the task was neither as wholesome nor as dull as some would like to believe.

CHAPTER FOURTEEN

Arrows of Desire

According to Bruno Bettelheim, the most important function of fairy tales is unconscious; they echo and give form to the fears, urges, and enigmas already lurking in a child's mind. Bettelheim thought the stories both expressed and brought coherence to children's inner lives and were essential aids in the challenge of growing up. When adults worry about exposing children to the monsters and violence in fairy tales, he cautioned, they underestimate the interior tumult with which children are *already* grappling. "Fairy tale imagery," wrote Bettelheim, "helps children better than anything else in their most difficult and yet most important and satisfying task: achieving a more mature consciousness to civilize the chaotic pressures of their unconscious."

Lewis would have agreed with Bettelheim that children can handle the scarier aspects of fairy tales, but that's about it. Lewis detested Freudianism and satirized it in an early prose allegory entitled *The Pilgrim's Regress*. He found Freud's theories reductive, arguing that if all artistic imagery can be boiled down to nothing more than symbols of infantile sexuality, then "our literary judgments are in ruins." It was not that he detected no sexual fantasies in art, but rather that there was so much else there as well that sex struck him as the least of it. Besides, Freudian criticism often engages in what Lewis rejected as "the personal heresy," the study of texts as glosses on the minds of their creators. "The poet," Lewis wrote, "is not a man who asks me to look at *him;* he is a man who says 'look at that' and points." This riposte, of course, sidesteps the question of what the poet communicates about himself—intentionally or otherwise—by his style of pointing and by the things he chooses to point at.

Psychoanalysis frequently assumes that a patient who passionately denies a motive or an anxiety is really concealing the presence of that very feeling. (This is the original clinical meaning of "denial.") As a therapeutic tool, this concept leaves a lot to be desired—as almost anyone would conclude from reading Freud's case histories. I first read *Fragments of an Analysis of a Case of Hysteria,* better known as *Dora,* in an undergraduate course on psychoanalytic criticism. Our young instructor wanted to move quickly past the basic Freudian principles so that he could get to the work of Jacques Lacan, then a relatively new and fashionable theorist. With unconcealed impatience, he let several of us (all women) vent our outrage over Freud's treatment of his patient, poor Dora, a young Viennese woman whose father was sleeping with the wife of a friend and who, his daughter suspected, was tacitly encouraging the friend to sleep with Dora by way of compensation. Freud validated Dora's suspicions (her father, not surprisingly, denied trading his daughter for his friend's wife), but he also betrayed her by insisting that, contrary to her protests, she really was in love her father's friend. It's always a good idea to bear in mind that Freud's theories usually failed at their primary, stated purpose: helping his patients.

But whatever Freud's shortcomings as a therapist (and they were considerable), he had remarkable acumen about the workings of the human mind. We *do* sometimes deny most fiercely what we covertly desire, and erect a rational skepticism against what we secretly fear to be the truth. A. N. Wilson believes that Lewis's animus toward Freudianism had personal as well as scholarly roots. Lewis was, Wilson writes, "obsessed not only by his father, but also by the possibility that his life could be interpreted in a purely Freudian way." This fear was well founded; Freudian psychology became a pervasive intellectual fad during his lifetime, and hardly anyone in educated circles escaped the occasional armchair analysis by amateur Freudians among their friends and colleagues. Lewis's religious conversion followed on the heels of his father's death and a flare-up of his guilt over having treated Albert so "abominably." Since Freud had argued that religious faith arises in part from a "longing for a father," the obvious conclusion in Lewis's case was that he converted to soothe his grief and loss.

Freudian literary criticism, especially the kind written during Lewis's lifetime, can be crude and simplistic. In the myopic attention it pays to the drives and fears of the individual, it often leaves out the social, cultural, and intellectual elements of artworks that are, after all, meant to be acts of communication with other human beings. But fairy tales — unlike, say, comedies of manners or epic poems or historical dramas — tend not to have much social, cultural, or intellectual content. They transpire in a dream landscape full of primal forces and totemlike people and objects: wolves, stepmothers, houses in the woods. This place, sometimes known as Faerie, is also called "The Perilous Realm," and the stories set there are, as Tolkien once put it, "plainly not primarily concerned with possibility, but with desirability." If any type of narrative invites Freudian interpretation, it is the fairy tale. And "fairy tales" are what Lewis said he wanted to write when he began the Chronicles. Quite possibly he assumed that psychoanalytic critics would take no interest in the sexless, critically ignored realm of children's fiction. But it is exactly the contexts in which our imaginations feel most relaxed and free — in dreams and in play — that most welcome the return of the repressed.

A few of the Chronicles' characters — the White Witch, Prince Rilian, and Aslan himself — do have the archetypal resonance of fairy-tale figures. Others are more psychologically realistic, like the Pevensies, Caspian, and the other children from our world. Lewis's familiarity with medieval allegory surely contributed to making the landscape itself psychological; Narnia is, more than anything else, the domain of his own imagination. When Lucy first discovers it, it has been frozen for years, dominated by an implacable female tyrant. With the arrival of Aslan comes the thaw, and the joyous restoration of all the countryside's natural beauty; this is the story of Lewis's conversion embodied in the land, and also the voice of his own hidden desire for liberation, written at a time when Janie Moore had become utterly impossible and was on the brink of requiring institutionalization.

But Narnia has its own unconscious, the place to which all its less acceptable desires are exiled, and that place is Calormen. Alan Jacobs is right when he observes that Lewis drew upon a "readymade source of 'Oriental' imagery" in creating Calormen. Lewis was far from the first Western writer to find it convenient to believe that the East had a concession on sophisticated depravity—or to regard that depravity with a thinly concealed fascination. In the 1920s and '30s, British writers indulged in a penchant for decadent Oriental pageantry, especially on the stage. Lord Dunsany, a pioneer of the fantasy genre and an author much admired by Tolkien, found early success writing stories and short plays about implacable gods and cruel potentates in curled slippers for Dublin's Abbey Theatre.

Lewis saw one such play, a drama in verse called *Hassan,* by James Elroy Flecker, performed by the Oxford University Dramatic Society in 1931. Forgotten today, *Hassan* is an exercise in bejeweled cynicism and languid savagery, in which the Caliph of Baghdad offers two illicit lovers a terrible choice: either separate forever or enjoy one day of perfect love to be followed by death in "merciless torment." (They choose the latter, and their ordeal takes place offstage, after enough paraphernalia has been paraded across the stage to fuel the audience's worst imaginings.) Lewis saw the play with his brother, and Warnie, presumably sickened by the implied torture, walked out. Lewis compelled himself to stay to the end, writing to Arthur Greeves that he considered it "almost a duty for one afflicted in my way to remain...the same principle on which one trains a puppy to be clean—'rub their noses in it.'"

Lewis was referring to his own sadomasochistic inclinations—specifically, his interest in erotic flagellation. A fetish for whipping or birching is sometimes referred to as "the English vice," supposedly encouraged by the British public school system and its lavish, ritualized use of corporal punishment. When they were in their late teens, Lewis and Greeves had confided in each other about their sexuality; Arthur admitted to being attracted to other men and Lewis to fantasizing about "disciplining" shapely young women. As an Oxford freshman, he once got very drunk at a party and loudly offered to pay a shilling a lash to whoever would submit to a whipping at his hands. Later, Lewis came to view such tastes as antithetical to his religion, and by the time he saw *Hassan* performed in Oxford, he was apparently striving to eradicate them.

At some point, Greeves went back though Lewis's old letters, burning some and in others crossing out the passages that refer to his friend's enthusiasm for "the rod." He was most likely worried that their correspondence would be published someday, and that the younger Lewis's wayward lusts might prove embarrassing. To his credit, Walter Hooper (briefly Lewis's secretary and currently a trustee of Lewis's literary estate, as well as a Roman Catholic priest) restored those passages in editing his mammoth, three-volume *Collected Letters of C. S. Lewis*. It can't be pleasant to learn of the unorthodox sexual predilections of an idolized religious mentor, but it probably helps that Hooper has chosen to regard the adult Lewis as having been cured of these "teenage lusts of the flesh" through the agency of faith.

Greeves no doubt knew better; few traits are more ineradicable than unwelcome sexual fantasies and desires, as the more candid participants in the Christian "ex-gay" movement have admitted. Behavior, on the other hand, can be controlled, and after his conversion Lewis probably put away any hopes of acting on his fantasies. (Although I like to think that in his marriage he found a willing partner for what strike me as fairly commonplace and innocuous bedroom games.) Repression tends to intensify sexual impulses, however, and as time went by, Lewis's must have come to seem monstrous to him; he probably thought them much worse than they really were. It took the extravagant, homicidal cruelties of *Hassan* to exceed his own "affliction"; only Flecker's wicked Caliph of Baghdad could go far enough to revolt him.

Imaginary (or real) atrocities set in the Near and Far East have for a long time both horrified and comforted Westerners who prefer to disassociate themselves from their own worst instincts. In 1932, Lewis wrote to his brother:

> When I have tried to rule out all my prejudices I still can't help thinking that the Christian world is (partially) "saved" in a sense in which the East is not. We may be hypocrites, but there is a sort of unashamed and *reigning* iniquity of temple prostitution and infanticide and torture and political corruption and obscene imagination in the East, which really does suggest that they are off the rails — that some necessary part of the human machine, restored to us, is still missing with them.

Europe's past, of course, was just as full of spectacular and ingenious sadism, committed by everyone from the ancient leaders of Greece and Rome to devout churchmen to the kings and queens of Lewis's beloved Britain. The people of Shakespeare's time routinely saw criminals, religious dissidents, and enemies of the crown publicly tortured, dismembered, and killed in the streets of London. On a more modest scale, if we are to judge from the diaries of Samuel Pepys, respectable bourgeois citizens customarily beat their misbehaving servants without a second thought. Swarthy people in turbans and harem pants by no means held a monopoly on this sort of abuse, but it was convenient — and also exciting — to think of them that way, especially when the imagined victims were young, pretty, and helpless.

Lewis's own life and fiction abound in less exaggerated and lurid scenarios of dominance and submission. From his obedience to the exacting orders of Mrs. Moore, to Prince Rilian "tied to the apron strings" of the Green Witch, to Lewis's own daily efforts to humble himself before God, he clearly found this dynamic fascinating, whether for ill or good. Most of these situations, real and imaginary, hinge on the abasement of a man before a woman; Rabadash's promise that he will drag Susan to his palace by her hair is one of the rare exceptions. It's even possible that Lewis saw his servitude to Mrs. Moore as a kind of penance for his own sadistic impulses.

But as Freud observed of sadomasochism in *Three Essays on the Theory of Sexuality*, "the most remarkable feature of this perversion is that its active and passive forms are habitually found together in the same individual...a sadist is always at the same time a masochist, although the active or the passive aspect of the perversion may be the more strongly developed in him and may represent his predominant sexual activity." Lewis admitted in one of his letters to Greeves that he had often fancied himself in the victim's role when he was young, but that he came to consider it "a feeling more proper to the other sex."

The Freudian view of human nature, which would regard a man like Lewis as falling short of some ideal masculinity, is woefully limited. Freud's preoccupation with individuals and their internal conflicts prevented him from seeing that relationships consist of more than the fantasies people have about each other, that a relationship between two people is really a kind of entity in itself. Freud interpreted both sadism and masochism as malformations of a normally "aggressive" libido; sadists exaggerate the innate aggressiveness in the sexual drive, and masochists turn the aggressiveness on themselves. For Freud, desire was like an arrow, either straight or bent, correctly aimed or overshot, striking the appropriate target or circling back like a boomerang toward the person who fired it.

But surely what the sadist or masochist craves most is a particular *dynamic,* generated by a theatrical imbalance of power, in which one player towers above, possessed of all the strength, glory, and authority, while the other cringes below in utter humility and dependence. The imbalance creates a charged emotional field; who plays what role matters less than the voluptuous contrast between them. Often no real violence and very little pain are involved. The sadomasochistic impulse seems to arise not from the urge to behave aggressively, but from the desire to be suspended in an ever-unfolding continuum of overwhelming feeling. And this, in turn, throws new light on the emphasis Lewis put on his submissiveness before God; for here was a man for whom piety and prostration were much the same thing.

I was recently holding forth on this topic to a friend, describing how Lewis chose to interpret interpersonal hardships—unfair or delusional scolding from Mrs. Moore, the felt obligation to respond to hundreds of letters from readers, and so on—as trials imposed on him by a God who demanded complete submission to his will. After a pause, my friend asked, "But isn't that the same as almost everyone's relationship to God? It's about bowing as low as you can before an incomprehensible power."

His observation stopped me in my tracks. Surely not every believer is a closet sadomasochist? On the other hand, perhaps sadomasochism is not as exotic as it's made out to be. Perhaps its devotees are merely people whose affinity for a particular dynamic takes a sexual rather than spiritual form? It only seems outrageously transgressive because we don't recognize its meaning as theater and ritual. The church where I fidgeted through countless Sunday Masses as a girl had an unsettlingly lifelike crucifix hanging over the altar. Whenever I got bored enough to study it, I saw the tortured body of a man, swooning in agony, blood dripping from his brow, hands, feet, and side. What would someone with no prior knowledge of Christianity conclude upon walking into *that* god's temple?

Religions have been known to demand great suffering from their adherents, ordeals ranging from fasting and other forms of self-denial to self-flagellation and hair shirts to outright martyrdom. Remove the overt sexuality and the paraphernalia from a sadomasochistic scene, and the emotional center of helplessness and dependency isn't so very different from the intense bond between parent and child or between a god and his worshipper. Perhaps all of these are facets of something universal that I, too, can recognize. It's the desire to be carried away by something greater than ourselves—a love affair, a group, a movement, a nation, a faith. Or even a book.

CHAPTER FIFTEEN

The Other Way In

During my freshman year at the University of California at Berkeley, I took a course called Rhetoric 1A. I sat in a small classroom with about twenty other undergraduates clutching beat-up copies of Albert Camus's *The Fall* and listened to a stout, cranky young man in a grubby T-shirt and a Yankees cap explain to us that we needed to learn a whole new way of reading. In high school, teachers were satisfied if we could point out that *The Fall* contains several scenes involving water or metaphors of water, which symbolized oblivion. But when we tentatively offered this sort of observation, the stout young man would sigh, and say, "OK, but what is it *doing* there?" At times, our obtuseness reduced him to simply repeating that same question over and over.

Even today, I'm sometimes not entirely sure that I know what he meant by this question. Most often, I think that he was telling us to look at the components of Camus's fiction and ask ourselves what strategy lay behind each choice the author made. The green light at the end of the pier in *The Great Gatsby,* for example, doesn't just stand for the doomed hopes and fantasies of the title character; it also marks Fitzgerald's novel as the kind of story that works through romantic symbols. A satirical novel written about a character like Jay Gatsby would never use such a motif, not when its intention would be to cast the bootlegger as a poseur and his dreams as ludicrous or deluded. The swoony, aching, soft-focus quality of the green light would be incompatible with the funny, often cruel specificity of satire.

But perhaps that's not what the stout young man was trying (and largely failing) to communicate to me and my fellow undergraduates. One day in Rhetoric 1A, feeling especially exasperated by the impasse, I asked him if he meant, "What the heck is *that* doing there?"—the sort of question you'd ask if you tripped over a garden rake in the corridor of a high-rise office building. I was being flippant, and he was not amused, but lately my interpretation seems more pertinent than not. It's a question worth asking, not just about the water imagery in *The Fall,* but also about *The Fall* itself. Why is this book here—in my hands, opened before my eyes? Why was it written to begin with and why was it printed, bound, and sold? Why am I reading it? Why read?

This is an immaterial question for most academic critics. However iconoclastic their approach to great books (or to the very idea of great books), however intently they seek to "interrogate" or "dismantle" the ideologies that imbue those books, for the English professor, books themselves are always a given, as the salt mine is for the salt miner. The common or recreational reader, on the other hand, has different questions flitting at the periphery of her mind: Why read this book? Why read any books at all?

A satisfactory answer is apparently hard to come by. Many, many people don't even bother to read; movies and television are easier and usually more fun, and athletics or spending time with friends and family are more healthful. In 2004, the National Endowment for the Arts published a report, "Reading at Risk," indicating that less than half of adult Americans read literature in their leisure time. (Since the survey defined "literature" as "any novels, short stories, plays or poetry," leaving out memoirs, histories, and other forms of literary nonfiction—such as this book—we'll have to assume the percentage is on the low side.) The results, the report maintained, "show the declining importance of literature to our populace."

If these ex-readers wanted it, they could find plenty of intellectual justification for their abandonment of books at the average university English department. Not long after I entered college, academic thinking underwent a series of transformations. The traditional, reverential study of canonical literature that prevailed in Lewis's day, and the revolution-mongering of the 1960s and 1970s that supplanted it, gave way to poststructuralist and postmodern theory. Books that past generations regarded as eternal monuments of genius were dragged into the courts of theory and indicted for their ideological inadequacies. Their authors' personal lives and political beliefs served as evidence against them. Racism, sexism, classism, and homophobia lurked everywhere, often in disguises that required expert decoding. If you wanted to explain why the world proved so resistant to the utopian designs of a fading radicalism—and that's exactly what many academics, having seen such dreams die, wanted to do—you could point to the poisonous bias embedded in even the most celebrated pillars of our culture.

For academics, seeing literature's former gods brought low doesn't constitute much of a dilemma—the salt miner keeps going to the mine every day whether or not he likes salt; that's his job. The common reader has different prerogatives. In a few unhappy cases, however, both readers are forced to exist side by side in the same person. In his academic satire, *The Handmaid of Desire*, the novelist John L'Heureux, who teaches creative writing at Stanford University, describes an English department under siege by a young firebrand professor who wants to turn it into a department of Theory and Discourse. But the firebrand has a secret stashed in a locked cabinet—a copy of Jane Austen's *Emma*. His professional reputation depends on hiding this forbidden passion from his colleagues; his own discipline, his livelihood, is dedicated to proving that the pleasures of old-fashioned novels are invidious, regressive, illusory.

The honest, educated reader, when tackling the towering literary works of the past, now faces a different, though no less precarious task: how to acknowledge an author's darker side without losing the ability to enjoy and value the book. Prejudice is repellent, but if we were to purge our shelves of all the great books tainted by one vile idea or another, we'd have nothing left to read—or at least nothing but the new and blandly virtuous. For the stone-cold truth is that Virginia Woolf *was* an awful snob, and Milton was a male chauvinist. The work of both authors can be difficult to read, but also immeasurably rewarding. Once upon a time, when people believed encounters with great art were morally uplifting, it was easier to summon the extra bit of initiative required to give the classics a try, and literature professors were expected to encourage them. Today, scholars are more likely to tell readers about the pernicious influence of the great books they used to revere.

In recent years, it's gotten easier to write off complaints about how an author portrays race, class, or gender as "political correctness," but that's just as facile as reducing every author to the sum of his political beliefs; hatred and injustice are wrong, not merely "incorrect." When it comes to a favorite author, the impulse to try to demonstrate that he wasn't really a racist, or at least wasn't so bad, can be nearly irresistible. C. S. Lewis's most devoted Christian readers regard his writings as, if not quite sacred, then at least sacralized. For them, the temptation to deny that he held a lot of objectionable opinions is very strong. Nevertheless, he did indeed hold those opinions, and they can't be rationalized away with talk of "ready-made" sources. The racism, sexism, and snobbery (of various types) lie pretty close to the surface in some parts of the Chronicles, and so do some less easily labeled faults like Lewis's knee-jerk objections to any kind of change or reform. He was, in many respects, what Neil Gaiman fondly describes as one of Britain's "old buffers, somewhere to the right of Genghis Khan."

But perhaps ethics are not all that counts, or even what really counts, when it comes to reading stories. I have hated some morally impeccable novels, and liked some reprehensible ones. I'm not convinced that either kind has altered the moral underpinnings of my own life. Like Lewis, I've noticed that the best-read people I know don't seem to be any more trustworthy, kind, honest, brave, or decent than the ones who scarcely read at all. And as Exhibit A to this particular argument, I hold up my own case. However much I may have been shaped by the Chronicles, I've remained impervious to the one ideology their author deliberately tried to instill in me: Christianity. Maybe even some of the lesser virtues that I like to think I've absorbed while reading about Narnia were there to begin with. Perhaps I did not so much learn from these books as recognize my better self in them.

When I returned at last to *The Lion, the Witch and the Wardrobe* and then to the rest of the Chronicles after my long estrangement from Lewis and his work, I could see, oh so clearly, all of the flaws I've detailed in the past seven chapters. I winced at the depictions of the Calormenes and understood for the first time that the White Witch is a dominatrix. Lewis's frankly stupid asides on the subject of Experiment House annoyed me. I realized that Corin and his taunting of Rabadash were among the reasons that *The Horse and His Boy* had never quite sat with me. And all these reservations were piled on top of my fundamental disinterest in the books' religious message, which to my adult ear arrives with the leaden thud of a Sunday newspaper full of ads.

While puzzling over how to understand this, I found guidance in an unexpected quarter: Philip Pullman. Pullman's trilogy of children's fantasy novels, His Dark Materials, is often regarded as an anti-Lewisian project, and he has made his own distaste for Narnia abundantly clear. When I interviewed him for a profile in 2005, I pressed him on this topic, and got him to concede that he did see the Chronicles as "grappling with real things, with salvation and damnation and temptation and trial....So although I dislike profoundly the moral answers Lewis finds, I respect the wrestle for truth, the struggle that he's undergoing as he searches for the answers." Nevertheless, Pullman considers Lewis's children's fiction to be, for the most part, "repellent" and "morally loathsome."

Still, it was in His Dark Materials that I stumbled upon a way to consider the Chronicles as an adult, neither grieving for my childhood capacity to immerse myself in a book, nor giving up that experience as entirely lost. Pullman's trilogy, inspired by Milton's *Paradise Lost,* takes the opposite of the traditional view of the Fall of Man; equally influenced by the poetry of William Blake, His Dark Materials is a paean to the value of experience over innocence.

Pullman's heroine, the twelve-year-old Lyra Belacqua, acquires an alethiometer, a dial-like device, resembling a compass or clock, with small images around the rim: a moon, a serpent, a lute, and so on. The alethiometer divines the truth about current, past, and future events, but reading it is difficult; like the figures in an allegory, the alethiometer's symbols have many layers of meaning. At first, Lyra proves to be a prodigy at reading the device; she does it by pure instinct or intuition. But as she comes of age and falls in love, this aptitude fades. Lyra, now an adult, has become self-conscious. At the very end of the trilogy, an angelic being tells her that her old skill with the alethiometer came by "grace," but she can "regain it by work." The work required to relearn how to use the alethiometer, however, will take "a lifetime....But your reading will be even better then, after a lifetime of thought and effort, because it will come from conscious understanding. Grace attained like that is deeper and fuller than grace that comes freely, and furthermore, once you've gained it, it will never leave you."

Pullman told me that he'd adapted this idea from an essay by the German playwright Heinrich von Kleist, entitled "On the Marionette Theater." Kleist's essay is presented as a conversation between two friends, one of whom marvels over the exceptional grace of some puppets he has recently seen performing. Without consciousness, the puppets, unlike human dancers, can never be self-conscious or affected. "We've eaten of the tree of knowledge," one of the men remarks. "Paradise is locked and bolted, and the cherubim stand behind us. We have to go on and make the journey round the world to see if it is perhaps open somewhere at the back."

Kleist leaves the possibility of finding an alternate entrance somewhat up in the air, but Pullman believes that it is attainable. Having lost our innocence, we must pursue understanding, knowledge, and experience to its furthest reaches. There, we can hope to regain not our lost grace, but perhaps a superior one. "You have to go all the way through human life," Pullman told me. "You have to go around the world and reenter Paradise through the back way."

This puts Pullman at odds with a long tradition of children's authors who regard childhood as a vanished Eden. Men like J. M. Barrie and Lewis Carroll preferred the company of children not (as the jaded modern mind sometimes presumes) because they were pedophiles seeking adult pleasures from children, but because they longed for childlike pleasures they couldn't share with adults. What they really wanted, what they tried to regain in playing pirates or planning outings with little boys and girls, was something truly impossible; they wanted their own childhoods back.

To want to be a child, however, is not childlike. As Lewis himself once observed, children almost always want to grow up, and why shouldn't they, since innocence (as grown-ups are prone to forget) is also powerlessness? Pullman, who worked as a schoolteacher for many years, has never forgotten this. He takes the child reader's side by celebrating the virtues of experience, and if I had had the chance to read his books as a little girl, I would have adored him for this. "You can't go back," he explained to me. "That's the point. You can't regain the grace you've lost. The only thing to do is go on through that and eventually acquire the other sort of grace, the conscious grace, the taught, the learned grace of the dancer." This idea runs against the grain of our sentimental notions about childhood, but as far as

Pullman is concerned, it's "a truer picture of what it's like to be a human being. And a more hopeful one."

Not long after this conversation, it occurred to me that I could apply the same principle to reading. I'd always assumed that I could never recapture the old enchantment I once found in books, especially the complete and total belief that I'd felt while reading the Chronicles. I know too much now: about Lewis's personality and intentions, about literary sources he'd raided, about his careless reflections of the world's injustices. But what if I decided to know even more, to learn more, about how the Chronicles came to be written and all the various ways they have been and can be read? Then I might arrive "somewhere at the back" and find a door open. Not the original one, not the wardrobe itself, but another kind of door, perhaps, with a different version of paradise on the other side.

Part Three

Songs of Experience

CHAPTER SIXTEEN

Castlereagh Hills

From the top of Slieve Ban, one of the peaks of the Mourne Mountains on the southern border of Northern Ireland, you can lie back in the grass and watch the blue shadows of clouds drift across the glinting surface of the Carlingford Lough while bees buzz nearby in the heather. It is otherwise utterly quiet, and the side of the slieve is so steep it seems to plunge directly down before your feet, as if a pebble you accidentally kicked over the side would land on the back of a cow grazing peaceably in a field by the shore, hundreds of feet below.

Across the lough, on Ireland's storied Cooley Peninsula, is Carlingford Mountain, which—I was told almost as soon as I arrived in the village of Rostrevor—is also said to be the giant Fionn mac Cumhaill (or Finn McCool) in profile. He's lying down for a nap, and the fog that rolls over the top of the mountain and sometimes refuses to burn off even on fine days is his coverlet. The Cooley Peninsula is where the hero Cúchulainn fought the rapacious Queen Medb over the brown bull of Cooley, a magnificent animal she wanted for her own, in the Old Irish epic "The Cattle Raid of Cooley."

Behind Slieve Ban, the long chain of granite mountains extends up along the eastern coast of county Down, beginning with Slieve Martin and the thickly wooded slopes of Rostrevor Forest. The trees on the higher ground are firs, their pointed tops like the spear tips of a mighty army. The trees are packed so densely it would be difficult to walk among them. No sunlight can get through, so nothing grows below, and beneath the top layer of silvery green needles there's a dim, silent, monochromatic realm of copper-colored trunks rising from a blanket of copper-colored needles. Lower down the mountain, you can walk through an older and more hospitable oak forest dating back to the eighteenth century, and at the very top of the mountains are heaths, open grass- and heather-covered uplands, soggy and riddled with pools of water stained as dark as tea.

This is the landscape that C. S. Lewis said reminded him most of Narnia. Or, rather, it might be, since that bit of information comes to us thirdhand, from Walter Hooper, who apparently had it from Warren Lewis sometime before he died in 1973. And if Lewis did, as reported, think of Narnia while walking with his brother through the hills around Rostrevor, I can't be entirely sure that the hills looked then—in the 1950s—as they do now. Those forbidding firs, so evocative of the "dark and seemingly endless pine forest" that Caspian rides through while fleeing his uncle's castle in search of the Old Narnia, are neither wild nor ancient. They were first planted in 1930, and to judge by appearances—from a distance you can see that the trees are laid out in unnaturally uniform patches of all the same height—they're occasionally harvested, as well. This place is steeper and more rugged than my own vision of Narnia. During my travels through England and Ireland I've seen fragments of *my* Narnia here and there; the whole thing, never.

For me, the Chronicles were first and foremost about a place. More than I wanted to meet Lucy or to romp with Aslan, I wanted to *go to Narnia*. In this, I was not alone. "The only problem I've ever had with Narnia is that I never got to go there," Tiffany Brown told me. Neil Gaiman said that as much as he liked Tolkien's tales of Middle-earth, he never really wanted to visit that world, or to have the adventures Tolkien described, either. But Narnia was different:

"Narnia, you felt, was just an infinite number of stories waiting to happen. If you went there, you would have adventures that were different but equally as cool. You would go to places that he hadn't mentioned on the map." As of this writing, there are more than seven thousand images on Flickr, a photo-sharing Web site, tagged "narnia"; most are shots of landscapes that reminded the photographers of a place that doesn't actually—or even approximately—exist.

Lewis's invented land, though far less sturdily elaborate than Tolkien's, felt every bit as real to these readers, just as it did for me. Rife with logical improbabilities in everything from its economics to its history to its agriculture, Narnia nevertheless remains palpable, a place you can almost see, almost smell, almost hear. Its reality is rooted in the sensual richness of the natural world, described by Lewis with ardor, care, and simple grace. Here, at length, is one of the best of these passages, from *The Lion, the Witch and the Wardrobe,* the part in which Edmund trudges through the woods as a captive of the White Witch and her dwarf henchman:

Every moment the patches of green grew bigger and the patches of snow grew smaller. Every moment more and more of the trees shook off their robes of snow. Soon, wherever you looked, instead of white shapes you saw the dark green of firs or the black prickly branches of bare oaks and beeches and elms. Then the mist turned from white to gold and presently cleared away altogether. Shafts of delicious sunlight struck down onto the forest floor and overhead you could see a blue sky between the tree tops.

Soon there were more wonderful things happening. Coming suddenly round a corner into a glade of silver birch trees Edmund saw the ground covered in all directions with little yellow flowers—celandines. The noise of water grew louder. Presently they actually crossed a stream. Beyond it they found snowdrops growing....

Only five minutes later he noticed a dozen crocuses grow-ing round the foot of an old tree—gold and purple and white. ...Close behind the path they were following a bird suddenly chirped from the branch of the tree. It was answered by the chuckle of another bird a little further off. And then, as if that had been a signal, there was chattering and chirruping in every direction, and then a moment of full song, and within five minutes the whole wood was ringing with birds' music, and wherever Edmund's eyes turned he saw birds alighting on branches, or sailing overhead or chasing one another or having their little quarrels or tidying up their feathers with their beaks....

There was no trace of the fog now. The sky became bluer and bluer, and now there were white clouds hurrying across it from time to time. In the wide glades there were primroses. A light breeze sprang up which scattered drops of moisture from the swaying branches and carried cool, delicious scents against the faces of the travelers. The trees began to come fully alive. The larches and birches were covered with green, the labur-nums with gold. Soon the beech trees had put forth their deli-cate transparent leaves. As the travelers walked under them the light also became green. A bee buzzed across their path. "This is no thaw," said the dwarf, suddenly stopping. "This is *Spring*."

Anyone who has done much reading aloud to children knows that long passages of environmental description can be risky. Even adults reading novels meant for adults tend to skim over scene-setting paragraphs devoted to geology or weather patterns. (At least, I do. I'm not sure how closely I would have read the first three para-graphs of this chapter, for example.) The passage I've quoted is, in the book itself, interspersed with action and dialogue: the abandon-ment of the witch's sledge, the binding of Edmund's hands behind his back, cracks of the dwarf's whip, the witch commanding the two of them to walk faster. Suspense over what will happen to the prodigal Pevensie does keep the story from bogging down in leaves and flowers, but Lewis's landscape descriptions are never merely ornamental; they are a story in themselves. Edmund's predicament seems to be getting more and more dire, but the counternarrative, reverberating in the forest around him, tells a different tale. The witch's power is ebbing with the melting of the snow.

For Lewis, a prodigious and enthusiastic walker, landscape *was* feeling. One of his clearest memories from childhood was of looking out the nursery window at "the Green Hills," Castelreagh Hills, a series of low, pasture-covered slopes to the southwest of Belfast. "They were not very far off," he wrote in *Surprised by Joy,* "but they were, to children, quite unattainable. They taught me longing— *Sehnsucht;* made me for good or ill, and before I was six years old, a votary of the Blue Flower." The blue flower is a key symbol in German Romanticism; it first appeared in a dream scene in an unfinished novel by the poet Novalis and it stands for unappeasable, mystic desire. Lewis christened this complicated emotion "Joy," and his autobiography is less about the prosaic details of his material life than about his search for Joy and its meaning.

Joy, as Lewis defined it, was "an unsatisfied desire which is itself more desirable than any other satisfaction." He first felt it in full while standing by a flowering currant bush as a little boy. He was reminded of the beauty of his brother's toy garden and flooded with a sensation he compared to the "enormous bliss" known to Adam and Eve in Milton's Earthly Paradise. It was a great longing, but not for the toy garden, nor for his own past, "though that came into it." Before he could ask himself what he wanted, "the desire itself was gone, the whole glimpse withdrawn, the world turned commonplace again, or only stirred by a longing for the longing that had just ceased. It had taken only a moment of time; and in a certain sense everything else that had ever happened to me was insignificant in comparison."

The first time I read this passage, I thought, naturally, of my own childhood longing for Narnia; *Sehnsucht,* apparently, is a communicable disease. Either that, or—and perhaps this is more likely—Lewis managed to bottle a goodly portion of Joy-inducing material into the Chronicles, and whenever someone of the same yearning temperament uncorks them, a swoon is sure to result.

Narnia, like the unreachable Castlereagh Hills, is elusive even in the Chronicles themselves. One book, *The Voyage of the Dawn Treader,* never sets foot there. Two more, *The Horse and His Boy* and *The Silver Chair,* merely pass through. *The Magician's Nephew* shows us Narnia's creation, but doesn't linger afterward. Of the three remaining Chronicles, *The Lion, the Witch and the Wardrobe* takes place in a Narnia that is cursed and frozen for most of the book; in *Prince Caspian* it is occupied by the disbelieving Telmarines, who have driven all the magical creatures into hiding; and, finally, *The Last Battle* gives us a corrupted Narnia slouching toward Armageddon.

The important thing to understand about Joy, Lewis insisted, is that "it is never a possession, always a desire for something longer ago or further away or still 'about to be.'" In some ways, it resembles the lethal nostalgia A. E. Housman described in *A Shropshire Lad:*

> Into my heart an air that kills
>   From yon far country blows:
> What are those blue remembered hills,
>   What spires, what farms are those?
>
> That is the land of lost content,
>   I see it shining plain,
> The happy highways where I went
>   And cannot come again.

Perhaps Lewis had these verses in mind when, in a 1929 letter to Arthur Greeves, he described *A Shropshire Lad* as a "terrible little book…perfect and deadly, the beauty of the Gorgon." But even then, Lewis would have made a distinction: Housman writes of "content" that's been lost; Lewis's Joy was the desire for something he had *never* had, and probably never could have had; it was also the desire for desire itself.

I can't read the words "yon far country" without experiencing a Narnian twinge. Even now, when trying to picture the place, the image that usually comes to mind is a distant prospect, green hills amid small groves of trees, with tiny, tantalizing figures moving here and there, impossible to make out in any detail, and the sea glinting at the horizon. If there's one thing you can be sure of about Narnia, it's that wherever you are, it isn't *here*. So perhaps it was quixotic to try to find the real places that inspired it. Nevertheless, Lewis's landscape descriptions are anything but gauzy and fantastical; you can feel them with all of your senses. This is one aspect of the Chronicles that calls to me now just as powerfully as it did in my childhood, perhaps even a bit more so. Narnia was a breeze on my face, the "sweet, rustling, chattering noise" of a stream (in *The Silver Chair*), the smell of the sea. It had to have been at least partly based on the real world, on places that Lewis knew intimately. If I couldn't get to Narnia, why not look for those?

CHAPTER SEVENTEEN

The Far Country

In the first chapter of *The Horse and His Boy,* set in Calormen, the foundling Shasta meets the warhorse Bree, who unbeknownst to the Calormen noble who owns him, is actually a talking Narnian beast. Bree persuades Shasta to escape with him by rhapsodizing about "Narnia of the heathery mountains and the thymy downs, Narnia of the many rivers, the plashing glens, the mossy caverns and the deep forests ringing with the hammers of Dwarfs."

Adam Gopnik, in an essay about Lewis for *The New Yorker,* calls the landscape Bree celebrates "clearly a British composite." Those might be taken as fighting words in some quarters, if it were more generally known that Lewis regarded Ireland as the inspiration for Narnia. He is so closely associated, though, with Oxford, where he lived for nearly fifty years, that most people assume that Narnia is essentially English. Perhaps Lewis would have quarreled with this notion (he would surely have identified "deep forests ringing with the hammers of Dwarfs" as a Germanic image), but even he admitted that, as much as he'd detested "this hot, ugly country" the first time he saw it as a schoolboy, by the early 1930s England had begun to feel like home. "I suppose I have been growing into the soil here," he wrote to Arthur Greeves. Lewis called himself Irish when it suited him, but otherwise passed for English, and in some ways Narnia is the same; Irish on the inside, because Ireland was the longed-for countryside of his childhood (his "land of lost content"), but English, too, because for Lewis England was immediate—touchable, smellable, audible, visible.

Narnia lay all around Lewis. There is a germ of the thaw in *The Lion, the Witch and the Wardrobe* in a passage from a letter he wrote to Arthur Greeves in 1945: "It is bitter cold this morning but lovely to see the green earth after all the snow and to hear the birds singing. I have just seen the first celandines." He spotted them along Addison's Walk, a footpath surrounding an island meadow on the grounds of Magdalen, named for the early eighteenth-century writer, editor, and politician who favored it when he was a fellow at the college. It was on Addison's Walk, late one autumn night in 1931, that Lewis engaged in the hours-long conversation with Tolkien and another don, Hugo Dyson, which led to his conversion to Christianity. The Walk's connection to Lewis's religious life makes it a pilgrimage site for his Christian devotees, but its celandines and crocuses were what captivated me the first time I strolled there on a raw day in early spring.

Lewis's own backyard was Narnia, too. He and Warnie decided to pitch in with Mrs. Moore to buy the Kilns even before they set foot in the house itself; for the brothers, the cottage's main attraction was the nine acres of sylvan land that came with it, climbing up the northern side of Shotover Hill. A path from the back of that land leads to the southern slope of Shotover, where a former royal forest has been converted into a country park, including, to the east, the four-hundred-year-old oaks of Brasenose Wood.

Not long after moving in, Lewis recorded sightings of gregarious "bright-eyed robins," squirrels, owls, and even a badger's burrow (which thrilled him to the bone) on the grounds behind the Kilns; all these creatures would eventually find their way into the Chronicles as talking beasts. Lewis made a habit of walking in his "little wood" in all seasons, and observed it with a care that never seemed to diminish with familiarity. "We had about a week of snow with frost on top of it," he wrote to Arthur, "and then the rime coming out of the air and making thick *woolly* formations on every branch. The little wood was indescribably beautiful. I used to go and crunch about on the crusted snow in it every evening—for the snow kept it light long after sunset. It was a labyrinth of white—the smallest twigs looking thick as seaweed and building up a kind of cathedral vault overhead."

After books, the natural world is the most frequent subject of the letters Lewis wrote before he became a celebrated apologist. (Once famous, he often exhausted his epistolary energy in theological correspondence with his readers.) He prided himself on his appreciation of all kinds of weather, even those that other people found harsh or dull; he was a connoisseur of skies, classifying for Warnie's benefit the three types of English overcast: "spring gray—long level clouds of white, silver, pearl, and dove-color…winter gray—ragged and pleated clouds of iron color [and] the hot summer gray or celestial damp blotting paper." The 1930s and early '40s were the golden age of Lewis's informal nature writing, after the conversion that loosened him up imaginatively and before the Second World War and Mrs. Moore's deterioration made any absences from home difficult. His letters from those years are full of long, vibrant descriptions of the epic walking tours he took in Wales, Ireland, Scotland, and western England with his brother or friends. But he could also extract remarkable impressions from the humblest things lying close to home:

I suddenly paused, as we do for no reason known to consciousness, and gazed down into a little ditch beneath a grey hedge, where there was a pleasant mixture of ivies and low plants and mosses, and thought of herbalists and their art, and what a private, retired wisdom it would be to go groping along such hedges and the eaves of woods for some herb of virtuous powers, insignificant to the ordinary observer, but

well known to the trained eye — and having at the same time
a stronger sense of the mysteries of living stuff than usual,
specially the mysteries twining at our feet, where homeliness
and magic embrace one another.

All that from staring at a ditch! Herbalism notwithstanding,
Lewis's interests were never especially botanical (unlike, say, Tolkien, who used to exasperate the Lewis brothers by interrupting the
"ruthless" pace of their country walks to stop and examine plants and
trees). For Lewis, the ivies and mosses evoked a way of life — earthy
and modest, yet not without enchantment; in other words, medieval — that he found appealing. Nature was a wellspring of moods
and reflections, an extension and magnification of his own sensibility and sense of history, not a realm apart from the human or an
object of science. He loved to exercise his literary skill in describing those clouded English skies and the subtle shadings of ambience
they suggested, but he never cared much about the meteorological
factors that distinguished the cumulus clouds from the stratus.

England is a good place for people of this inclination; few landscapes have been so continuously worked and shaped by human
hands, and so it makes sense to see the natural world there as profoundly integrated with human affairs. Stories as well as trees are
rooted in the earth of Britain, and every major landmark, it seems,
is encrusted with tales and rumors. At Shotover Country Park, on
the other side of the hill from the Kilns, I wandered over to a kiosk
to pick up some photocopied leaflets from a box, expecting guides
to the plants and animals around me. I wasn't disappointed in that,
but in addition to a map of the park and lists of notable trees, I also
found a handout called "Myths and Legends on Shotover."

The local tales attached to the hill feature an Oxford student who
fended off a wild boar with a volume of Aristotle, a fugitive empress
who disguised herself as a corpse, highway robbers, Robin Hood,
and Oliver Cromwell. Few Britons would find the little leaflet in

any way remarkable. But I stood puzzling over it, under a suitably damp blotting-paper sky, realizing that I'd just experienced one of those moments of unexpected cultural dissonance that pop up every so often between Americans and the British. There are many state parks where I grew up on the southwest coast of the United States, most of them much bigger than Shotover, and in none of them are visitors regaled with local "myths and legends." The original inhabitants of western American parks, if any, were wiped out in the not so distant past, along with whatever stories they might have told about those places. No wonder England seemed almost as strange and magical to me as Narnia did when I was a child.

One of Shotover's legends concerns a giant who lived in the forest and was said to be buried in the barrow that once stood on the top of the hill. (The barrow was destroyed by tank-testing operations during World War II.) When bored, the giant played marbles with the small boulders that can still be found scattered over a sandpit at the park's center. Did Lewis know this story? It seems likely, given that he loved folktales, lived at the foot of Shotover for thirty years, and had regarded giants with a "queer fascination" since childhood.

It doesn't seem too great a leap to conclude that the giants Jill, Eustace, and Puddleglum encounter on the moors beyond the northern border of Narnia in *The Silver Chair* owe something to the Oxford giant. Lewis's giants, idle and stupid, lean with their feet at the bottom of a river gorge, resting their elbows on the edge, "just as men might stand leaning on a wall—lazy men, on a fine morning after breakfast" (or men propped up against a bar in a pub presumably, though that wouldn't have been a suitable comparison for a children's book). The giants commence a game, throwing large stones at a nearby cairn. This makes a dangerous situation for the travelers; Puddleglum mutters that they would be a lot safer if the enormous dolts were actually trying to hit them.

Giant notwithstanding, Shotover Hill, full of picnicking families and strolling couples, is no vast and lonely moor like the one
at Narnia's northern frontier, and however pretty the celandines of
Magdalen may be, they cannot persuade you that you are in a forest instead of the grounds of a stately institution. The little wood
behind the Kilns (it has, with the addition of a parcel of land from
a neighbor, been turned into the tiny C. S. Lewis Nature Reserve),
is one of the few places I saw in Oxford that looks almost entirely
Narnian. At its exact center, under a canopy of ash and lime trees,
you can blot out the impression of the suburbs that lie all around and
imagine you are in Narnia's Lantern Waste, but take one step closer
to the park's edge, and that illusion will soon evaporate.

Much of Oxfordshire matches one storybook image of the English
countryside: velvety green fields trimmed with a fat braid of hedgerow
and the occasional puff of trees. The hills are low, easy, upholstered.
Nothing could be gentler or more curvaceous. Near the Thames River
footpath, the route Lewis and his friends would take from Oxford to
a riverside pub called the Trout, cows and canal boats move drows-
ily. The land is flat and prosperous. Although I can see a certain resemblance to Tolkien's Shire, this region is nothing like Narnia, since
Narnia, as any reader of the Chronicles can attest, is *wild*.

Everyone imagines that Narnia looks like England, but England
lost its forests hundreds of years ago, and when Lucy, Peter, and Susan first arrive at Aslan's How in *The Lion, the Witch and the Wardrobe,*
they find themselves on a hill looking out over "a forest spreading
as far as one could see in every direction." This, I realized only after
reading it for what must have been the thirtieth time, was a fact I had
never entirely absorbed before. When I conjure up a mental picture
of Narnia, I see something like a park, rolling turf broken by a few
rocks and pleasantly scattered trees. Neither farmland nor woods,
my Narnia falls somewhere in between—not cultivated, exactly, but
not the forest primeval, either.

During my travels in England, the closest approximation to this mental image I found wasn't in Oxford at all. It was a view of the park at Chatsworth, the seat of the Duke of Devonshire in the Peak District of Derbyshire, where I had stopped off to visit Susanna Clarke and her partner, Colin Greenland, on my way to Ireland. Susanna had also loved Narnia as a girl, and I wanted to talk with her about how it might have influenced her own work, particularly her witty, opulent fantasy novel, *Jonathan Strange & Mr. Norrell,* set in early nineteenth-century England.

Driving back from the train station, Colin and Susanna suggested a stop at Chatsworth. We'd already begun talking eagerly about the Chronicles, and as we stood just behind the enormous seventeenth-century mansion and looked out over the grounds, I was startled to find that here, at last, the right balance between nature and culture had been struck. I asked Susanna if she agreed that Chatsworth's park resembled Narnia.

"Yes, I think it does," she replied. "In the same way that Narnia was an idealized view of the English countryside, this is, too. Of course, it's man-made, you know."

"What do you mean, man-made?"

"Well, for one thing, originally, you could see the village of Edensor from here." She pointed to a notch between two slopes in the near distance. "One of the dukes had the entire village moved in the 1800s. To 'improve the view.' There was a famous eighteenth-century landscape architect called Capability Brown who had the river straightened and changed a lot of other things. Back then, they had an ideal landscape in mind. They got it from French landscape painters who were painting their idea of a *Greek* landscape, but of course they had that all wrong."

"Actually, the word that springs to mind when I look at it is 'Arcadia,' and that was supposedly in ancient Greece, wasn't it? But having been to Greece, I know now that it never could have been as lush as this. It's much too dry there."

"Right, it doesn't look like this at all! With the eighteenth-century English ideal, what you want is a series of very gentle green hills with occasional stands of trees. Of course, Capability Brown would have rather that it be deer under the trees instead of those cows over there."

"So, right now, we're admiring a landscape that's been overhauled to look like paintings from another country that were meant to depict still another country that doesn't remotely resemble them. And what you and I are both reminded of by all this is a *fictional* country. But, tell me, do you remember that Lewis describes Narnia as almost entirely forested?"

"Does he? That's not how I imagined it."

"I didn't either, but it's true. Chatsworth might look like Narnia to us, but it doesn't match the descriptions in the books, so add that to the general confusion."

Eventually, Susanna and I determined that our picture of Narnia had come as much from Pauline Baynes, the illustrator of all seven Chronicles, as it had from Lewis. It is Baynes's Narnia we saw in Chatsworth, the low hills carpeted with green grass and studded with oaks and pine, laid out under the hooves of Fledge, the winged horse on the cover of *The Magician's Nephew*. Lewis's landscape descriptions bewitched me as a child, but I grew up in a desert, and for images of much that he describes — snow, heather, even a genuine spring — I had to rely on Baynes. Her illustrations showed me how Narnia looked, and it looked like no place I'd ever been to myself.

As a child, it would never have occurred to me that the illustrations for any book could be at odds with the text. To me, the words and pictures were inextricable, each as true in its own way as the other, so I never noticed the discrepancies between Baynes's Narnia and Lewis's. In my mind, I suspect, the pictures almost always won out. (Susanna, however, maintains that from an early age she had serious reservations about Caspian's "stupid-looking" haircut in *The*

Voyage of the Dawn Treader: proof, for her at least, that Baynes's illustrations were not infallible.)

Baynes's style, with its flattened perspective and fine decorative
patterns of branches, vines, flowers, and leaves, is meant to recall
medieval illuminated manuscripts and tapestries. Plants get as much
of her attention as animals and people. In the little exterior spot illustrations in particular, she defines the edges of the drawing using
lines (often tree trunks or vines) curving outward like parentheses,
balanced by figures that stand in exaggerated contrapposto, so that
everything in the picture appears to be dancing or swaying in place.
The characters are almost always drawn in full figure, often from a
distance and placed so as to set off the landscape, as when the Pevensies appear as little details in the corner of a drawing of the island
at the beginning of *Prince Caspian*. Baynes's illustrations are merry,
delicate, fluid, and droll, but also, like Narnia itself, a little elusive. We
seldom feel as if we're inside them.

Before working on *The Lion, the Witch and the Wardrobe*, Baynes
had done the drawings for a short book of Tolkien's called *Farmer
Giles of Ham,* much to that author's delight. Lewis, however, claimed
that he'd first discovered her work not through his friend, but by
walking into an Oxford bookstore and asking the clerk to recommend someone who could produce good pictures of children and
animals. As it turned out, he was rarely satisfied with her renderings
of either. Baynes had yet to turn thirty when she began illustrating
the Chronicles, and although she always spoke respectfully of Lewis,
she was more tactful than honest when she described him as offering "no remarks or criticism" except when prompted.

It greatly frustrated Lewis that his collaborator was a "timid,
shrinking" young woman who reacted to his critiques as if he'd
pulled her hair or blackened her eye. He had plenty of reservations
about her work. He believed, for instance, that Baynes had deliberately drawn the Pevensie children "rather plain—in the interests
of realism," for *The Lion, the Witch and the Wardrobe,* and asked if she

could "pretty them up" in the later books. It's a baffling request, unless you happen upon an edition of one of E. Nesbit's children's books with the original illustrations and compare them to Baynes's work. Lewis had grown up with H. R. Miller's drawings of Nesbit's child characters, conventionally attractive by Edwardian standards: thick-haired, pinafored girls with long-lashed eyes, and neatly combed boys in sailor shirts and short pants.

Lewis could be gracious to Baynes (when he won the Carnegie Medal for *The Last Battle,* he wrote to her, "Is it not rather 'our' Medal?"). Privately, however, he felt that her illustrations were often insufficiently accurate, complaining to his friend Dorothy Sayers about her "total ignorance of animal anatomy" and her lack of "interest in matter—how boats are rowed, or bows shot with, or feet planted, or fists clenched." Most of his letters to Baynes have an air of barely concealed impatience; her sensitivity was an irksome restraint on his natural inclination to let others know, without reservation, exactly how they could improve their artistic efforts. His imperfectly pulled punches and backhanded compliments probably wounded her as much as a full-scale attack, or even more so, if she was insecure enough to start imagining what he'd refrained from saying. "You have learned something about animals in the last few months," he wrote Baynes after seeing the illustrations for *The Magician's Nephew,* the penultimate book in the series. "I mention the beasts first because they show the greatest advance." It is the sort of remark guaranteed to make an uncertain artist wonder what he really thought of all those animals she'd drawn for the *previous* five volumes.

And how wrong Lewis was! True, a drawing of people in a rowboat really ought to have the rowers facing toward the stern, not the bow, but his insistence that Bree be drawn with the "big fetlocks" typical of a warhorse suggests that sometimes Baynes understood the tone of his tales better than he did. Her dainty, stylized lines match the lyricism of Lewis's invention in a way that hearty naturalism and fidelity to animal anatomy never could. But then,

Lewis's own appreciation for the visual arts had never been well developed; a colleague who visited the Kilns recalled being dismayed
by the absence of pictures or anything else created solely to please
the eye. Otherwise, Lewis might have recognized that Baynes's fanciful "Arabesque" style (as he dismissively called it) was ideally suited
to depict a "wild" land—"not men's country," as Trufflehunter the
badger puts it—that was, in truth, deeply infused with humanity
and its dreams.

Narnia is *wildness,* not *wilderness,* a humanized vision of nature,
drenched in imagination and stories, which is one of the reasons
it seems so English. I found more evidence of this while retracing
another of Lewis's favorite Oxford walks, the climb over Hinksey
Hill, which now lies on the far side of the thundering A34 bypass
from the city center. Atop Hinksey in 1922, Lewis felt a brief stab
of "the old joy" while (he wrote in his diary) sitting in "a patch of
wood—all ferns and pines and the very driest sand" on the day before he took his final exam in Greats. Like a lot of the countryside
where Lewis once roamed, Hinksey retains only a tiny portion of
wood and farmland, hemmed in by new houses, highways, and a
golf course that has claimed the summit of the hill. (It seemed that
almost every time I tried to follow in Lewis's footsteps, I found myself confronted with a golf course.) William Turner painted a bucolic
view of Oxford from the top of Hinksey Hill in the early nineteenth
century, and that probably gives a better sense of how it looked to
Lewis in the 1920s than does visiting the place today.

Nevertheless, a tiny wedge of relatively unspoiled land on the
hill has been set aside as a nature preserve, with a walk laid out for
schoolchildren. At intervals along the path, placards have been set
up next to representative trees, explaining that this is an elder, said
to be the home of witches, or a hawthorn, said to be a harbinger of
death. Farmers, visitors are informed, used to be afraid to invite bad
luck by cutting down a holly and would leave the tree standing in
the middle of their plowed fields. Another sign announces that this

oak is a tree whose forebears brought "your" forebears to this island. Furthermore, a green man lives inside the oak, and every May he dances through the streets of Oxford. Most of the placards are illustrated with drawings of human figures personifying the various trees, a long-haired maiden for the birch and a crooked hag for the elder. The text on the signs is written in the first person, as if each tree were telling its own story.

The hippieish whimsy of the Hinksey Hill nature walk (the first placard promises an "enchanted forest" with "whispering trees") must, I think, be due to the influence of Lewis and Tolkien. British folklore attaches great significance to trees, but (as Susanna Clarke assured me) rarely suggests that they contain anthropomorphic spirits or that a tree might also be a person. "Kat Godeu," a poem from the fourteenth-century Welsh *Book of Taliesin,* describes a war fought by trees, but this seems to be a singular, magical event. The personified tree is a Greek idea, and in the Chronicles, the dryads and the hamadryads go by their classical names.

One of Lewis's tree women looks after Jill in the castle of Cair Paravel at the beginning of *The Silver Chair.* She is "a delightful person…graceful as a willow, and her hair was willowy too, and there seemed to be moss in it." (Jill doesn't realize that her attendant is a tree nymph, but anyone who has read the other Chronicles will instantly recognize her as such.) Lucy, walking through the awakening woods in *Prince Caspian,* recalls the human forms of the silver birch—"it would have a soft, showery voice and would look like a slender girl"—and the oak—"he would be a wizened, but hearty old man with a frizzled beard and warts on his face and hands, and hair growing out of the warts"—exactly like the drawings on the Hinksey Hill placards.

The images are so appealing, such a pleasing blend of the homely and the otherworldly, it's no wonder people would like to think that their ancestors believed in them long ago. According to historians, anthropologists, and archaeologists, however, what we regard as age-old "traditional" lore is often a more recent invention. Take the Green Man, who supposedly lives in an oak and has come out to dance in the May Day parade since time immemorial. The authors of the Hinksey Hill placards make a common mistake in identifying the Green Man as an ancient legend; in fact, the name was invented in the 1930s by a folklorist interested in British church architecture. It refers to a type of architectural ornament often found in Romanesque and medieval churches, a carving of a male face surrounded by foliage and sometime sprouting leaves and vines from its mouth and ears. This Green Man (which may or may not have stood for a character from folklore) has sometimes been confused with a pantomime figure called Jack in the Green. Jack in the Green, a local man who covers himself with foliage until he looks like a walking shrub, does indeed march in May Day parades, but he has been doing so only since the eighteenth century and he has no known connection to the Green Man motif.

Who is the Green Man? Is he a modern approximation of a pre-Christian nature elemental like the god Pan, recreated from clues found here and there — a village festival, a carving on an altar screen, the mysterious forest dweller from the medieval poem *Sir Gawain and the Green Knight*? Or is he an example of wishful thinking, a concoction invented by modern Britons who want to reconnect with an indigenous religion that has been lost forever? Lewis and Tolkien thought they were woefully out of step with their time when they wrote fiction voicing their yearning for the old ways and a deeper imaginative connection with the land; instead, they turned out to be speaking for millions. It was in the 1970s, at the same time that *The Lord of the Rings* gained its first great success, that English villages began to revive the long-abandoned Jack in the Green processions, along with traditional morris dancing on May Day.

All this was the culmination of what the historian Ronald Hutton has called "a powerful tendency on the part of the English to search for a timeless and organic relationship with their country." That desire's roots lie in both the universal tug of nostalgia and the very real trauma of industrialization. Its modern manifestation, in the search for, say, the historical site of Camelot or the emergence of modern-day Druids, began not long after Lewis and Tolkien were born.

Of course, neither Narnia nor Middle-earth are real countries, even if some of Tolkien's most fanatical readers seem to know more about the history of his invented world than they do about the one they actually inhabit. Unlike a real country, Lewis and Tolkien's imaginary lands are literally built of stories, and stories, unlike rocks and soil and trees, are always *about* something. Part of what Narnia and Middle-earth are about is Britain, but not the Britain of the A34, electric teakettles, and New Labour, the Britain I tromped through, in an ultimately vain search for the original of Narnia. I suspect they are not even really about the idyllic Britain where both men grew up, or the Britain of the fourteenth century, the period Lewis might have chosen for his own if he were given the opportunity. That far country is a Britain of the mind, part real, but mostly fantasy, and, like Narnia itself, it remains always just out reach.

CHAPTER EIGHTEEN

Northern Lights

Lewis met J. R. R. Tolkien in 1926, but they didn't become close until a few years later, when Lewis would write to Arthur Greeves describing Tolkien as "the one man absolutely fitted, if fate had allowed, to be a third in our friendship in the old days." Back in Belfast, Lewis and Greeves had come together over a mutual fascination with Norse legends. Someone suggested that the fifteen-year-old Jack Lewis ought to drop in on the boy across the street, who was convalescing (Greeves suffered from a heart condition that prevented him from working for most of his life), and there he discovered a copy of *Myths of the Norsemen* by H. A. Guerber. "Do *you* like that?" Lewis asked, and "Do *you* like that?" came the response from Greeves. So began the longest and most intimate friendship of Lewis's life, initiated by the revelation that "both knew the stab of Joy, and for both it was shot from the North."

"The North" played a role, too, in Lewis's friendship with Tolkien, who in 1926 was a professor of Anglo-Saxon at Oxford. They met at a gathering of the university's English faculty, but several factors conspired against their immediately becoming allies, let alone friends. First, Tolkien was a Roman Catholic, and second he belonged to an opposing faction in their discipline. "At my first coming into the world," Lewis wrote in *Surprised by Joy,* "I had been (implicitly) warned never to trust a Papist, and at my first coming into the English Faculty (explicitly) never to trust a philologist. Tolkien was both." As a philologist, Tolkien wanted the English syllabus to be redesigned to put more emphasis on Anglo-Saxon and Middle English texts; he belonged to what was known as the "Language" camp. Lewis, at that time, favored the "Literature" camp, which preferred to keep the focus on more recent works, effectively limiting English to the study of literary art, rather than regarding it as a language like Greek or Latin. (Eventually, Lewis came over to Tolkien's side in that dispute.)

At the time, Lewis patronizingly described Tolkien as "a smooth, pale, fluent little chap....No real harm in him, only needs a smack or so." To make matters trickier, Tolkien hated Edmund Spenser, the Elizabethan poet Lewis adored and whose reputation he would eventually revive in *The Allegory of Love*. Tolkien's stated objection to Spenser at the time was "the forms," that is, Spenser's mangling of the language in an effort to simulate old-fashioned diction; he also resented Spenser for maligning Catholics in his masterpiece, *The Faerie Queene*.

What the two men shared, however, was a passion for what Lewis called "northernness." Tolkien had formed a club dedicated to reading the Icelandic source texts for Norse mythology—the *Elder Edda* and the *Younger Edda*—in the original Old Norse (also known as Old Icelandic); he called the group the Kolbitar, after an Icelandic term for old men who sit close enough to the fire to gnaw on the coals. Lewis, intrigued by the idea of acquainting himself with the roots of his youthful obsession, joined, and soon he was writing to Arthur, enthusing about "what a delight this is to me, and how, even in turning over the pages of my Icelandic Dictionary, the mere name of a god or giant catching my eye will sometimes throw me back fifteen years into a wild dream of northern skies and Valkyrie music: only they are now even more beautiful seen thro' a haze of memory—you know that awfully *poignant* effect there is about an impression *recovered* from one's past."

Lewis's passion for northernness began with a scrap of cryptic verse; throughout his life he was always particularly susceptible to fragments of poetry or prose that hinted at things unknown and perhaps inexpressible. At the age of nine, he encountered one of Henry Wadsworth Longfellow's poems written in imitation of the Norse sagas, entitled "Tegnér's Drapa." The first stanza catapulted him into a strange ecstasy:

> I heard a voice, that cried,
> "Balder the Beautiful
> Is dead, is dead!"

He didn't know who Balder was or who mourned him, but this handful of words, all by itself, made Lewis feel "uplifted into huge regions of northern sky, I desired with almost sickening intensity something never to be described (except that it is cold, spacious, severe, pale, and remote) and then...found myself at the very same moment already falling out of that desire and wishing I were back in it." Northernness was from the very beginning a primary source of Joy.

Nevertheless, Lewis's enthusiasm for things Norse went through a dormant period during his boyhood, his "dark ages" of "rubbish" and "twaddling school stories." Then, in a schoolroom, at the age of thirteen, he stumbled upon a magazine that had reprinted some of Arthur Rackham's illustrations for Wagner's *Ring* cycle and with them the title *Siegfried and the Twilight of the Gods*. "Pure 'Northernness' engulfed me," Lewis writes of this moment in *Surprised by Joy*, although he still had no idea who Siegfried was and assumed that the twilight of the gods described some shadowy realm where they lived. Now, however, he was prepared to pursue these alluring hints to their source.

Rackham's watercolor illustrations of the *Ring* legends (you can get them in a Dover Publications paperback) are autumnal, redolent of Lewis's favorite of the four seasons, all stone and fallen leaves, white skies and gray water. In the early plates, Siegfried appears as a little savage, bare-legged, bare-armed, and shoeless, wearing only his animal skins, and until he discovers the sleeping Brünnhilde, he's surrounded by nothing but caves, gnarled trees, and stunted, hairy dwarves. Rackham's Fafnir is particularly earthy and well imagined, as much frog as lizard, with an amphibian's thin, leathery skin and the nasty, flat head of a pike. The illustrations summon a hard, primitive world of cold nights and few comforts, and they filled Lewis with "a vision of huge, clear spaces hanging above the Atlantic in the endless twilight of Northern summer, remoteness, severity."

Lewis always described "northernness" in such terms: it was cold, "severe," even empty, yet beautiful: not a widespread aesthetic taste, though not a rare one, either. But, tellingly, the language Lewis uses to characterize his rediscovery of the Norse myths, while also environmental, calls upon another, very different, set of images. When he first laid eyes on Rackham's pictures, "It was as if the Arctic itself, all the deep layers of secular ice, should change not in a week nor in an hour, but instantly, into a landscape of grass and primroses and orchards in bloom, deafened with bird songs and astir with running water." The Novemberish paintings, paradoxically, hit Lewis like the first day of spring. The result was a spiritual awakening of sorts, very much like the thaw that announces Narnia's liberation from the White Witch.

"You will misunderstand everything unless you realize that, at the time, Asgard and the Valkyries seemed to me incomparably more important than anything else in my experience," Lewis wrote in *Surprised by Joy*. His long walks and bicycling excursions through counties Antrim and Down became a quest for settings that struck him as worthy haunts for Siegfried, the Niebelungs, and Fafnir. The landscape he inhabited became doubly enchanted. He had heard about the creatures of Celtic folklore—fairies, leprechauns, and giants—as a little child, from his Irish nurse, Lizzie Endicott; "northernness" added the suggestion of something less familiar and indigenous.

From Arthur Greeves, Lewis learned to appreciate the virtues of "homeliness," the word the two of them used for the humble and comfortable, what Americans might call "cozy." The two of them took long walks and sampled the scenery like oenophiles sipping wine: "Best of all," Lewis wrote in *Surprised by Joy,* "we liked it when the Homely and the unhomely met in sharp juxtaposition; if a little kitchen garden ran steeply up a narrowing enclave of fertile ground surrounded by outcroppings and furze, or some shivering quarry pool under a moonrise could be seen on our left, and on our right the smoking chimney and lamplit window of a cottage that was just settling down for the night." However hearty and healthy their expeditions might appear to the casual observer, they were part of a dedicated pursuit of aesthetic rapture.

For Tolkien, northernness was a far more complicated proposition. The Norse culture that the young Lewis made the center of a semispiritual, imaginative, but mostly private inner life was, for him, tangled in feelings about his family, his religion, his ancestry, and his profession. Where Lewis's Anglo-Irish national identity could be fluid, allowing him to be English or Irish as the spirit moved him, Tolkien believed very strongly in his own Englishness. His father's name, true, had come over from Saxony in the eighteenth century, but Tolkien insisted that his paternal forebears had been instantly absorbed into the English soil, and besides, it was his mother's people he regarded as his real ancestors. "Barring the Tolkien (which must long ago have become a pretty thin strand)," he once wrote to his son Christopher, "you are a Mercian or Hwiccian (of Wychwood) on both sides," referring, with a characteristic degree of specificity, to two of the kingdoms in what historians once called the Anglo-Saxon heptarchy.

To understand the significance of Tolkien's deeply felt national identity, it helps to know a little of the ethnic history of Britain (a term that, for the sake of simplicity, I'll use to include Ireland, Scotland, and Wales, as well as England, acknowledging that there's much controversy over that usage). The islands have been peopled for hundreds of thousands of years, apart from the Ice Age interludes during which glaciers and a frozen climate rendered them uninhabitable. Theirs is a history of successive migrations or invasions and settlements, with the loose grouping of British tribes we customarily call the Celts absorbing their nameless prehistoric predecessors, followed by a period of Roman occupation, an influx of Germanic tribes, including the Angles and Saxons, and finally the Norman Conquest in 1066, which installed a French-speaking elite. With each addition, the lingua franca of the islands changed and adapted.

The first time Tolkien encountered the language called Old English or Anglo-Saxon (a schoolmaster loaned him a primer when he was a boy), he felt that he recognized it immediately, not just as the basis of the English spoken all around him, but in his *bones.* Tolkien thought, as many do, that races and ethnicities have certain inherent traits, but he also believed, more firmly than most, that a people's essence and history are captured in their language. Tolkien responded to languages intensely, as aesthetic objects—but, really, "objects" is not an adequate word for it. For Tolkien, languages were aesthetic *realms,* lovely (or not) in detail, on the level of particular words, and in the larger structures of grammar. As his skill in philology, the study of languages, grew, a single word in an old manuscript or the name of a place—what might seem like inert nuggets of letters or sound to most people—could tell Tolkien all kinds of stories: about a god who used to be worshipped at this stone, a Roman villa that used to stand in that hamlet, the history of how a certain animal first appeared in a certain region.

Tolkien admired several languages—Finnish, Spanish, and Welsh, for three—but Anglo-Saxon was his home. And home was a fragile construct for Tolkien, whose father died in South Africa of rheumatic fever when he was four, and whose mother succumbed to complications resulting from diabetes when he was twelve. Mabel Tolkien had converted to Roman Catholicism not long after her son was born, and she had been cut off financially and emotionally by her family as a result. She struggled to support herself and her two children (John Ronald Reuel Tolkien had a younger brother named Hilary) on the limited funds left to her by her husband, but there were a few idyllic years spent in villages in Worcestershire. The area not only served as a model for the Shire in Middle-earth, but came to figure prominently in Tolkien's sense of himself as an Englishman. He was, he maintained, "a West-Midlander, at home only in the counties upon the Welsh Marches," and this, he felt, explained both his personality and his love of Anglo-Saxon.

For Tolkien, Anglo-Saxon was the heart of Englishness, and the Norman Conquest initiated the shameful decay of that noble tongue by introducing Continental borrowings and other forms of linguistic pollution. He felt the defeat of the Saxon King Harold by the Normans at the Battle of Hastings in 1066 as a fresh wound, and he held this against the French language and culture to the end of his days.

Tolkien was acutely susceptible to viewing life in this fashion, to seeing it as a tragic drift away from some past ideal. He had lost his perfect country home when his mother was forced by her financial woes to move to the city of Birmingham. Then he lost Mabel herself, a catastrophe he blamed on her family, who in his view had subjected her to "persecution, poverty, and largely consequent, disease" because of her religion. For the rest of his life he would cling fiercely to his Catholicism, a commitment his biographer, Humphrey Carpenter, attributes to loyalty to Mabel's memory: "after she died his religion took the place in his affections that she had previously occupied." (Tolkien was still invoking his mother's sufferings in 1965, when reproaching his children for drifting away from the Church.)

But if Tolkien saw his Catholicism as an unbreakable bond with his lost, beloved mother, the religion also suited his disposition. It was the first, the most ancient, the Mother Church, from which the wayward, venal world insisted on straying; however, Tolkien (a man who knew the value of ancient things and of mothers) would remain true to it. There's a certain gloomy strain in Catholicism, preoccupied with the Fall and the corruption of this earthly existence, that jibed with Tolkien's own temperament. "It is a fallen world," he wrote to his son Michael, sounding a theme that resonates through his letters, "and there is no consonance between our bodies, minds, and souls. However, the essence of a *fallen* world is that the *best* cannot be attained by free enjoyment, or by what is called 'self-realization' (usually a nice name for self-indulgence, wholly inimical to the realization of other selves); but by denial, by suffering."

All this explains why Tolkien was inclined to envision the Anglo-Saxon language (and, by extension, Anglo-Saxon culture) as an embattled underdog, ebbing away into the past. He knew that many precious works of Old English literature, particularly from the first half of the six-hundred-year reign of the Anglo-Saxon kings in England—which would necessarily include most of the pre-Christian texts—had been lost. Of the culture's heroic tradition, little more than *Beowulf* remains. "One sees," writes Tom Shippey, a professor of Anglo-Saxon himself and a champion of the philological aspects of Tolkien's work, "that the thing which attracted Tolkien most was darkness: the blank spaces, much bigger than most people realize, on the literary and historical map, especially those after the Romans left in A.D. 419."

Passages in *Beowulf* and other surviving works allude to legends and entire epics that have vanished, in part because Christianizing Crusaders in the latter days of Anglo-Saxon rule ordered some materials destroyed, but also because the Anglo-Saxon poetic tradition was primarily oral. The arrival of the French-speaking Normans eventually put an end even to that. "Modern English," Tolkien wrote to the poet W. H. Auden of the language we speak today, this polyglot mixture of words adopted from many other tongues, "is very remote from my personal taste." Whereas the conventional scholarly opinion is that English literature begins with Chaucer,

Tolkien thought it ended with him (or a little later—Spenser was certainly a death knell!).

An entire body of heroic epics and legends, stories that were, in Tolkien's opinion, *purely* English, had vanished, leaving his motherland bereft. Unlike the Scandinavians, whose ancient stories had been preserved in the *Eddas,* and the Finns, whose oral traditions were collected in a book called the *Kalevala* (another favorite of Tolkien's), the English had forgotten their native "mythology," and even the humblest of folklore had been neglected; England had no equivalent to Germany's Brothers Grimm, dedicated to preserving her fairy tales. Of the old, pre-Norman English world, only a handful of hints remain in the surviving Anglo-Saxon texts, primarily in the epic Tolkien loved and studied all his life, *Beowulf.*

Beowulf, the story of a great warrior who defeats a monster, the monster's mother, and finally a dragon, is the oldest extant example of Germanic literature, the only intact remainder of a vanished world. A pagan tale related by a Christian poet, it was most likely composed sometime in the 700s, but the concentration of pagan elements in the mixture is strong. Although written in Old English, *Beowulf* describes events that happen in Denmark, and its eponymous hero is a Geat—that is, from a part of Scandinavia that would eventually become Sweden.

Tolkien's conception of English identity revolved around language, and that made it essentially Germanic. Anglo-Saxon polytheism was derived from Norse mythology: the king of the Norse gods, Odin, was the Anglo-Saxon Woden; Thunor, a version of the Norse thunder god Thor, and so on. The Icelandic *Eddas,* the works that the Kolbitar was dedicated to reading, interested Tolkien in their own right, but their special value to him lay in the fact that they are the most extensive collection we have of Old Norse myth and legend and therefore offer us a shadow of what he thought his own ancestors believed.

While both Lewis and Tolkien were entranced by Norse myths, they came to the old stories with very different yearnings. For Lewis, "northernness" was something distant and austere, a call from far away that fed his appetite for transcendence. For Tolkien, the old tales had some of that frosty charm — "very remote and strange and beautiful" is how he described the passage in Anglo-Saxon that inspired his first imaginings of Middle-earth — but northernness was also "homely" to him, if not quite in the same way that Lewis defined that word; it was home, his roots, a fundamental part of his identity, even if he could see it only through a Scandinavian glass, and darkly. Still, what survived of Norse paganism did not really fill the gap Tolkien felt in his nation's imaginative past — or in his own. And finally he felt the urge to supply the missing stories himself.

CHAPTER NINETEEN

The Builder and the Dreamer

By 1929, Tolkien was meeting with Lewis in Lewis's rooms at Magdalen every Monday morning. They drank (tea and beer), talked, and read to each other from their work. Lewis loved to be read to, and excelled at off-the-cuff literary criticism; Tolkien needed someone with whom to share his love of Anglo-Saxon, Old England, and eventually, the secret, handmade world he had begun inventing during the war: Middle-earth. It was from the seed of these meetings that the informal institution of the Inklings would eventually grow.

The friendship between the two men was a complicated, fruitful affair; Tolkien would affirm to the end of his days, even after their connection had withered, that he never would have written *The Lord of the Rings* without Lewis's constant nudging and encouragement. They had much in common, and several significant differences. It's hard to contemplate their relationship without slipping into comparisons that would have distressed Lewis. He saw Tolkien and himself as cronies and collaborators—surely they fought for the same cause and in the same way? Lewis was the type to get swept up in a friendship, especially a new one, and to envision his friend as an ideal companion, brushing aside or simply ignoring any dissonance.

Tolkien, however, was a stickler by nature, the kind of person who feels compelled to raise objections to every observation and to dismiss every suggestion of influence on his own work, including that of Lewis. Not every one of Tolkien's quibbles is completely convincing; at times, his protests seem more like a reflex than anything else. According to Carpenter, Tolkien's children remember that, despite claiming to "disapprove" of drama, he seemed to enjoy the theater greatly. He was fond of saying that he disliked Shakespeare "cordially," but his letters contain several Shakespearean analogies suggesting that he was on a familiar basis with the plays, comparing, for example, Sam Gamgee's treatment of Gollum in *The Lord of the Rings* to the way Ariel behaves toward Caliban in *The Tempest*. (By contrast, Tolkien never makes such references to the artists he *really* hated, Wagner being the prime example.)

Lewis's Narnia seems a wispy caprice compared to Tolkien's imaginary land. There has never been another creative endeavor quite like Middle-earth — beginning with the extensive, fully elaborated languages Tolkien devised, and then the maps, genealogies, history, literature, and mythology that sprung from them. In the same way that certain people love movies so much they cannot rest until they get to make them, Tolkien's passion for languages led him, at an early age, to formulate languages of his own. And because his understanding of language was profound and organic (rather than the arid pedantry often assumed to motivate philologists), he knew that languages can't exist without someone to speak them; even a dead language was spoken and shaped by living people once. So Tolkien resolved to animate his handiwork by devising a world and a time in which the elvish tongues Sindarin and Quenya could be spoken. "I made the discovery," he explained to a reader, "that 'legends' depend on the language to which they belong; but a living language depends equally on the 'legends' which it conveys by tradition."

Tolkien often spoke of Middle-earth as partly of his own devising and partly received from a mysterious other source. From the first, when he began to write verses about an ancient mariner named Earendel in 1914 and showed them to a friend, the border between his own imagination and some variety of semirevealed truth was blurred. The friend asked Tolkien what the verses "really meant," and Tolkien's response was "I'll find out."

He soon came to think of the myths, legends, and epics he concocted in his spare time as a suitable replacement for the forgotten mythology and legends of the Anglo-Saxons. (His first efforts at writing *The Silmarillion* were compiled in a notebook entitled "The Book of Lost Tales.") "Imaginatively this 'history' is supposed to take place in a period of the actual Old World of this planet," he once told his publisher. He had fashioned a fictional past for a real country. In his later years in particular, Tolkien felt compelled to clear up minor discrepancies in Middle-earth's history by "finding out" obscure "facts" that would explain one thing or another.

To his lasting astonishment, Tolkien's "private and beloved nonsense" (as he called it), when unleashed upon the world, became immensely popular. His complete conviction in his own creation — one of the most comprehensive and steadfast cases of authorial conviction known to literature — was transmitted to many of his readers. They set about studying and speaking his languages and designing all sorts of time-consuming ancillary versions of Middle-earth, games like Dungeons and Dragons or gatherings where people dressed up like wizards or hobbits. He had created a new world; they packed their bags and moved in. Tolkien had a term for the practice of inventing worlds: "sub-creation." It was, he believed, in the construction of consistent, believable alternate realities that human beings paid the highest tribute to their Creator — by imitating him. Eventually, for the would-be denizens of Middle-earth, the professor himself became not unlike a god.

Tolkien's books were not among my own childhood favorites. With the vague notion that it was esoteric and dense, I put off attempting *The Fellowship of the Ring* until I was almost ready to leave for college. Even *The Hobbit* had, among owlish eleven-year-olds, a reputation for being a "hard" book; *The Lord of the Rings* was considered an intellectual Everest. I tried *The Hobbit* too soon, attempting it a couple of times before giving up at age eight or so. The copy we had lying around the house (presumably my father's) was a small, thick drugstore paperback, and its tiny type, combined with the story's uninspiringly middle-aged hero and all those odd names, contributed to make the story seem stuffy and impenetrable. By the time I acquired the patience for it, I was embarked on a jag of reading plays: Shakespeare, Wilde, Tennessee Williams, and (because my father had a shelf of these) George Bernard Shaw.

Besides, I much preferred fantasies whose main characters were children from this world. Yet even taking that into account, my own resistance to Middle-earth puzzles me. I loved Mr. Tumnus, yet somehow didn't recognize that Bilbo Baggins, with his cozily appointed hole, was the same type (and probably an inspiration for Tumnus, I now realize). I had trouble, I think, with *The Hobbit*'s longish passages of description. I couldn't visualize any of these places, and although Tolkien was even more devoted to the natural world than Lewis, his style was less lyrical and he didn't have Lewis's knack for suffusing scenery with human emotions. He wouldn't have wanted to, since he thought human beings already got far too much attention as it was. That was the nub of his objection to drama and to those critics whose taste ran toward "dramatic" fiction: they are, he wrote, "likely to prefer characters, even the basest and dullest, to things. Very little about trees as trees can be got into a play."

Just before leaving home, however, I finally tackled *The Lord of the Rings,* burning through it over the course of a summer. (It is the perfect long book to read before you set off on an ambitious and incomprehensible adventure.) I approached it then with a diligence that now strikes me as bizarre; it wasn't until I was in my late twenties that I was able to read it for pure, escapist pleasure. By that point, I recognized that, much as I liked it, Tolkien's freakishly prodigious powers of invention could not supply the book with what four years of studying English literature had led me to expect from a great novel. I relished *The Lord of the Rings,* and have reread it several times since then. I awaited each installment of Peter Jackson's three-part film version with excitement and even delved into the "mythological" texts collected in *The Silmarillion*—the province, really, of the hardcore fan, the geek. But by the time I left college I had read *Tess of the D'Urbervilles* and *Absalom, Absalom!* and *Crime and Punishment*—to name just three books with related themes—and knew they sounded depths that Tolkien never touched.

This is a delicate subject. Tolkien has many, many devotees who fly into a fury when anyone suggests that he is not, as Tom Shippey put it in the subtitle to his book on Tolkien, the "Author of the Century." Long stretches of Shippey's text are given over to sniping at Tolkien's less appreciative reviewers. The archenemy, the Sauron of the literary press in the eyes of Tolkien's champions, is the late American critic Edmund Wilson, who dismissed *The Lord of the Rings* as "juvenile trash." This, understandably, rankles the faithful, and whenever they encounter any objection like it, they rise to Tolkien's defense. Their counterarguments usually involve testy lectures on the unparalleled complexity, consistency, and thoroughness of Tolkien's imaginary world. He invented entire *languages,* for crying out loud: what contemporary novelist, however gifted, had done—or could do—that?

This reasoning never succeeds in winning over critics and readers who just don't have a taste for such things, the kind of people for whom Middle-earth looks like nothing more than the biggest model-railroad setup of all time. To the contrary: For those with an allergy to the fantasy genre, all this talk of the vastness of Tolkien's invented world proves that his fans don't really understand what makes literature *literature;* they think it's a matter of the quantity, rather than the quality, of invention.

Philip Pullman, while best known for his critique of Lewis, takes an even dimmer view of Tolkien on this count. Having concocted his own alternate universe in which to set *His Dark Materials*, he finds himself bemused by readers who want to explore it. "This is a particular kind of interest that I've never had," he told me, "and it's not a literary interest. I could never care less how many miles Middle-earth is from the Shire or whatever it is, or what's the past participle of a certain word in Klingon." When readers ask for explanations of the finer points of his imaginary cosmology, he's flummoxed. "I haven't got an answer because I'm not interested. It doesn't matter. What I'm interested in is telling a story. The world is there for me to tell a story in, not for its own sake."

Several decades of inept, derivative fantasy novels and the nerdy reputation of Tolkien fandom have fortified the ranks of Tolkien naysayers. A lot of them find the whole Middle-earth ambience icky and a little sad. (I have a friend who refuses flat-out to read anything involving elves.) Tolkien has had many admirers of considerable intellectual stature—Auden was his great champion in the press, and the novelist Iris Murdoch sent him fan mail—but this, too, doesn't go very far in persuading other intelligent people who can't abide his books. Murdoch perhaps chose the wisest course when her husband, the Oxford professor John Bayley, would demand to know how she could be so enthralled by books that were so "fantastically badly written": she'd stare at him in amazement and insist that she didn't know *what* he was talking about.

Lewis and Tolkien certainly felt that they were surrounded by hostile forces. Explaining his own love of "fairy tales" may not have been as central a project for Lewis as was defending the faith, but he gave the cause plenty of energy all the same. Tolkien, too, attempted an apologia, although criticism was really not his forte. His essay "On Fairy Stories," apart from introducing the concept of "sub-creation," isn't much more developed than Lewis's own writings on the topic—just harder to follow; Tolkien's expository writing has none of Lewis's limpid clarity. "I am not a critic," he once wrote to Lewis, and "On Fairy Stories" is evidence that he understood the limits of his own talents very well. He wrote it in part because he felt that he'd been "unnaturally galvanized" into the critical role during all the time he'd spent with Lewis and "the brotherhood."

"On Fairy Stories" emerged in large part from the long conversations the two friends had in Lewis's rooms. Lewis had a fathomless appetite for informal debate, the honing and teasing out of philosophical positions and arguments. He had, remember, aspired to a fellowship in philosophy before settling for English. It was via that late-night talk with Tolkien and Hugo Dyson in 1931 that he'd converted (or at least that's what he chose to believe), and the arguments that convinced him were related to ideas that he and Tolkien shared about the merit of fairy tales.

Lewis had been leaning back toward Christianity for a while, but he needed someone to help him dismantle the intellectual apparatus he'd constructed, years earlier, to justify his agnosticism; he was too stubborn, and too convinced of his own rationality, to toss all that away without a fight. Tolkien handed him the concept that did the trick, an idea that in one fell swoop redeemed his lifelong enthusiasm for pagan legends and conclusively refuted the naysayers who accused the two of them of playing about with a lot of childish moonshine.

Tolkien persuaded Lewis that the stories he'd thrilled to all his life—about sacrificed and reborn gods like Balder or Dionysus—were really like echoes moving backward and sideways and sometimes even forward in time, reverberations of the one occasion when God actually sacrificed himself for mankind. The other stories, made by men, weren't "lies" (or, as Lewis liked to call them, "lies breathed through silver"); they were shadows of the single instance when the myth "really happened." People had kept on inventing

such shadows, conjuring up imaginary worlds, because human beings were made in the image of a God who was above all a creator,
an artist. With this in mind, Lewis could believe in Christ as the Son
of God and not give up the other myths he loved so much — the
fairy tales, the epics, the "northernness." Those stories, like Middle-
earth itself, were not "real," but they were nevertheless "true." They
were reflections of the one and only myth that had actually unfolded
in history, the one instance when the eternal, transcendent truth of
God and the fallen world of reality had been one and the same.

CHAPTER TWENTY

The Second Love

Not long after Lewis had that momentous conversation with Tolkien and Dyson on Addison's Walk, Tolkien wrote a poem entitled "Mythopoeia," putting into verse his conviction that creating "mythic" art was a more authentic means of pursuing truth than the "dusty path" of science and progress. The poem is addressed from "Philomythus" ("Myth lover"—Tolkien) to "Misomythus" ("Myth hater"—Lewis), but what it has to say is less revealing than the fact that it was written at all. Why write a poem arguing points with a man you've just spent hours talking to directly, a friend you speak to at least once (and usually several times) a week?

The practice of poetic conversation between close friends reached its zenith with the Romantic poets of the early nineteenth century, and with William Wordsworth and Samuel Taylor Coleridge in particular. Some of their most famous poems were extensions of their conversations; the autobiographical impulse of the early Romantics often transformed poetry into a higher form of letter. Wordsworth's "A Complaint," for example, written in 1806, is just that, a protest against "a change in the manner of a friend," after Coleridge returned from a long journey withdrawn and preoccupied; Coleridge's "To William Wordsworth," written not long afterward, voices his renewed awe at his friend's gifts and his own fears of artistic inadequacy.

Although Tolkien had very little interest in "modern" (i.e., post-Chaucerian) poetry, and had remained impervious to the charms of Keats despite the best efforts of one of his old school friends, he could hardly help soaking up at least a little of the late-Victorian notion of the poet's life, epitomized by the Romantics.

As Paris in the twenties was to young writers and other bohemians of the late twentieth century, so were Romantic friendships like that between Wordsworth and Coleridge to literary men from Lewis and Tolkien's generation. The Romantics provided a model for a certain kind of relationship (and by extension, community) based on shared creative dreams and the desire to get beyond conventional manners and roles. As often happens with all-pervading cultural fantasies, even if you're too embarrassed, too modest, or even too cynical to invoke the model openly, it's still hard to escape it entirely. Writing is a lonely profession, especially when you feel out of step with your time, whether you believe you're ahead of it (as Wordsworth and Coleridge did) or behind it (Tolkien and Lewis). The later Romantics—Keats, Shelley, and Byron—may have racked up more dramatic, glamorous histories than Wordsworth and Coleridge, but none of them could claim a more consuming, fertile, or tempestuous collaboration. In their heyday, these two friends managed to make writing an almost communal activity.

They met in 1795, and for a little less than a decade they were united in an effort to revolutionize English poetry. At the peak of their friendship, Coleridge and Wordsworth worked side by side at the same table in various rural cottages throughout England, but especially in Coleridge's cottage in Somerset. They read their work aloud to each other, exchanged criticism, and even contributed lines or entire stanzas to each other's poems. The foundation of their bond was Coleridge's certitude that in Wordsworth he had found the consummate literary genius of their time, the man destined to write a long, comprehensive, philosophical poem that would champion a new way of life and in doing so change the world. With Wordsworth's sister,

Dorothy, and a rotating selection of sympathetic friends, the two men went on epic walks through the countryside, fervently talking of ideas and poetry and opening their hearts and minds to the natural world in search of the same emotional and spiritual transport that, a hundred years later, Lewis would name Joy.

While their talents weren't of the caliber of Wordsworth's and Coleridge's, Lewis and Tolkien were as susceptible to this template of literary friendship as anyone; both certainly had thought of themselves as poets rather than novelists in their youth. Furthermore, Lewis had been calling himself a "Romantic" since long before he met Tolkien. He had devoured the poetry of Shelley and Keats as a boy. After pooh-poohing Wordsworth through his youth, Lewis came to admire and identify with the poet in his twenties; when asked late in life to list the ten books that had most influenced him, Lewis included *The Prelude,* Wordsworth's epic, autobiographical poem (addressed, naturally, to Coleridge).

Like Lewis, Wordsworth looked back on a youth when "meadow, grove, and stream,/The earth, and every common sight" inspired a kind of ecstasy, "the glory and the freshness of a dream," only to realize that this capacity had withered in adulthood: "there hath past away a glory from the earth." Eventually, Lewis found the solution to what he called his "Wordsworthian predicament" in religion, and he believed that the author of *The Prelude* would have found renewal in Christianity, too, "if only he could have believed it." Even the title of Lewis's autobiography, *Surprised by Joy,* is taken from a Wordsworth sonnet.

In other aspects, however, Lewis played Coleridge to Tolkien's Wordsworth. He was a great talker—if not so great as Coleridge, who bedazzled everyone who heard him—and he had a tendency to monopolize conversations. (Tolkien, like Wordsworth, was the more reserved and saturnine of the pair.) The popularity of Lewis as an Oxford lecturer, radio essayist, and apologist paralleled Coleridge's success during his occasional stints as a public speaker; "the people here absolutely *consume* me," Coleridge complained to a friend after a bequest enabled him to resign a position as a minister. Both Lewis and Coleridge cared little for clothes and their own appearance, and both relished herculean walks that would have exhausted mere mortals; Coleridge was known to cover forty miles in a day without thinking much of it.

Coleridge, like Lewis, was a precipitator, very keen on pulling groups of like-minded friends together to see what happened, and he had a knack for caricature and social satire that he sometimes exercised to his own disadvantage. And while Coleridge never went through a period of serious religious doubt (he was always a passionate Christian, if often an unconventional one), he shared Lewis's conviction that the splendors of nature must necessarily point toward something beyond it. "My mind," he wrote to a friend, "feels as if it ached to behold & know something *great*—something *one & indivisible*—and it is only in the faith of this that rocks or waterfalls, mountains or caverns give me the sense of sublimity or majesty!—But in this faith *all things* counterfeit infinity!"

Above all, Coleridge was an enthusiast; he devoted himself to encouraging and celebrating Wordsworth when his friend was still a relatively untried poet with a lesser reputation. Lewis tirelessly coaxed Tolkien to finish and publish his writings; Tolkien, like Wordsworth, tended to fuss interminably over small imperfections and would have kept much of his work to himself if not prodded to let it go. As it was, *The Prelude* (which Wordsworth originally conceived of as an *introduction* to the great work Coleridge expected of him—the great work itself, to be called *The Recluse,* he never completed) was not published until after Wordsworth's death. Tolkien described himself as "a notorious beginner of enterprises and non-finisher," and blamed this on the difficulty he had in concentrating. Yet he could spend days fretting over the astronomical details in *The Lord of the Rings,* worrying about getting the phases of the moon just right instead of thinking about how to get to the next scene. If the result feels more persuasive because of his meticulousness, it's only due to Lewis's nagging that we have an end product at all.

Coleridge is probably the greatest "non-finisher" in English literature, more famous, perhaps, for what he didn't do (complete "Kubla Khan" or "Christabel") than for what he did. This is an occupational hazard for artists whose efforts are fueled exclusively by gusts of creative inspiration; gusts are by definition brief. In Coleridge's case, his changeable nature was compounded by opium addiction, a habit he fell into partly for medical reasons (laudanum was routinely prescribed by physicians in those days) and partly to escape from an unhappy marriage. The drug ruined his life, aggravating all the traits that made him uniquely exasperating even to his best friends. "He talks very much like an angel," said one of the poet's patrons toward the end, "and he does nothing at all." Opium magnified Coleridge's tendency toward self-pity and kept him from dealing sensibly with what he regarded as the great torments of his later years: his unrequited love for Wordsworth's sister-in-law and his eventual estrangement from Wordsworth.

Finishing certainly wasn't Lewis's problem; considering the incessant demands and disruptions of his domestic situation, he was superhumanly productive, even during the worst days of Mrs. Moore's decline. He wrote all seven of the Narnia books in a little over two years. During the same period he was hospitalized with a streptococcal infection (the one attributed by his doctor to exhaustion) and coped with a crisis in Mrs. Moore's health that required moving her to a nursing home. He handled that task alone; Warnie, as was his wont when the going got tough, was off recovering from one of his inopportune alcoholic binges.

Lewis dealt with all this on top of the regular duties of an Oxford tutor. Over the previous two decades, he had produced *The Allegory of Love,* the three science-fiction novels known as the "Space Trilogy," several books of apologetics and the radio talks that spawned them, and many articles and (often unsigned) reviews for newspapers and other popular publications. Tolkien, by contrast, had published only *The Hobbit,* which was a success—but not on the level of, say, *Mere Christianity*—and he kept getting stuck in the midsection of *The Lord of the Rings.* The two of them had cooked up a scheme in the early 1930s to write a "thriller" apiece (Lewis picked space travel as his theme; Tolkien's was time travel), and whereas Lewis had fulfilled the plan in triplicate, Tolkien had only "a fragment" of a novel to show for himself.

This, the two men's various biographers agree, bothered Tolkien. That is the problem with literary friendships: the commonalities that foster them can also lead to comparison, competition, friction. The fastidious Tolkien was further annoyed by Lewis's authorial sloppiness, his uncorrected mistakes and inconsistencies, which were, like many of Coleridge's faults, the result of an endearingly wholehearted forward momentum that blithely swept over the sort of minor problems that would inevitably trip up Tolkien.

Lewis was "a man of immense power and industry," Tolkien wrote to a reader who had noticed some correspondences between the space trilogy and *The Lord of the Rings,* "but at last my slower and more meticulous (as well as more indolent and less organized) machine has produced its effort." Until it did, however, only a writer of angelic forbearance could have witnessed his friend's blossoming career without a twinge of envy. It didn't help that when Lewis incorporated some little element of Tolkien's mythology into his own fiction, he'd often get it wrong, such as misspelling "Númenor" (an Atlantean civilization from the distant past of Middle-earth) as "Numinor." That, and the elvish-inflected names that Lewis invented for the supernatural entities in his science-fiction novels, irritated his friend, though he knew Lewis intended it as a tribute.

What sustained the Tolkien and Lewis friendship was their affection for old things and old ways of life, and above all their love of old literary forms. This, too, was something they had in common with the Romantics. In the preface to *Lyrical Ballads,* a groundbreaking collection of poems by both Wordsworth and Coleridge, published in 1798, Wordsworth spoke for both men in denouncing "poets, who think that they are conferring honor upon themselves and their art in proportion as they separate themselves from the sympathies of men, and indulge in arbitrary and capricious habits of expression in order to furnish food for fickle tastes and fickle appetites of their own creation." This expresses pretty well how Lewis felt about modernism, personified for him by the poet T. S. Eliot, whose work he once repudiated as "a very great evil."

Lewis, it must be said, never took the time to understand the modernist writers properly; he didn't think that he needed to. He was sure that Eliot's "poems of disintegration" were morally dangerous: "I contend that no man is fortified against chaos by reading *The Waste Land,*" he declared, "but that most men are by it infected with chaos." As Wordsworth had in his own time, Lewis believed that the literary establishment (for that is what he considered the modernists to be) had instituted and then slavishly followed an assortment of highfalutin fashions that cut them off from "the sympathies of men."

Lyrical Ballads returned to songs and legends rooted in English folk culture for inspiration, rejecting the mannered, elaborate classical allusions that reigned in the poetry of the previous generation. Lewis and Tolkien weren't as convinced as Wordsworth and Coleridge were that they had "the sympathies of men" on their side, but they knew that the stories they preferred—whether fairy tales, heroic sagas, or pulp adventure yarns—were the sort of thing people had been writing and enjoying for millennia. The modernists, by contrast, prided themselves on being original, on discarding obsolete literary forms and subject matter that imposed a false coherence on the tumult of twentieth-century life. Indeed, modernism defined itself in part by its rejection of the nineteenth-century cult of Romanticism, whose focus on the transcendent self embodied in the artist Eliot dismissed as sentimental and solipsistic. Romantic individualism, Eliot wrote, could lead its disciples "only back upon themselves."

Lewis believed that the modernists were both snobs and parvenus. While he certainly championed "the masters" against the assaults of such upstarts, he was not a social critic in the contemporary vein of Alan Bloom, the author of *The Closing of the American Mind*. Lewis would never have defined himself as a defender of high culture against the crass rabble, the kind of conservative who trumpets "Great Books" and the work it takes to read them. Instead, he saw himself as an antimandarin, a defender of old-fashioned readerly pleasures. He had, after all, read most of the English-language classics, even the ones that make today's undergraduates groan and reach for the Cliffs Notes, purely for the fun of it.

Modernist novelists who wanted to abandon conventional storytelling as an oppressive, arbitrary, and outdated convention, were, in Lewis's eyes, the real enemies of both the literary classics *and* the common folk. They were the same sort of people who sneered at him for liking *The Wind in the Willows* and H. G. Wells. Reading Virginia Woolf's *Orlando,* he admired her "astonishing power of rendering the feel both of landscapes and moods, rising sometimes to real loveliness" but complained of "a total absence of any matter on which to use the power." He thought he detected in the modernist project a debilitating fear of vulgarity. "The reason why they don't like either the narrative elements or low comedy," he wrote to Dorothy Sayers, "is that these have obvious immediate entertainment value. These prigs, starting from the true proposition that great art is more than entertainment, reach the glaring *non sequitur,* 'entertainment has no place in great art.'"

But while Lewis took it upon himself to defend Shelley from the critical disapproval of Eliot and his coterie, there was one aspect of Romanticism for which he had no use: its revolutionary fervor. Shelley was a notorious atheist, Coleridge a would-be socialist, and even Wordsworth had been exhilarated by the French Revolution before it went off the rails. At no point in his life would Lewis ever have written, as Wordsworth once did, "I disapprove of monarchical and aristocratical governments, however modified. Hereditary distinctions and privileged orders of every species I think must necessarily counteract the progress of human improvement." Lewis and Tolkien didn't believe in progress or "human improvement." Man had fallen and only God could fix that.

CHAPTER TWENTY-ONE

Marvelous Journeys

Tolkien's intellectual battles were more esoteric than his friend's—he had, for example, a serious quarrel with anyone who regarded Anglo-Saxon poetry as no more than a means to study the Old English language, rather than as literature in its own right. But where he and Lewis coincided most happily was in their affinity for the venerable literary form known as the romance. (This was, of course, before the term "romance" was adopted as a label for the genre of pulp fiction devoted to fantasies of courtship.) Much that frustrates and baffles certain readers about their work has to do with confusion over what the two men intended to write. Their books may look like novels, but in essence they are romances.

When critics complain, as Edmund Wilson did, about the morally simplistic characterization in *The Lord of the Rings,* or its focus on mere adventure, or the pervasive unreality of its heroic deeds and magical beings, they are pointing out that Tolkien's book is not a very good novel, and there is truth to that. *The Lord of the Rings* has no character to equal Jane Eyre or Raskolnikov, none of the sophisticated moral humanism of *Huckleberry Finn*—and certainly nothing approaching the stylistic bravado of *Lolita.* But if *The Lord of the Rings* doesn't excel in any of these novelistic arenas, that's largely because it isn't trying to. "My work is not a 'novel,'" Tolkien wrote testily to one would-be student of his book, "but an 'heroic romance,' a much older and quite different variety of literature." As for Lewis, although he called the Chronicles "fairy tales" rather than romances, he saw the genres as deeply related, at times indistinguishable.

One "modern" author whom both Lewis and Tolkien held in esteem was William Morris. This Victorian dynamo was the founder of the Arts and Crafts movement, a political activist, historical preservationist, member of the Pre-Raphaelite Brotherhood, fine-press publisher, translator, travel writer, poet, painter, designer, architect, and, in his final years, the author of eight "prose romances," works of fiction that made him the "great author" of C. S. Lewis's youth and first gave Tolkien the idea to write romances of his own. Morris is now best known for his textile and wallpaper designs, rich, intricate botanicals inspired by medieval tapestries, many of which you can still buy today. His role as pioneer of the socialist movement in Britain makes him interesting to political historians. The prose romances are probably the most dimly remembered of all his accomplishments; they have often been regarded as a kind of holiday he took from more significant pursuits. Nevertheless, it may well be through Morris's tales of questing knights and valiant Germanic heroes that he has had, indirectly, the greatest influence of all.

Morris and the Pre-Raphaelites celebrated the art and literature of the Middle Ages at a time when conventional wisdom held up the Renaissance as the pinnacle of European culture and Raphael as the quintessential Renaissance master. The centuries between the Fall of Rome and the rediscovery of classical antiquity were at that time (as they occasionally still are now) dismissed as the "Dark Ages." This was sheer bias, in Morris's opinion, rooted in the eighteenth century's overvaluation of the disciplined, balanced formality of classical art. Historians were wrong, he wrote, when they portrayed the medieval period as "lawless and chaotic; its ethics a mere conscious hypocrisy, its art gloomy and barbarous fanaticism only, its literature the formless jargon of savages."

Like many of the Romantics, Morris saw vigor and truth in the eccentricities of individual expression, which, he argued, had been allowed freer rein in the Middle Ages than in the Renaissance. You could see this in the very objects that filled the medieval world: the chairs and wall hangings, the pitchers and illuminated books, each with its own handmade beauty. The Renaissance cathedral is an orderly, Palladian symphony of columns and arches, speaking persuasively of reason. The walls of a Gothic church, by contrast, teem with carvings of saints, allegorical figures, gargoyles, and other grotesqueries climbing improbably upward until they vanish into the shadowy mysteries of pointed vaults. Where the quintessential Renaissance structure—St. Peter's Basilica or the Campidoglio in Rome—presents a refined, controlled ideal, orchestrated by a single master, the medieval public building is the work of dozens of unnamed craftsmen, each adding his own idiosyncratic touch.

With the Renaissance came not only the institution of a uniform classical style of beauty but—and worse yet in Morris's view—the dawn of capitalism. Compared to the industrial workers of his own century, Morris felt, even medieval serfs had more varied, less alienating work and more free time. But it was the artisans who most captivated his imagination. A medieval guild craftsman, he wrote, was "master of his time, his tools, and his material, was not bound to turn out his work shabbily, but could afford to amuse himself by giving it artistic finish; how different that is from [the] mechanical or trade finish some of us, at least, have learned." A world furnished with a few cherished possessions made in the old, authentic ways was an infinitely healthier and more joyful place to live, he believed, than one cluttered with cheap, mass-produced junk built by bored, miserable workers.

If, for inspiration, Morris looked even more intently to the past than the earlier Romantics had, he still shared their belief in the possibility of a redeemed future. His own infatuation with Norse legends and sagas (several of which he had translated) led him to visit

Iceland; there he had seen people living in simple, wholesome (if sometimes harsh) circumstances and in communities without great disparities in wealth. This experience further fired his interest in socialism, and when not designing furniture or directing the publication of the Kelmscott Chaucer (one of the most beautiful books ever printed), Morris could be found on the streets of London attempting to rally the proletariat. His time-travel narrative, *News from Nowhere,* imagines a twenty-first-century England that has restored the virtues of the fourteenth century with a few key alterations. In fact, Morris's utopian vision resembles the Shire — a cheerful, unassuming, agrarian society with few machines and a reverent respect for the natural world and its rhythms — but unlike Tolkien's hobbits, the inhabitants of Morris's future England have organized their economy along strictly communal lines.

In Morris's prose romances, the politics are much more subdued (though perhaps no more detached from reality). Lewis first came across a copy of Morris's *Well at the World's End* on a shelf at Arthur Greeves's house when he was in his early teens. The book single-handedly revived his childhood penchant for "knights in armor," and soon "the letters WILLIAM MORRIS were coming to have at least as potent a magic in them as WAGNER." Tolkien wasn't much older when he used a small cash prize he'd won in an academic competition to buy a copy of *The House of the Wolfings.* That book, the story of a tribe of pre-Roman Goths, gave him the idea of adapting a tale from the *Kalevala* "along the lines of Morris's romances" (as he put it in a letter to his wife-to-be). His prime candidate for this adaptation was the Finnish legend of Kullervo, a hapless young man who winds up inadvertently committing incest and precipitating other catastrophes during an attempt to avenge the massacre of his family. (This idea, transplanted to Middle-earth, eventually became the story of Túrin Turambar, a cursed hero who endures a string of similar misfortunes, published posthumously in 2007 as *The Children of Húrin.*)

My copy of Morris's *Well at the World's End* comes in a double volume, bound together with a similar work, *The Wood Beyond the World,* and published by Inkling Books, a one-man concern in Seattle. The collective title given to this volume by its conservative Catholic publisher, *On the Lines of Morris' Romances,* is taken from Tolkien's letter to his fiancée, and the subtitle is *Two Books That Inspired J. R. R. Tolkien.* If that's not sufficient to get the point across, a back-cover blurb appeals directly to "Tolkien fans who long for more of the same delight that they get from *The Lord of the Rings.*" (In truth, the stately, rambling narratives of Morris's romances are unlikely to beguile any but the most patient and scholarly aficionados of Middle-earth, and even then their interest will probably be more historical than anything else.) The introduction to *The Wood Beyond the World* takes pains to assure readers that this "uncomplicated romance" contains "no hidden messages about contemporary social issues," presumably a reference to Morris's politics. Lewis and Tolkien, too, were more than capable of reading selectively, extracting what they liked from the romances, while leaving Morris's socialism on the plate.

What they liked was something that had never quite been attempted before. *The Well at the World's End* and *The Wood Beyond the World,* written in the 1890s, are entirely original stories, set in imaginary lands that resemble the mystical Britain of the Arthurian tradition combined with the timeless noplace where fairy tales transpire. Morris was the first writer to do this—devise a whole new world for his romances, rather than setting them in "Faerie Land" or a semimythologized version of a place that actually existed. From his example grew Tolkien's concept of the secondary world and, eventually, Middle-earth itself. In a way, the socialist Morris was the grandfather of a vast and highly lucrative genre of popular fiction, even though what he'd set out to do was revive a beloved, forsaken form.

The heroes in Morris's romances, like the heroes in the medieval romances he emulated, are knights who set forth in search of adventure, passing through castles, towns, and isolated cottages, battling other knights, rescuing ladies, swearing loyalty to leaders and companions, and encountering supernatural wonders like giants or sorceresses. They become embroiled in complicated questions of honor and often struggle to figure out who among the strangers they meet can be trusted and who cannot. A beautiful maiden might turn out to be a foul crone or even a serpent in disguise; a magnificent palace might conceal an ugly secret. As is often the case in romances, the Morris hero pursues a quest; he searches for a kidnapped lady, or a magical object or place. In *The Well at the World's End,* Ralph, the youngest son of the king of Upmeads, leaves home without a particular goal in mind, but soon decides to seek the eponymous well, whose waters will renew a drinker's youth and fortitude.

All of these elements are as familiar to us as cops and robbers, even if we've never heard of Thomas Malory's *Morte d'Arthur* or *Sir Gawain and the Green Knight.* The iconography of medieval romance is woven into our world and our language. The knight in shining armor, the damsel in distress—these are half-mocking labels we use to tease people for acting out roles from an idealistic, outdated notion of chivalry. The Holy Grail or the dragon that requires slaying are metaphors invoked in newspaper or magazine articles to indicate that a particular goal or challenge has some extraordinary significance. Four hundred years ago, Cervantes mercilessly parodied the clichés of the romance in *Don Quixote,* but his mockery didn't slow it down; romance mutated and evolved, manifesting in dozens of new forms: the gothic tale, magic realism, the road novel. It lives on in comic books, science fiction, movies and television series, even video games. Once you learn how to recognize it, you see it everywhere, especially in narratives (whatever the medium) that speak to the young.

Northrop Frye, one of the last great literary critics to flourish before the advent of structuralism, defined the classic romance as belonging to "the mythos of summer," in which the essential element is "adventure." This observation comes from *Anatomy of Criticism*, Frye's attempt, in 1957, to devise a systematic, objective catalog of literary modes and forms. As a student at Oxford in the 1930s, Frye attended Lewis's famous lectures on medieval literature, and I can't help wondering if he recognized in himself the two qualities Lewis listed as the defining traits of the medieval thinker. The medieval scholar was "bookish," Lewis wrote, and above all "an organizer, a codifier, a builder of systems. He wanted 'a place for everything and everything in the right place.'"

Frye took this mentality to its logical extreme by devising a codification for all books, slotting the vast, multifarious body of English literature into a gridlike system of classifications. He called his approach "archetypal criticism." Although it has since fallen out of fashion and at times seems almost pathologically optimistic (Frye describes his project as based on "the assumption of total coherence"), the aerial view it offers of literature's evolution shows us connections not visible from any other angle.

Since the romance's essential element is adventure, Frye observed that it is "necessarily a sequential and processional form." Travel is its central metaphor. A beginning that involves the hero "setting forth" is more crucial to making a story a romance than whether that hero is a young man in armor, or a young man at all. "Of all fictions," Frye wrote, "the marvelous journey is the one formula that is never exhausted, and it is this fiction that is employed as a parable in the definitive encyclopedic poem of the mode," which is Dante's *Divine Comedy*.

The *Divine Comedy* is a rare romance of middle age, beginning with its narrator midway through "the journey that is our life," lost and desperately in need of someone to show him the path forward. Most romance, however, belongs to youth and speaks to the desire to get out in the world and prove oneself, which may be why the form proliferates most luxuriantly and in some of its purest strains in children's fiction. I knew as a little girl that there were really two kinds of readers: those who liked *Little Women* and those who preferred *The Phantom Tollbooth,* but it wasn't until I was much older and learned to think like a critic that I understood exactly where the difference lies: *Little Women* is a novel; *The Phantom Tollbooth* is a romance. *Little House on the Prairie* is a novel; *The Wizard of Oz* is a romance. Magic is, without a doubt, a fictional device you almost never see outside of romance, but not all romances are magical. *Island of the Blue Dolphins* has neither magic nor a traveling protagonist, but the main character's journey from helpless child to self-sufficient adult, a destination reached via a series of often desperate but also exhilarating adventures, makes it a kind of romance, the romance of survival.

Frye defined his literary modes (they are: myth, romance, high mimetic, low mimetic, and ironic) according to the relationship between the main character and the reader. A hero who is superior "in kind" to the reader—in other words, a divine being—marks the story as a myth. A hero who is human, but possessed of superior rank and qualities, a king or other leader, is the sign of a high mimetic narrative, usually a tragedy or epic. The low mimetic hero, the figure at the center of most realistic novels and comedy, is the reader's approximate equal. The ironic portrays characters we look down upon or pity. The classic hero of romance is human, like the high mimetic hero, but capable of "marvelous" actions. He inhabits "a world in which the ordinary laws of nature are slightly suspended," and is assisted or hindered by "enchanted weapons, talking animals, terrifying ogres and witches, and talismans of miraculous power."

Narnia and Middle-earth are worlds of this kind, and so is the Land of Oz and the wizarding community of the Harry Potter series. But the main characters in these books are not always capable of marvelous actions or singled out from the ordinary run of mortals. Harry, it's true, has much in common with King Arthur in his boyhood; he is a hero with a special destiny as well as a past shrouded in mystery. But Dorothy Gale is no more than a plucky little American girl of unexceptional descent, and Milo, the listless hero of *The Phantom Tollbooth,* is distinguished only by the enigmatic package he receives at the moment when his chronic boredom seems about to blossom into full-fledged depression.

As for the Pevensie siblings, we do learn of a prophecy in *The Lion, the Witch and the Wardrobe,* a poem predicting that evil won't be driven from the land until "Adam's flesh and Adam's bone" sit at "Cair Paravel in throne." However, Lewis believed people ought to be discouraged from thinking of themselves as singled out for an extraordinary, exalted fate; that way lies the deadliest of the seven deadly sins, pride. In the Chronicles, it's the selfish villains like Jadis and Digory's uncle Andrew who talk of having "a high and a lonely destiny." Narnia is meant to be ruled by human beings, and the Pevensies are simply the human beings who happen to come along to do it. Peter, Susan, Edmund, and Lucy are ordinary children, much like the readers for whom the Chronicles were intended; it is Narnia that makes kings and queens out of them. In Frye's terminology, the Pevensies are low mimetic characters, the kind of people routinely found in novels, but somehow they have stumbled into the realm of romance.

The same could be said of Tolkien's hobbits. They aren't technically human, but they're more like us, really, than the majestic human heroes of Middle-earth. Tolkien used the hobbits as a way of, as he once expressed it, "putting earth under the feet of 'romance,'" injecting "colloquialism and vulgarity" into a story otherwise dominated by "the highest style of prose." "High" was the word Tolkien used to describe the sort of thing he most enjoyed writing and reading, the lofty myths and epics of *The Silmarillion.* Characters like Aragorn and the elves belong to this part of his legendarium, and so does the grand dialogue that readers like Edmund Wilson find so silly.

The result, Tolkien's trilogy, is a hybrid, a winning formula combining the low mimetic characters that readers had grown comfortably accustomed to in novels with the grandeur and archetypal mystery many of them missed from the old romances. Morris hadn't thought of this when he attempted to revive the romance, but in children's fiction the combination was less remarkable; Lewis Carroll and E. Nesbit had already inserted modern, middle-class English children into magical lands and situations. Tolkien himself had created an irresistibly bourgeois protagonist in his children's book, *The Hobbit,* and sent him off on a Wagnerian quest involving dwarves, dragons, and a magic ring.

The main point Tolkien tried to get across in "On Fairy Stories" was that he saw no reason to restrict such fictions to an audience of children. "Fairy stories," he wrote, "have in the modern lettered world been relegated to the 'nursery,' as shabby or old-fashioned furniture is relegated to the playroom, primarily because the adults do not want it, and do not mind if it is misused." He recast the hand-me-downs as newly desirable antiques.

But this mixture of literary modes does not sit easily with everyone. For some it will always seem fatally juvenile, and for others merely dissonant. When a friend wrote to Tolkien complaining of the way certain characters in *The Lord of the Rings* spoke, he responded as a philologist, by explaining that King Theoden of the Rohirrim (for example) *must* say things like "I myself will go to war, to fall in the front of the battle, if it must be. Thus shall I sleep better," instead of the less archaic "I should sleep sounder in my grave like that rather than if I stayed home"; Theoden speaks differently from people like us because he *thinks* differently. The events and actions that occur in *The Lord of the Rings* could happen only in a world where people talk, and therefore think, in the way Theoden does. The kind of man who would say something like "Not at all, my dear Gandalf" would never behave with the Rohirric king's doomed nobility when confronting certain death in battle: "'Heroic' scenes do not occur in a modern setting to which a modern idiom belongs," Tolkien insisted.

This means that the hobbits, who speak like Edwardian country-folk, not only talk differently from the elves, but also think differently

—they live, in effect, in another world. They resemble the denizens of the twentieth century enough to provide the modern individual with a sympathetic bridge to Middle-earth. They *are* us, much like the contemporary reader in Tolkien's eyes: anti-Romantic, inflexible, incurious, unimaginative—a reader, like Eustace Scrubb, of the wrong kind of books, but secretly attracted to the old magic. As Tolkien imagined the distant past of Europe, time went by and the invented history of Middle-earth segued into the real history of our own world; hobbits and men became more and more alike and eventually merged. The last of the elvish blood is by now almost gone from the human race and the hobbitish mind-set has become universal. The age of romance ended. The age of the novel began.

This transition is a source of the great sorrow underlying *The Lord of the Rings;* the world it describes is on the cusp of a transformation; its heroic past is slipping away and another era, one of "colloquialism and vulgarity" is taking its place. "Associations with sunset and the fall of the leaf linger in romance," Frye writes, and this decline "evokes a mood best described as elegiac…often accompanied by a diffused, resigned, melancholy sense of the passing of time, of the old order changing and yielding to a new one." This so exactly describes the tone of *The Lord of the Rings* that I half suspect Frye of having Tolkien in mind when he wrote those words. But, in truth, it is the mood of all heroic epics. As a form, the romance is retrospective. The epic poet is forever lamenting that the titans of the past—Achilles, Odysseus, Beowulf—have left this earth. We shall not see their like again.

Frye writes further of the "extraordinarily persistent nostalgia" of the classic romance, "its search for some kind of imaginative golden age in time or space." Deliberate archaism comes with the territory, which is why Spenser (however objectionably in Tolkien's eyes) adopted an old-fashioned diction for *The Faerie Queene*. Though very fond of his hobbits, Tolkien did much prefer writing lays and sagas, like the ones collected in *The Silmarillion,* stories written in "the highest style of prose." His publishers, however, didn't regard this material as salable, and they were probably right. Nearly everyone who reads *The Silmarillion* comes to it only after being smitten with *The Lord of the Rings,* and many are disappointed. What they find are old-fashioned epics very much like the prose romances of William Morris. If it were not for the popularity of Tolkien's trilogy, *The Silmarillion,* if published at all, would now likely be as obscure as *The Well at the World's End.*

Tolkien's publishers, however, wanted him to repeat the success he'd had earlier with *The Hobbit,* a story that, when very first conceived, had not been set in Middle-earth. It was hobbits that sold, hobbits like Bilbo Baggins that readers loved and identified with; *The Lord of the Rings* was for a long time referred to by Tolkien and Lewis as "the new *Hobbit,*" as if it were merely the sequel to the earlier children's book. Tolkien had to be pushed into presenting his private mythology as the backdrop to further hobbit adventures. The hybridization that has made the romance so resilient, that has allowed it to return in new forms and to triumph again and again with new audiences, did not come naturally to him. He was no great reader of novels.

But Lewis was. As much as the defensive Tolkien fan dislikes comparing Middle-earth to Narnia — *The Lord of the Rings* is not a children's book, the author himself would have to insist, over and over again — it was children's fiction, with its giddy disregard of genre boundaries and other forms of decorum, that first showed writers how to cross the line. The Chronicles cross the line so often that they effectively rub it out. And that, for Tolkien, was a problem.

CHAPTER TWENTY-TWO

A Too-Impressionable Man

Tolkien began with *The Hobbit,* and then backed his way into the solemnity of *The Lord of the Rings.* Narnia, of course, was different. *The Lion, the Witch and the Wardrobe* and its sequels were begun and remained books for children, their background a gossamer and sometimes contradictory improvisation. These were mere "fairy tales," as Lewis freely called them, although there was nothing "mere" about fairy tales as far as he was concerned. Still, classic fairy tales are set in a world that's everywhere and nowhere, and in fairy tales it is always *now.* As Lewis continued to write more Chronicles, Narnia inevitably acquired a history, a geography, even a national identity of sorts, if never so extensive a one as Middle-earth's.

The Chronicles are not elegiac — what could be more pointless than trying to arouse nostalgia in children? — but from the very beginning Narnia had at least a sketch of a past. The good old days that Mr. Tumnus reminisces about with Lucy are a woodland idyll that the Pevensies help to restore and then get to live in. Their reign as kings and queens becomes Narnia's golden age, and by the time they find themselves grown up and back at the lamppost, they no longer speak as they once did. Even the narrator adopts the shift in diction: "'Sir,' said Queen Lucy. 'By likelihood when this post and this lamp were set here there were smaller trees in the place, or fewer, or none. For this is a young wood and the iron post is old.' And they stood looking upon it."

This is how aristocrats in chivalric romances talk, and the hunt that brings the siblings to the Lantern Waste (for a white stag who gives wishes to whoever catches him) is just the sort of pastime Chrétien de Troyes's characters would pursue on a summer afternoon. The Pevensies have graduated from fairy tale to romance. The transition is natural because the genres enjoy a familial relationship. When Lewis writes of one of his favorite books, *The Faerie Queene,* "what lies beneath the surface in Spenser's poem is the world of popular imagination: almost, a popular mythology," he refers to a common technique of the great romances: the combination of folk traditions with the sophisticated literary amusements of aristocrats. Why does the lady Una, when she first appears with the Redcrosse Knight in *The Faerie Queene,* lead a "milkwhite lambe" on a string (hardly a practical companion for a long trip by horseback)? Because in Spenser's time, English village pageants celebrating Saint George always included a local woman who played the part of the lady rescued by the saint, and she would customarily lead a white lamb.

From its early days, the romance, like the novel, was promiscuous and adaptive, read for entertainment more than the elevation of the soul. It blended religious symbolism with love poetry, instructions on manners for elegant courtiers with folklore borrowed from old wives and nursemaids. The great Italian romances of the Renaissance—Ludovico Ariosto's *Orlando Furioso* and Matteo Maria Boiardo's *Orlando Innamorato*—were, Lewis observed, written by educated men who approached traditional fairy tales with "a smile half of amusement and half of affection, like men returning to something that had charmed their childhood," only to find that "their pleasure is not only the pleasure of mockery. Even while you laugh at it, the old incantation works."

Tolkien did not agree, at least not when it came to the mockery. He took fairy tales very seriously. Mutual friends of the two men have offered various explanations for why Tolkien disliked the Narnia books so much, and this is one likely reason. Tolkien himself rarely elaborated on the subject. In a letter he wrote the year after Lewis died, he simply laments that "all that part of CSL's work" had remained "outside the range of my sympathy."

Roger Lancelyn Green recalls running into an indignant Tolkien in Oxford not long after both men had read the manuscript of *The Lion, the Witch and the Wardrobe*. "It really won't do!" Tolkien fumed. "I mean to say: *Nymphs and Their Ways, The Love-Life of a Faun!* Doesn't he know what he's talking about?" The note of parody in the titles of Mr. Tumnus's books seems to have particularly irked Tolkien, to have struck him, even, as improper. There is no book called *The Love-Life of a Faun* mentioned in *The Lion, the Witch and the Wardrobe* (that's a joke no child could be expected to get), but Tolkien's mistake is revealing. His memory nudges Lewis's gentle teasing closer to raciness than his friend would ever have come himself. To Tolkien, *Nymphs and Their Ways* was just as bad as a mildly smutty joke, really, tantamount to desecration.

"I have a very simple sense of humor (which even my appreciative critics find tiresome)," Tolkien once wrote to a reader. There's not much comedy in *The Lord of the Rings,* but what there is comes mostly from the hobbits, sticking to their comfort-loving, yokel ways in the midst of all the "high" adventures and noble speeches. Theirs is a rustic humor but not an earthy one, and in that *The Lord of the Rings* does feel very much a children's book.

By contrast, the wit of the Chronicles is positively worldly. There are the excerpts from Eustace's shipboard diary that appear in *The Voyage of the Dawn Treader,* shrewdly drawn little cameos of deluded self-justification ("Heaven knows I'm the last person to try to get an unfair advantage but I never dreamed that this water-rationing would be meant to apply to a sick man"). Reading those passages was my first experience with that refined literary device, the unreliable narrator, and with irony. Irony was a specialty of Lewis's. The most successful of his books during his own lifetime, *The Screwtape Letters,* is entirely ironic. Purporting to be the advice sent to a trainee devil by his supervisor, it is instruction by inversion, in which the reader comes to understand the lineaments of Christian virtue by flipping everything the demonic narrator says on its head.

Irony—especially the ironic social comedy Lewis relished (he was a great admirer of Jane Austen)—is a cultured humor. You can find amusement in the differences between what we would like to happen and what usually *does* happen only if you are already in possession of a variety of stories, official and otherwise. Austen's *Northanger Abbey,* a particular favorite of Lewis's, is about a young woman who has read too many gothic novels too credulously but who inhabits the world of a novel of manners; only an author familiar with both types of narratives could have written it. Irony, satire—Tolkien didn't care much for this kind of thing; he had invented an alternative world in part to escape a society that struck him as repellently cosmopolitan and complex. The broad humor of the hobbits was a plain dish that suited him just fine. Still, hobbit humor is curiously lacking in what most people would regard as an indispensable ingredient of broad, rustic jokes around the world: sex.

Tolkien, it must be said, was a terrible prude. There is more eroticism—however peculiar and sublimated—in the Chronicles than in *The Lord of the Rings,* even though Lewis was purposely trying to avoid sex in deference to the youth of his readers. The White Witch and the Lady of the Green Kirtle are evil, but they are also unmistakably alluring; Susanna Clarke, in response to complaints about the "misogyny" in those depictions, says, "I see it as [the witches] being *too* attractive, as if he were saying, 'If someone were to tempt me to do bad things, it would be a woman like *this.*'" The old romances often took the power and danger of sexual desire as one of their major themes; that's one reason why the modern romance genre inherited the label. *The Lord of the Rings* may be intended for adults, but the rare occurrences of romantic love in the book are bloodless and melancholy affairs. If Lewis often gives the impression that he's having a hard time keeping eroticism *out* of the Chronicles (it swirls below the surface), Tolkien never seems quite able to get it *in*.

This discomfort with sex was really only another facet of Tolkien's fastidiousness, his preoccupation with purity and corruption. Languages, in particular, could be either virginal or defiled. Once, when fantasizing about some pocket of Anglo-Saxon culture that might have survived unsullied by the francophone Normans, Tolkien pictured a community speaking a language that "had never fallen back into 'lewdness', and has contrived in troubled times to maintain the air of a gentleman, if a country gentleman." How a language can be "lewd" is a puzzle, but that image of a good country gentleman signifies a lot: he is a man free of both the decadence of urbanity and the coarseness of the peasant. This is a pretty narrow strip of territory to occupy. It also bespeaks a delicacy you would hardly expect to find in human societies like those of Middle-earth, which Tolkien himself described as existing in the "simple 'Homeric' state of patriarchal and tribal life." He must have forgotten that *The Iliad* begins with two heroes squabbling over a concubine.

Beowulf was the standard Tolkien aspired to. In that poem, the women characters make only brief appearances, and then as dignified or tragic queens. Loyalty between a chieftain and his followers is the emotion that most interests the *Beowulf* poet, far more so than erotic passion. A sentimental reader of *The Lord of the Rings* wrote to Tolkien in the 1960s, expressing dismay at how quickly the warrior maiden Éowyn abandons her unrequited love for Aragorn and pairs off with another man at the book's conclusion. Tolkien wrote back, "This tale does not deal with a period of 'Courtly Love' and its pretenses; but with a culture more primitive (sc. less corrupt) and nobler." Courtly love, after all, was an invention of the detested

French, an adulteration of the heroic epic perpetrated by the middle and late medieval romancers who came after the *Beowulf* poet. It was yet another example of the deplorable tendency of cultures to intermingle, forsaking their immaculate roots.

No wonder, then, that Tolkien objected to *The Lion, the Witch and the Wardrobe,* which mixed up classical and Northern mythologies, canonical fairy tales and slangy modern schoolchildren, myth and satire, all with such cheerful indiscrimination. He was not entirely alone in that sentiment. Even Green, who had liked the first draft of the book, tried to get Lewis to cut the scene where an incongruous Father Christmas appears to the Pevensies and the Beavers during their cross-country flight from the Witch, bearing magical gifts and a steaming pot of hot tea. Lewis ignored him. If Spenser could get away with it, why shouldn't he?

What was Tolkien to think? Lewis had delighted in Middle-earth. He had eagerly read and extravagantly praised all of the literary manifestations of Tolkien's private world. He referred often and admiringly to his friend's essay on the value of fairy tales and imaginative fiction. And, even after the two men had grown apart, he happily fulfilled a promise to the publisher of *The Lord of the Rings* to "do all in my power to secure for Tolkien's great book the recognition it deserves." That included providing a back-cover blurb, two (unsigned) rave reviews in newspapers, and urgent recommendations to all of his correspondents and friends.

But when it came to creating his own imaginary land, Lewis disregarded Tolkien's exacting formula for making a "secondary world." Narnia was not self-enclosed and consistent. It lifted figures and motifs in whole cloth from a motley assortment of national traditions, making no effort to integrate them into any coherent mythos. Tolkien had carefully revised later editions of *The Hobbit* to remove a reference to tomatoes (if Middle-earth is meant to be an early version of Europe, then tomatoes, a New World import, would be anachronistic), while Lewis thought nothing of giving Mrs. Beaver a sewing machine!

Tolkien could also hardly fail to notice that, as highly as this friend—his *best* friend—thought of him, Lewis remained indifferent to other distinctions that lay very close to Tolkien's heart. The religious conversion that Tolkien had worked so hard to bring about had led Lewis not to Roman Catholicism, as Tolkien had hoped. Instead, his friend turned back to the Church of England, an institution Tolkien regarded as degenerate. Tolkien's Catholicism had always contained a strain of paranoia (although ordinarily quick to spot and condemn a tyrant, he supported the fascist general Francisco Franco in the Spanish civil war because some of Franco's left-wing opponents had persecuted priests and nuns), and here Lewis had blithely gone and joined the ranks of the enemy.

Tolkien concluded that Lewis, try as he might to purge himself of old prejudices, had never really succeeded. At heart, his friend remained an Ulster Protestant and a member of the church whose only real foundation, in Tolkien's opinion, lay in its hatred and persecution of "Papism." Lewis preferred to believe that his apologetics spoke for traditionally minded Christians everywhere, that his theology transcended denomination. But this ecumenical stance amounted to asserting that the differences between Protestants and Catholics (as well as among Protestants themselves) didn't really matter. And as far as Tolkien was concerned, they most certainly did.

The chief reason Tolkien offered publicly for the fading of his friendship with Lewis in the 1940s was the influence of a third man, the novelist Charles Williams. Lewis read Williams's *Place of the Lion* in 1936 and promptly wrote a fan letter to the author, declaring the novel "one of the major literary events of my life." Williams, who worked at the Oxford University Press in London, had in turn recently read the manuscript of *The Allegory of Love* and felt something similar. They quickly became fast friends.

During World War II, the offices of the OUP were moved to Oxford, and Williams came with them. Lewis enthusiastically incorporated his new friend into the Inklings. He adulated Williams, not just as a writer, but as a great soul. Lewis informed one acquaintance that should he happen to see Williams walking down the street he would instantly recognize him, "because he looks godlike; rather, like an angel." Williams had this effect on people. In Williams's company, W. H. Auden remarked, he felt himself to be "for the first time in my life . . . in the presence of personal sanctity." And T. S. Eliot wrote, "He seemed to me to approximate, more nearly than any man I have known familiarly, to the saint."

Tolkien always maintained that he liked Williams personally; his writing and thinking, however, were another matter. "Our minds remained poles apart," he informed his American publisher when asked about the connection. *The Place of the Lion,* a very strange novel, describes the unfolding of a sort of Platonic apocalypse in modern-day Britain; the ideal manifestations of things (their "forms," as Plato called them) begin to materialize, absorbing all their imperfect iterations in the real world. One character witnesses the appearance of the ideal butterfly, into which all of the ordinary butterflies are sucked, as if by a vacuum cleaner.

Tolkien had no use for intellectualized, quasi-allegorical stories of this ilk, but Lewis was a dyed-in-the-wool Platonist—this element of his thinking sometimes seems to eclipse the Christian—and he found *The Place of the Lion* inspiring. (The enormous lion that stalks the British countryside in Williams's novel is surely one of Aslan's inspirations.) Tolkien was convinced that Williams's influence had spoiled the final novel in Lewis's space trilogy, *That Hideous Strength,* and he lamented this as further evidence that his old friend was "a very impressionable, too impressionable, man."

Near the end of his life, not long after Lewis's death, Tolkien related to a journalist how Lewis had sparked the invention of a major chunk of Middle-earth's legendarium by one day announcing, "Tollers, there is too little of what we really like in stories. I'm afraid we shall have to try and write some ourselves." Hence, their vow to write a "thriller" apiece. Tolkien never finished that particular book, but in the years that followed, "the most lasting pleasure and reward for both of us has been that we provided one another with stories to hear or read that we really liked—in large parts." What Tolkien liked, however, were the first two books of the space trilogy; for Narnia, the imaginary land that many readers naturally associate with Middle-earth upon learning that the two men were friends, he felt only disdain.

That close friendship and its disintegration, and Narnia's role in the sad conclusion, continue to invite comparisons of the two men's imaginary worlds. It was much the same with Wordsworth and Coleridge, whose intimacy and estrangement have long prompted readers to "side" with the poetry of one or the other. For many years, Wordsworth routinely came out ahead; *The Prelude* was weightier, more philosophical, more overtly "serious" than any of Coleridge's verse. Lately, now that Victorian sobriety has gone thoroughly out of fashion, Coleridge's visionary idiosyncrasy has gained the edge over Wordsworth's poetic essays. Perhaps Lewis would be due a similar reassessment if most of the people making the comparison weren't still primarily interested in trying to vindicate the fantasy genre itself. They tend to be Tolkien fans, and they are upset that he is not taken as seriously as they feel he ought to be. His masterpiece should not be equated with a handful of derivative children's books!

Perhaps for this reason, Tolkien's alleged objection to the rampant syncretism of the Chronicles, and to his friend's deficiencies at "world building," has been given extraordinary weight. Even people who don't respect either man's fiction—critics like John Goldthwaite and Philip Pullman—repeat the complaint that Narnia is thin and miscellaneous, a patching together, seams out, of various mythologies and narrative tones. *The Lion, the Witch and the Wardrobe* is a version of the Christian Passion, set in a variation on the Renaissance notion of Arcadia, populated by figures from classical and Norse legend, mingling as incongruously as the costumed actors on a film studio back lot. Furthermore, it borrows its voice from the children's fantasies of E. Nesbit and *Peter Pan,* its talking animals from Beatrix Potter, its chivalric trappings from Malory. Goldthwaite calls Narnia a "Platonic 'shadowland'" constructed with "an utter disregard for the laws of consistency that must be observed when writing any fantasy."

At least Tolkien could be thankful that by the time Narnia came along, Lewis knew better than to work bits of Middle-earth's mythology into his new invention. Or perhaps Tolkien had to ask him not to. Such a request might indeed have been necessary, because although Tolkien could have found no better audience for his lost tales and histories, no reader more willing to enter into his imaginary world, no mind better equipped intellectually to appreciate it, Lewis simply didn't subscribe to Tolkien's preoccupation with cultural integrity.

Why should he? Behind the two men's shared fondness for medieval literature, for romance, for England, lay some important differences. Lewis had long understood the Middle Ages to be a period not of pristine simplicity but of rampant cultural admixture and amalgamation. Christianity and pagan mythology, science and theology, history and poetry, were all wrestled by those great medieval codifiers into a single, overarching system. Everything went into the pot; everything had to, to validate God's plan. It never seems to have occurred to Lewis to regard the result as polluted. There's little evidence that, whatever his youthful prejudice against the French, he shared Tolkien's view of the Norman Conquest as a tragedy. Lewis adored his friend's "private mythology" but gave no sign of agreeing that it represented the true, immaculate soul of England. And on that count, Irishman though he was, he came closer to the truth.

CHAPTER TWENTY-THREE

The Old Religion

On the second floor of the British Museum in London is a small chest known as the Franks Casket. Made of whalebone ivory, it's roughly the size of two small cigar boxes stacked on top of each other and elaborately carved on all four sides as well as on the lid. The Franks Casket dates from the eighth century and is thought to have been made for a prince of Northumbria, a northeastern kingdom in Anglo-Saxon England, although the carvings suggest a theme of exile, so it may not have been made there. Perhaps whoever first owned it used it to store rings and other golden items, the sort of treasure with which the leaders of the Danes and Geats secure the loyalty of their men in *Beowulf*. The casket is about the same age as the poem, made at the moment in English history that Tolkien idealized. The runes inscribed on the casket include some of the oldest surviving lines of Anglo-Saxon poetry, and the images resemble Pauline Baynes's illustrations for *Farmer Giles of Ham*.

The Franks Casket is also unabashedly syncretistic. The right side depicts a Germanic warrior meeting a strange animal goddess, possibly the spirit of a sacred grove, possibly a Valkyrie, but in any case a figure from Norse paganism. The left side shows Romulus and Remus, the twin brothers who founded Rome. The Adoration of the Magi shares the front panel with images of Weland the Smith, a semidivine artisan figure from Norse mythology who resembles the great elvish metalworkers of *The Silmarillion*. On the back is carved the siege of Jerusalem by the Roman general Titus. The images on the lid portray an archer, probably from the Norse sagas. The maker of the casket apparently found it advisable to cover every religious base, pagan as well as Christian, with a dash of lore from the receding empire thrown in for good measure. This mélange commemorates a particularly fluid time in England's religious history, a period when a new faith was replacing an older one.

Such moments were hardly rare in Britain. A few hundred years after the Franks Casket was carved, the ascendant Catholicism of the eighth century would become "the Old Religion," persecuted by the officials of the new Church of England and practiced in secret by families forced to build priest holes in their houses in order to hide "recusant" Catholic clergymen. Before the Anglo-Saxons, the Celtic Britons had their own polytheistic beliefs, with gods called Lugh, Sulis, and Toutatis; the occupying Romans would summarily rename these Mercury, Minerva, and Mars. Long ago, before even the Celts arrived, there were the Neolithic peoples who erected Stonehenge ("the oldest place in the old," as Lewis once described it in a letter) and left Britain and Ireland peppered with their tombs and standing stones. What gods they worshipped, we will never know. According to *Beowulf*, it is one of their earthwork tombs or barrows—built, the poet explains, by "somebody now forgotten"—that houses the dragon whose venom will ultimately kill the epic's aging hero. After defeating the monster, the poisoned warrior king stares up at the stone arches supporting the barrow's inner chamber, ancient even then, realizing that his own end, too, is near.

The first time I visited England I went for a walk with a friend over the headlands of the Isle of Wight off the southern coast. We happened upon a group of barrows, and hiked over the edge of the tallest. The top of the mound had collapsed long ago, leaving a grassy bowl. We lay down inside and listened as the wind blew up over the hill from the sea, while in that small shelter all was still. I tried to imagine the people who'd built the mound, thousands and thousands of years ago, a race whose very name has been lost, but who, like people everywhere, made a ceremony of burying their dead. I felt a sensation of plunging, not through space but through time, a feeling both giddy and solemn. I may even have held my breath for a while. When the moment passed, I turned and began to describe it to my friend, who, I learned to my surprise, had experienced much the same thing.

Lewis grew up amid sites like this one; the remains of the oldest man-made structures in Britain are in Northern Ireland. When I hiked to the top of Slieve Martin in Rostrevor, I found, as promised in a park brochure, a stone with fading petroglyphs and, not far off, a cairn, or pile of rocks, marking an ancient grave. A prodigious country walker like Lewis must have happened upon hundreds of such remnants as he and his friends tramped through the hills of England, Ireland, Wales, and Scotland.

Those experiences inspired the opening of *Prince Caspian,* a favorite scene among Lewis's readers. The Pevensies, after being magically yanked from a railway platform in England onto a deserted island, make their way from the shore to the island's center. There, amid the trees, they find a crumbling stone wall with an arched opening; through it, they walk into "a wide open place with walls all round it. In here there were no trees, only level grass and daisies, and ivy, and grey walls. It was a bright, secret, quiet place, and rather sad." The children soon recognize this for the ruins of a castle, but it isn't until Susan finds a solid gold chessman (an echo of Norse gods' golden game pieces, found in the grass by the survivors of Ragnarok) that they realize that this is *their* castle, the remnants of Cair Paravel. Because of the incongruities in the passage of time between Narnia and our world, they've returned hundreds of years after their own reign.

Energetic promoters of Northern Ireland as a site for C. S. Lewis tourism have claimed that Dunluce Castle on the Antrim Coast was the model for Cair Paravel. Lewis himself never said as much, although he knew the place; his family often vacationed along the northern coast of Ireland in the summers when he was a child. Built on a tall, steep rock outcropping surrounded by rough surf, accessible only by a narrow bridge, Dunluce is gloomier than I ever imagined Cair Paravel being. (If you happen to have an old LP of Led Zeppelin's *Houses of the Holy*, you can see for yourself; Dunluce is the background for the gatefold photograph.) What's left of the castle looks stolid and houselike, not especially evocative of the spires and gables that Pauline Baynes drew for *The Lion, the Witch and the Wardrobe*. I was, however, won over to the idea of Dunluce as Cair Paravel (sentimentally, if not rationally) by something far below the castle itself, at the foot of its massive basalt base: a little grotto, washed by the waves, called the Mermaid's Cave. Mermaids and mermen, as some readers of Narnia will recall, sang at the coronation of Lucy, Edmund, Peter, and Susan in *The Lion, the Witch and the Wardrobe*.

Like the remains of Cair Paravel, Dunluce Castle is roofless, and its floors have been replaced by a carpet of grass. You can see a similarly carpeted ruin beside the Thames footpath in Oxford, the route Lewis and his friends took on their frequent walks to the Trout pub in Wolvercote. These walls, what's left of Godstow Nunnery, are older even than Dunluce. Henry II's popular mistress, Rosamund Clifford, was once buried in the convent's church choir. That was too close to the altar for the liking of Saint Hugh, the Bishop of Lincoln, who had her tomb removed in 1191 as part of a campaign against "superstitious and magical abominations everywhere," according to his hagiographer. The tomb was later destroyed in another religious purge when Henry VIII dissolved the Catholic orders and established the Church of England in the 1530s. At that point, the building was converted to a private house and occupied by a well-off local family — until the English civil war, when it was badly damaged during the fighting between Puritan revolutionaries and Anglican royalists.

Eventually, the ruins became a picnic spot favored on sunny afternoons by, among others, Lewis Carroll, Alice Liddell, and her sisters.

Look deep enough and many such places in England become spiritual palimpsests; each faith is written over the one that came before, leaving traces of the "Old Religion" still visible beneath. This was true back in the days of the *Beowulf* poet; even the dragon is a squatter in a structure built by somebody long dead. The difficulty with Tolkien's plan "to restore to the English an epic tradition and present them with a mythology of their own" was that by conceiving of that mythology as essentially Anglo-Saxon, rather than British, he tried not only to freeze a moment in that history but to airbrush out the past. The Anglo-Saxons, coming as they did somewhere in the middle of the long succession of peoples that have settled in Britain, never established an entirely "pure" culture there.

As for what Lewis called "England's national epic," Thomas Malory's *Morte D'Arthur*, well, Tolkien had reservations about *that*. The Arthurian tradition was Celtic in origin and it was primarily preserved in the chivalric romances written by French poets in the Middle Ages. As a result, Tolkien disdained the stories of King Arthur and his knights on no less than three counts: first, for their Christianity, which, for complicated reasons, Tolkien felt compromised their mythic integrity; second, for the French elements (especially the "corrupt" code of courtly love), about which the less said the better; and third, for their Celtic roots.

Tolkien's attitude toward Celtic culture was ambivalent to say the least. When, in the 1930s, his British publisher sent an early manuscript of *The Silmarillion* to a reader, a report came back that complained of the "eye-splitting Celtic names" and described Tolkien's tales as conveying "something of that mad, bright-eyed beauty that perplexes all Anglo-Saxons in the face of Celtic art." Tolkien, naturally, protested. His names and stories were not Celtic! "I do know Celtic things (many in their original languages, Irish and Welsh)," he wrote in reply, "and feel for them a certain distaste: largely for their fundamental unreason. They have bright color, but are like a broken stained glass window reassembled without design. They are in fact 'mad' as your reader says—but I don't believe I am."

The distinction is charged—politically, historically, personally, and (for Tolkien at least) linguistically. Tolkien believed, as did just about everyone at that time, that the English were descended mainly from the Anglo-Saxons. The rest of Britain—Wales, Scotland, and (especially) Ireland—constituted a "Celtic fringe," whose ancestors had been pushed to the so-called outskirts by the invading Germanic tribes who overran the heartland after the Romans abandoned their British colonies in the fifth century. This idea had many uses for the English, all springing from the widely held conviction that the Anglo-Saxons and the Celts had fundamentally different temperaments as well as cultures.

The Celts were "mad": moody, whimsical, flighty, and often charming, but prone to superstition, to drink, and to melancholy. The Anglo-Saxons were practical, energetic, and efficient, in accordance with the common stereotype of Germans. Anglo-Saxons got things done and hewed to a noble code of honor inherited from their warrior past. This explained why the Anglo-Saxons (that is, the English) rightfully dominated the people of the Celtic fringe; they were inherently superior and capable, uniquely fitted for leadership. Lewis himself subscribed to this view at times, characterizing his father's Welsh family as "sentimental, passionate, and rhetorical."

This doctrine of the two temperaments flourished in the nineteenth century, when prominent English experts equated Celtic ancestry with Catholicism and a general lazy backwardness that would have to be eradicated if the Irish (in particular) could ever hope to equal their English rulers. The prominent naturalist Robert Knox thought the Irish were incurable, and wrote, "The source of all evil lies *in the race,* the Celtic race of Ireland. There is no getting over *historical facts....* The race must be forced from the soil; by fair means, if possible; still they must leave. England's safety requires it. I speak not of the justice of the cause; nations must ever act as Machiavelli advised: look to yourself. The Orange club of Ireland is a Saxon confederation for clearing the land of all papists and jacobites; this means Celts."

Tolkien would never have condoned this sort of racism, even if it hadn't come laced with a large dose of anti-Catholicism, but he was prone to the fantasy of racialism all the same. Each language has a distinct flavor, as he saw it, and his own immediate recognition of Anglo-Saxon constituted, in his opinion, "as good or better a test of ancestry as blood-groups." Blood explained why he "took to early West-Midland middle English as a known tongue as soon as I set eyes on it."

In this belief, incidentally, Tolkien was almost certainly wrong. Recent advances in the analysis of DNA have made it possible to determine the distant genetic roots of contemporary individuals. Samples taken from the population of Britain revealed, to the surprise of many, that the modern English are mostly *not* of Anglo-Saxon ancestry. "Overall," wrote the Oxford geneticist Bryan Sykes, who oversaw the studies, "the genetic structure of the Isles is stubbornly Celtic, if by that we mean descent from people who were here before the Romans and who spoke a Celtic language." In some parts of England, the proportion of people who can claim Anglo-Saxon ancestry does run as high as twenty percent, but that is along the eastern coast. Tolkien's beloved homeland, the West Midlands, is almost entirely populated by the descendants of Celts, and on his mother's side (the only branch of his family that mattered to him, and the source of his perceived Anglo-Saxonism) he too was most probably a Celt.

Tolkien did waver in his "distaste" for things Celtic. As a boy, he found the Welsh names painted on the sides of railway cars both mysterious and evocative, and the elvish language Sindarin is based on Welsh, one of his favorite tongues. He wrote (or at least began) a few poems on Arthurian subjects, despite his apprehensions about the non-English

roots of the tradition. And one of the major works of his career as a
scholar was a translation, with E. V. Gordon, of the fourteenth-century
Middle English Arthurian poem *Sir Gawain and the Green Knight*. Tolkien's introduction (with Gordon) to that work praises it for not being
as "rambling and incoherent" as "older Celtic forms."

As for his own tales, Tolkien wrote that he intended them to convey "the fair elusive beauty that some call Celtic (though it is rarely
found in genuine ancient Celtic things)." Most likely, he found the
Celtic legends preserved in the Irish cycles and the Welsh *Mabino-
gion* — rife as they are with promiscuous women, arbitrary violence,
and bodily fluids, as most myths tend to be toward the root — too
coarse for his taste. His new mythology for England would instead
be "'high,' purged of the gross, and fit for the more adult mind of a
land long now steeped in poetry."

Lewis, of course, would sometimes count himself among the
Celts, but that did not necessarily keep him from agreeing with his
friend on the problematic aspects of Celtic culture. He did, however,
draw the line between the "flavors" of Celtic and Germanic myth
with a greater, less punitive delicacy, in a letter to Arthur Greeves:

> I noted that the Celtic was much more sensuous; also less
> *homely*: also, entirely lacking in *reverence*, of which the Ger-
> manic was full. Then again that the Germanic *glowed* in a sense
> with the rich somber colors, while the Celtic was all transpar-
> ent and full of nuances — evanescent — but very bright. One
> sees that Celtic is essentially Pagan, not merely in the sense
> of being heathen (not-Christian), as the Germanic might be,
> but in the sense of being irredeemably pagan, frivolous under
> all its melancholy, incapable of growing into religion, and — I
> think — a little heartless.

Some of these words — "transparent and full of nuances — eva-
nescent — but very bright" — could well describe Narnia, while the

"rich somber colors" and "reverence" of the Germanic sounds more like Middle-earth. At times, Narnia does feel like a heroic and not entirely successful attempt to inject "religion" (that is, Christianity) into an "irredeemably pagan" (pan-pagan, really) realm that its convert author cannot bear to leave behind. But harping on the division between Germanic and Celtic (or for that matter, classical) paganism was characteristic of Tolkien, not Lewis. Lewis never felt the need to choose between the two mythologies, for as he went on to say in that letter to Arthur Greeves, "I don't want to give up either: they are almost one's male and female soul."

CHAPTER TWENTY-FOUR

Riches All About You

L ewis's magpie aesthetic made Narnia a grab bag of every motif that had ever captured his fancy. Susanna Clarke told me that she'd once heard Narnia called just that, a "fancy," in comparison to Tolkien's fully articulated "fantasy." The distinction, she said, originated with an academic critic of contemporary genre fiction, Gary Wolfe, author of the book *Critical Terms for Science Fiction and Fantasy: A Glossary and Guide to Scholarship*. I wrote to Wolfe to find out more, and he kindly replied, explaining that although he'd never actually applied the distinction to Lewis and Tolkien, he could see how someone else might. He'd based it on Coleridge's conception of the difference between fancy and imagination, as described in *Biographia Literaria,* the philosophical and aesthetic autobiography Coleridge published in 1817.

According to *Biographia Literaria,* imagination "dissolves, diffuses, dissipates, in order to re-create; or where this process is rendered impossible, yet still at all events it struggles to idealize and to unify. It is essentially vital even as all objects (as objects) are essentially fixed and dead." Fancy, by contrast, only rearranges preestablished "fixities and definites," and is really no more than a "mode of Memory emancipated from the order of time and space." It is the difference between rearranging the furniture in your mind and building it from scratch. "So by these standards," Wolfe wrote in his e-mail to me, "you could make an argument that Tolkien inventing a new world and language that is not a direct mirror or allegory, is a better representative of Coleridge's 'imagination' than Lewis, who employed Christian allegorical elements and familiar figures from myth and folklore in a way that more or less equates with 'fancy.'"

Here we come to one aspect of the Romantic creed that Lewis found myopic: the cult of individual genius and its corollary preoccupation with originality. Lewis knew that the high valuation placed on artistic novelty was itself fairly recent. The writers he studied regarded new material and ideas as precarious; far better to found your text on established *authorities,* as the great writers of the past were called. But contrary to what a modern reader might conclude, Lewis believed that this attitude didn't necessarily reduce the work of medieval writers to the mere parroting or imitation of other authors.

When Chaucer "works over" a poem by Boccaccio, Lewis writes in *The Discarded Image,* his delightful book on the medieval mind, "no line, however closely translated, will do exactly what it did in the Italian once Chaucer has made his additions. No line in those additions but depends for much of its effect on the translated lines which precede and follow it." As he saw it, the miracle of medieval literature was that its great writers, without attempting to do anything unprecedented, and in the act of what appeared to be no more than touching up some venerable source, nevertheless transfigured their material: "they handled no predecessor without pouring new life into him."

Lewis took the defense of the Middle Ages as the great cause of his academic career. *The Allegory of Love* aimed to unlock the riddles of the medieval romances for modern scholars, and the same could be said of his critical magnum opus, *English Literature in the Sixteenth Century Excluding Drama,* a volume in *The Oxford History of English Literature* series (semiaffectionately nicknamed *OHEL*). Lewis described the supreme English poet of the 1500s, Edmund Spenser, as "neo-Medieval." What was good about English literature in the sixteenth century, Lewis firmly believed, had its roots in the world-view, the style, and the tastes of the Middle Ages.

The brilliance of the Renaissance (if by "Renaissance" we mean the revival of classical forms of art, literature, and philosophy in Europe beginning in Italy in the fifteenth century), Lewis felt, was not just overrated, but possibly nonexistent. "My line," he wrote to a colleague, "is to *define* the Renaissance as 'an imaginary entity responsible for anything a modern writer happens to approve in the 15th or 16th century.'" According to then current intellectual fashion, whatever the modern observer liked—such as Dante, a poet Lewis considered completely medieval—would be chalked up to a manifestation of the Renaissance; everything unappealing would be labeled as typical of the Middle Ages.

Like most students, I was taught to think of the years between the fifth and the fifteenth centuries as the Dark Ages. Historians have by now virtually abandoned that term, and even when it was more commonly used, it was meant to describe only the period before the eleventh century; the "darkness" refers to the lack of contemporary historical records from those years. But from the perspective of my Renaissance-adulating sixth-grade teacher and our social studies textbook, the metaphorical shadow fell over all of the Middle Ages. Those were ignorant and backward times as far as we were concerned, and not worth much attention. Perhaps this was true of, say, the visual arts in Italy. But, as Lewis observes in *OHEL,* it doesn't make much sense to regard the bulk of sixteenth-century English literature as a major improvement on Chaucer.

It would also be a mistake, he insists, to give too much credit for the flowering of Elizabethan literature in the late 1500s to "humanism." The English humanists—those thinkers who read, taught, and emulated classical authors—were, in Lewis's opinion, far more influenced by Latin than by Greek (which in any case most of them barely knew). And that influence was not necessarily salubrious.

The English writers of the early sixteenth century made the mistake of attempting to mimic Latin prose and verse styles in their own language. This was a bad idea, partly because Latin is inflected and English is not, and it led to stiff, drab writing.

If only the humanists had been as familiar with Greek as many people seemed to think they were! Then their writing might have escaped this Latinate deadliness; Lewis felt that it was impossible to be "marmoreal" in Greek. Latin, alas, permits endless pomposity. "The desire [among early sixteenth-century British writers] was for order and discipline, weight, and decorum," Lewis writes in *OHEL,* and this affectation produced prose and verse that was ponderous, artificial, and abstract. "Nothing is light, or tender or fresh" in the literature of the early 1500s, he complains. "All the authors write like elderly men."

Only when English writers got over their aspirations to classical dignity did English literature recover, and when it did, "fantasy, conceit, paradox, color, incantation" returned. Spenser and Philip Sidney brought back these qualities by taking up that quintessentially medieval form, the romance, in *The Faerie Queene* and *Arcadia.* Even Shakespeare's vitality as a dramatist, Lewis insisted, was tapped from popular art forms that had survived from the Middle Ages, unsullied by the fashions of the lettered classes. The literary rebirth in the Elizabethan era occurred, he argued, not because of classicism, but in spite of it. It happened because the great artists of the period revived the inherently medieval flavor of English, a language that is particular, intimate, diverse, and lively, rather than grand and abstract. Few English writers could successfully reproduce the stately gravitas of Latin verse (only Milton ever excelled at it, Lewis felt), and as long as they kept trying, they generated nothing but bad poetry and the rationales to justify it. "The more we look into the question," he wrote, "the harder we shall find it to believe that humanism had any power of encouraging, or any wish to encourage, the literature that actually arose" under Elizabeth I.

With this unconventional argument, Lewis completely reversed the commonly held view of the Middle Ages as a cultural lull, and placed them at the center of the English imagination and sensibility. If modern readers have difficulty appreciating this truth, he felt, it's because our world is so different from that one; we have to learn to imaginatively project ourselves into the medieval universe in order to read medieval books properly. Doing this requires more than just picturing a life without combustion engines or penicillin; you have to slip into the consciousness of someone with an entirely different conception of the cosmos. And you can't just think your way into it by, say, intermittently reminding yourself that the author you're reading believed that the planets are embedded in a series of nested crystal spheres and play music as they revolve. You had to try to *feel* what that world felt like to that man or woman. "The recipe for such realization is not the study of books," Lewis wrote. "You must go out on a starry night and walk about for half an hour trying to see the sky in terms of the old cosmology."

Lewis regarded the medieval model of the universe as a great collective work of art and science, a conceptual cathedral built of the thoughts and words of many people. Not all of these were Christians by any means; the medievals respected the classical philosophers they knew about almost as much as they revered scripture, and even the "barbarians" (that is, nonclassical pagans) had some influence. "The Model," as Lewis refers to it, was both beautiful to contemplate and reassuring to inhabit; everything had its proper place in a perfectly ordered hierarchy proceeding from unformed matter at the bottom of the scale to God at the pinnacle. All things were known, or at least knowable; all ideas could be made to fit into the whole, which was one reason why innovation for its own sake seemed superfluous.

If Lewis himself couldn't entirely believe in this "finite" yet melodious universe, he felt its attraction. "The 'space' of modern astronomy may arouse terror, or bewilderment or vague reverie," he wrote; "the spheres of the old present us with an object in which the mind can rest, overwhelming in its greatness but satisfying in its harmony....This explains why all sense of the pathless, the baffling, and the utterly alien — all agoraphobia — is so markedly absent from medieval poetry when it leads us, as so often, into the sky."

The medieval universe, however, was also extremely intricate. The angelic population alone consists of three hierarchies of beings, divided into three species apiece, each with its own name, duties, and native powers. This complexity was yet another result of the incorrigible bookishness of the time, compounded by the sheer credulity of medieval scholars whenever dealing with venerable texts. "They find it hard to believe that anything an old *auctour* has said is simply untrue," Lewis observed drily. If it was written down, it had to be correct, and therefore must be accommodated into the model.

As a result, medieval intellectuals devoted themselves not only to compiling, but also to reconciling the whole, diverse panoply of known printed information, pagan and Christian, much of it seemingly incompatible. This task called for great feats of imaginative metaphysics. The medievals' conception of astronomy may be the most eloquent example of their ability, à la Lewis Carroll's White Queen, to believe several impossible things before breakfast. They regarded the stars as physical objects *and* as supernatural intelligent beings bearing the names of pagan gods (although ultimately emanations of, and subordinate to, the Supreme God) *and* as disembodied forces, exerting great influence over human affairs — all at the same time. It's easy to see why allegory became the signature literary form of the period.

It was to help readers grasp this convoluted system that Lewis wrote *The Discarded Image: An Introduction to Medieval and Renaissance Literature.* He conceived of this long essay (or short book) as a Baedeker to the past, intended for readers who, like cultivated travelers, prefer to visit a foreign country with some sense of what "those ways of life, those churches, those vineyards, mean to the natives."

Ideally, reading is a kind of collaboration: the more a reader brings to the book, the more he has to contribute to the experience and the richer it will be. In another text with similar ambitions, *A Preface to Paradise Lost,* Lewis remarked that while Milton's poetry is often compared to organ music, "it might be more helpful to regard the reader as the organ and Milton as the organist. It is on us he plays, if we will let him." No musician can play well on a faulty or inadequate instrument; the ideal reader responds to the work on every octave it sounds.

It's difficult for moderns like ourselves, steeped in the Romantic veneration of individuality, to think of the closed, structured medieval universe and the period's slavish veneration of "authorities" as anything but conformist and oppressive. But, as the writers of sonnets often claim, artistic constraints can be paradoxically liberating. In this case, Lewis argued, they steered writers away from pretense and hot air. When you choose from a list of presanctioned subjects and themes, you need not justify the material as important or worthy; it supplies all the required weight on its own. As a result, the best authors of the Middle Ages wrote humbly, clearly, gracefully, unselfconsciously. "The glory of the best medieval work," Lewis wrote, "often consists precisely in the fact that we see through it; it is a pure transparency."

Not coincidentally, this sounds very much like Neil Gaiman's description of what he likes about Lewis's prose: "It's clean, it's beautiful, it makes sense," he told me. "It doesn't do anything but what it's meant to do." When I finally found my way to Lewis's criticism, I discovered that it had the same clarity as his children's fiction (a genre in which lucid writing is required). Even Lewis's great detractor, Philip Pullman, aspires to the same, very English, ideal of a transparent style: novelists like James Joyce and Vladimir Nabokov, he told me, write books in which "a lot of the interest and sometimes all the interest, is in the surface of the prose [but] my main interest is in the things that you can see through the window of the prose."

The great beauty Lewis found in medieval literature lies in its effort-less integration of precise, modest detail—the "homely," as he and Arthur Greeves called it—with the vast, comprehensive grandeur of the medieval cosmos. In such a scheme, every small thing—the fall of a sparrow, as Hamlet put it—plays its own, essential part. To demonstrate this, Lewis liked to pluck plainspoken, endearing little touches of realism out of old poems and hold them up to the light for his readers' admiration. One of his favorites was the moment in Chaucer's "Summoner's Tale" when the itinerant Friar John pauses to "droof awey the cat" before sitting down on a patron's bench. Lewis was also fond of the passage in Layamon's *Brut,* a Middle Eng-lish poem about the history of Britain, in which the fifteen-year-old Arthur is told by a party of Britons first that his father is dead and then that he must assume the throne; they observe the prince sitting "full still;/one while he was wan, and in hue exceeding pale; one while he was red."

To this list, he might also have added, from the famous scene of the Redcrosse Knight's battle with the dragon in *The Faerie Queene,* the poor grass "bruised" by the monster's huge, hot body and the startlingly bourgeois observation that the blood gushing from its wound was forceful enough to "drive a water-mill." This sort of "viv-idness," as Lewis called it, the deployment of the telling, concrete detail, has in our time become "every novelist's stock-in-trade." The medievals, however, more or less invented it, and "it was long before they had many successors."

Lewis himself embraced the same technique, and it served him particularly well in the writing of the most medieval of the Chron-icles, *The Voyage of the Dawn Treader.* Eustace Scrubb, blundering into the dying dragon's valley, finds the floor "grassy though strewn with rocks, and here and there Eustace saw black burnt patches like those you see on the side of a railway embankment in a dry summer." It is an image that any child of Lewis's time would have instantly rec-ognized, and an observation particularly well suited to Eustace, who knows so much more about modern machinery than he does about dragons. (Like steam engines, dragons have flaming innards.) The story is about to move toward a mystical transformation, but those black, burnt patches keep its feet on the ground, rooted in the idle perceptions of a schoolboy waiting for a train.

Of all the Chronicles, *The Voyage of the Dawn Treader* most resembles a traditional medieval romance. It tells the story of a journey, specifically the quest by Prince Caspian to find the seven lost lords of Narnia, friends of his father's who were sent off on an exploratory mission by the usurper Miraz. In this book, the visitors from our world—Lucy, Edmund, and Eustace—have mostly just come along for the ride. Like Lancelot or Gawain, the Narnian voyagers are motivated by worldly honor and a thirst for adventure, but there is a spiritual aspect to their quest, too, for at least one member of the party; he is out to fulfill a prophecy uttered over his cradle and intends to present himself on God's doorstep.

In Reepicheep, the talking mouse who is, ironically, a "parfait knight" to rival Galahad himself, Lewis manages to tweak the tradition of the chivalric paragon and to celebrate it at the same time. The mouse is both comical and admirable, his gallantry and unfailing physical courage ("no one had ever known Reepicheep to be afraid of anything") all the more impressive in someone so small:

"While I can, I sail east in the *Dawn Treader.* When she fails me, I paddle east in my coracle. When she sinks, I shall swim east with my four paws. And when I can swim no longer, if I have not reached Aslan's country, or shot over the edge of the world in some vast cataract, I shall sink with my nose to the sunrise and Peepiceek will be the head of the talking mice in Narnia."

Perhaps the most obvious literary ancestor of the third Chronicle is *The Voyage of St. Brendan the Navigator,* the story of a semilegendary Irish monk who, with a crew of sixty pilgrims, set sail across the Atlantic in search of the Land of Delight. This fabled paradise of eternal life, perpetual summer, and bountiful food and

drink is in turn derived from the old Celtic legend of the Isle of the
Blessed or Tír na nÓg. Brendan was an actual sixth-century Christian churchman, but his adventures were imaginary and they carried him into territory that is essentially pre-Christian. So, too, the
Dawn Treader arrives at last at the rim of the earth (Narnia's world
is flat) and partakes of pagan allegory. The sweet seawater that Caspian drinks, tasting of "light more than anything else," is an echo of
the liquid light drunk by the soul of Pompey when he reaches the
outermost layer of the cosmos, the realm of pure aether, in the first-
century epic of Lucan, *Pharsalia*.

The *Voyage of the Dawn Treader* is a long, glittering chain of such
citations and borrowings, beginning with a premise derived from
Homer and Dante as well as Saint Brendan. The deathly pool that turns
whatever touches it to gold is a variation on the Midas fable. There is
Jesus's expulsion of the moneylenders from the temple in the overturn-
ing of Governor Gumpas's paperwork-laden table on Doorn. The
albatross from Coleridge's *The Rime of the Ancient Mariner* appears in
the bird that leads the *Dawn Treader* away from the Dark Island; Saint
Brendan again in the encounter with the sea serpent; *The Tempest* in
the magician who oversees the thick-witted Dufflepuds and regrets
the need to rule them with "rough magic;" and, last but not least, the
conversion of Saint Paul on the road to Damascus in Eustace's ordeal as a dragon. That was the parallel, Neil Gaiman reports, that first
alerted *him* to the Chronicles' Christian subtext.

Lewis even wove bits of his own critical work into the story. The
horrors of the Dark Island (where dreams, "not daydreams — dreams,"
come true), for example, touch on something Lewis was writing at
the same time, in a very different context, about the disturbing nature
of nighttime dreams. In *OHEL,* he remarked that it is "at once so
true and so misleading" for people to call Spenser's poetry "dreamlike." Although *The Faerie Queene* has none of the quality of "waking reverie" we usually associate with the term, the poem's vivid,
often gory imagery has "a violent clarity and precision which we

often find in actual dreams." Ramandu, the convalescent star the companions meet near the end of their journey, even offers an epigrammatic version of medieval cosmology when Eustace informs him that "in our world...a star is a huge ball of flaming gas." "Even in your world," Ramandu replies, "that is not what a star is, but only what it is made of."

Do these appropriations, these borrowings and quotations, diminish *The Voyage of the Dawn Treader* in some way, make it less bewitching because we can track down the sources of its shining wonders? Do the fragments of Christian mysticism, classical cosmology, and Celtic legend rattle against one another gratingly, as Tolkien would probably have protested had he bothered to read the book? No writer can entirely avoid borrowing, of course—Tolkien himself put some of Tír na nÓg into Valinor, the paradise of the elves in the Uttermost West of Middle-earth. Tolkien, however, took more care to transfigure those origins, anodizing them in the solvent of his own mythos; only then would his work meet his own standard of true sub-creation.

If Lewis meant to do the same thing with Narnia, he obviously failed. But why assume that Tolkien was his model, or ought to have been? Perhaps he was no more interested in sub-creation than he was in the formal innovations of Woolf or Joyce. Why should he cast aside all the books he'd read and loved when he sat down to write—why not summon them instead? That's what Chaucer and Malory and Spencer did. "I doubt if they would have understood our demand for originality or value those works in their own age which were original any the more on that account," Lewis wrote of the medievals in *The Discarded Image*. "The originality which we regard as a sign of wealth might have seemed to them a confession of poverty. Why make things for oneself like the lonely Robinson Crusoe when there is riches all about you to be had for the taking?"

This choice was, in part, a matter of faith; if all myths were shadows of the one true myth, then, in a sense, they were all telling the same story. The really powerful myths had a fundamental unity that transcended the superficial dissonances that so irritated Tolkien. Still, it was not always possible to make everything fit properly with everything else, a dilemma medieval scholars regularly faced. The lumber room of Lewis's imagination contained a vast collection of ideas, images, and stories constructed according to different systems, rather like a pile of building materials cut to both metric and Old English measurements. And in addition to all that, there remained some odds and ends that defied systemizing entirely. Some of these were items he'd stashed away before his conversion, things belonging to his old "secret, imaginative life," treasures he wished to keep even though they couldn't be reconciled to the new regime. Their recalcitrance was part of their charm, the really wonderful thing about them. They would find a place in Narnia, too.

CHAPTER TWENTY-FIVE

The Third Road

There is an old Scottish border ballad called "Thomas the Rhymer." The eponymous Thomas is lying under a tree when a lady in a green gown approaches. Astonished by her beauty, he kneels, hailing her as the "Queen of Heaven," whereupon she corrects him, explaining that she is instead the queen of "fair Elfland." She carries Thomas off to her splendid court, where he obeys her injunction not to speak to anyone. When he returns to his "ain countrie," he discovers that seven years have passed, and in some iterations of the story Thomas acquires the gift of prophecy. One thing common to nearly every version is a moment in which the lady points to a narrow road "beset wi thorns and briers," naming it as the path to righteousness, and then to a broad, lily-lined road that is the path to wickedness — shades of *The Pilgrim's Progress*. But then the queen shows Thomas a third way, a "bonny road," twisting through fern-covered hillsides. That is the road to "fair Elfland."

By Lewis's own admission, the medieval model of the universe, though resplendently harmonious, was "a shade too ordered." Although there is something very human about the desire to inhabit such a comprehensible system, there's also something very human in finding it suffocating from the inside. "For all its vast spaces," Lewis wrote of the model in *The Discarded Image*, "it might in the end af-

flict us with a kind of claustrophobia. Is there nowhere any vagueness? No undiscovered byways? No twilight? Can we never really
get out of doors?"

The first time I read those lines, a few years after I wrote my
first piece about *The Lion, the Witch and the Wardrobe,* I experienced a
jolt of recognition. This had been exactly my own complaint about
Narnia as a teenager, after Lin Carter's *Imaginary Worlds* had clued
me in to Lewis's Christian agenda. The road that had once seemed to
lead to free and open country had in reality doubled back to church.
Now I was trying to explain why my damning adolescent assessment of the Chronicles wasn't entirely sufficient, either. As an adult,
I'd discovered that I could follow Lewis pretty far without feeling
obliged to return to Christianity, and that the old sensation of freedom, of wildness in Narnia, remained. Where did it come from?

The books I'd read about Lewis hadn't helped much; in fact, they
only made me doubt my own response. Today's Lewis scholars might,
as Walter Hooper does, caution others against succumbing to "the mistaken notion that if you have found a biblical or literary 'influence'
behind a work there is no more to be said about it," but this is in fact exactly what nearly all of them do. If glosses on scripture are really all there
is to Narnia, I don't believe I could have ever mistaken it for a glimpse of
far horizons. The true believers' Narnia is monolithic, black-and-white,
closed. It has no byways or twilight. There is no out-of-doors.

Now, at last, I had found Lewis himself writing wistfully of a third
road, like the bonny road that leads to Elfland, which is also Fairy-
land or Faerie, as the place was known of old. A better name for it
now might be the Otherworld, since the word "fairy" has, in the last
150 years, become tainted. Originally, a fairy was neither an animate
Barbie doll with wings nor an adorable urchin wearing a petunia
for a dress, but a creature belonging to one of many supernatural species in northwestern European folklore. Some were beautiful, some
were ugly, some common, some rare. Many looked like human beings,
others did not, and while some fairies were indeed small, others were

larger than men, and still others could be big or small, depending on how they felt at the moment. The fairies in the folktales of the British Isles are most often the same size as human beings; in fact, some of them may once have been human beings. Specifically, they may be the dead, or people thought to be dead who perhaps aren't after all. Vagueness is their brief.

Lewis devotes an entire chapter to these creatures in *The Discarded Image,* calling them Longaevi after the pagan author Martianus Capella, who with that word encompassed those beings who "haunt the woods, glades, and groves, and lakes and springs and brooks; whose names are Pans, Fauns, Satyrs, Silvans, Nymphs," a list that includes almost all of the anthropomorphic population of Narnia. The importance of what I will have to call the fairies (Longaevi is a bit much) lies, as Lewis wrote, in their unimportance. "They are marginal, fugitive creatures. They are perhaps the only creatures to whom the Model does not assign, as it were, an official status. Herein lies their imaginative value.... They intrude a welcome hint of wildness and uncertainty into a universe that is in danger of being a little too self-explanatory."

Tolkien, too, was fascinated by the notion of Faerie and its inhabitants. These creatures, he wrote, are "not primarily concerned with us, nor we with them. Our fates are sundered, and our paths seldom meet. Even upon the borders of Faerie we encounter them only at some chance crossing of the ways." The third road pointed out to Thomas the Rhymer, the road to Elfland ("elf" was one synonym for "fairy"), leads neither to heaven nor to hell, and it promises a place where the relentless moral weighing that Christianity imposes upon every action in this world simply doesn't apply. It is not a safe place — to the contrary, the traditional beliefs hold that the less a human being has to do with fairies and their business, the better — but then the real out-of-doors has never been very safe, either.

Lewis, as an Irishman, knew fairies more intimately than his friend. The housemaid who helped raise him and his brother had seen them near Dundrum in county Down, where their aunt lived, and as a man Lewis had vacationed in a bungalow on Ireland's northern coast which the locals wouldn't approach after dark. It was haunted, but according to Lewis, the ghost didn't frighten the neighbors nearly as much as "the Good People" also known to frequent the spot: "They are greatly dreaded," he reported, "and called 'the good people' not because they *are* good but in order to propitiate them." In Celtic legend, they are known as the Sidhe (Gaelic for "peace," another placating euphemism), local spirits who fiercely guard their favored sites and are sometimes said to be descendants of the Tuatha Dé Danann, a mythical race of gods and heroes who were expelled from Ireland by human invaders before relocating to the Otherworld.

In his legendarium, Tolkien transformed these beings into the noble, ethereal elves who are migrating out of Middle-earth throughout *The Lord of the Rings.* (He conceived of his elves as a real historical race, of which Celtic myths and legends are a fanciful, degraded memory.) But in folklore, the Otherworld was never entirely detached from this one; it was like an alternate Britain, a different layer of reality, often contiguous with our own and occasionally accessible at certain points of convergence: a rabbit hole, perhaps, or a mirror, or a wardrobe.

Sometimes the Otherworld was said to be underground, its entrances in the barrows and other prehistoric sites that dotted the countryside. Most of these legends probably arose from attempts to explain how the ruins got there in the first place and from ancient rumors of the people who preceded the Celts. The stone spearheads found near their old haunts were called "elf-shot," and the fairies were reputed to fear cold iron, possibly a memory of Stone Age natives subsiding before better-armed invaders. According to the peculiar mythology of Ireland, the land was home to a succession of five different "races" (some human, some giants, some much like gods) before the ancestors of the present occupants arrived.

The closest relation to the Sidhe in the Chronicles is the Lady of the Green Kirtle in *The Silver Chair.* Her dress is the same color as both the Queen of Elfland's gown and the sash worn by the Green Knight, who, acting under the secret orders of Morgan Le Fay (whose surname means "the fairy") tests Sir Gawain's honor. The Lady of the Green Kirtle abducts Prince Rilian from Narnia and carries him off to her underground kingdom, where she detains him by enchantment, a typical act of fairy mischief. She is also a shape-shifter, specifically a lamia (a monster originating in Greek mythology), a child-devouring serpent that can transform itself into a beautiful woman. The Lady of the Green Kirtle is called a witch, but in many old tales the figures we now know as witches were originally described as fairies. She seems fair, but plays foul, tricking Jill, Eustace, and Puddleglum into seeking shelter with the giants of Harfang, who intend to eat them at their Autumn Feast.

If *The Voyage of the Dawn Treader* is the most medieval of the Chronicles, *The Silver Chair* has the most in common with traditional fairy tales. It shares their primal preoccupations with giants, kidnapping, and the prospect of being devoured, anxieties that are, if not peculiar to small children, then at least the most intense in them. Rereading the scenes at Harfang, where the giants are among the few characters in any of the seven books to treat the child characters like children, I was reminded of the time my three-year-old friend Corinne looked at me appraisingly and announced, "I don't *think* you'll eat me." Until then, it hadn't occurred to me just how menacing the world must sometimes look from her perspective or that I myself might constitute a kind of giant.

The Lady of the Green Kirtle does differ from traditional fairies in her imperial ambitions; she plans to conquer Narnia with her army of enslaved gnomes and to install Rilian as a puppet monarch. Why she should need to do this when he is already the rightful heir to the throne is never explained, and it would be more fairylike of her to simply capture the prince on a whim, much as a human being would decide to keep a caged bird as a pet. This is how the capricious "gentleman with the thistledown hair" in Susanna Clarke's *Jonathan Strange & Mr. Norrell* collects certain choice Londoners, exceptionally attractive human specimens whom he forces to attend exhausting nightly balls at his decrepit castle. The rest of humanity doesn't interest him much. The Lady of the Green Kirtle is deliberately, rather than incidentally, wicked. A Narnian dwarf, upon learning of the lady's scheme, pronounces her "doubtless the same kind as that White Witch....those Northern Witches always mean the same thing, but in every age they have a different plan for getting it."

In truth, the White Witch—either how she first appears, as a variation on Hans Christian Andersen's Scandinavian Snow Queen in *The Lion, the Witch and the Wardrobe,* or as the vaguely Babylonian Empress Jadis in *The Magician's Nephew*—seems at best a remote relative of the Lady of the Green Kirtle, who is so entirely British. To the Green Witch, Lewis gives the most persuasive argument against faith in all the Chronicles, making her the mouthpiece of both his own youthful skepticism and the materialist beliefs held by the modernist contingent at Oxford. Though she is less overtly menacing than Jadis, this makes her a much more dangerous figure.

Realizing that the children and Puddleglum have broken her spell over the prince, the lady casts a drugged powder into the fireplace, strums a mandolin, and commences to argue away not only their god, but the entire aboveground world: "You have seen lamps, and so you imagined a bigger and better lamp and called it the *sun.* You've seen cats, and now you want a bigger and better cat, and it's to be called a *lion.* Well, 'tis a pretty make-believe....Look how you can put nothing into your make-believe without copying it from the real world, this world of mine, which is the only world."

The heroes are saved when Puddleglum stamps out the fire, cutting the incense with the pronounced smell of "burnt Marsh-wiggle."

He announces that the witch may very well be right, but so what? "Four babies playing a game can make a play-world which licks your real world hollow."

The Marsh-wiggle's defiance affected me profoundly as a child—not as a defense of theism, of course, but as a defense of fairy tales; I agreed that sometimes make-believe really did lick real life. As an argument for religion, however, Puddleglum's speech is feeble; he is saying, in effect, I don't know whether what I believe is true, but I'd rather live in a world where it is than in a world where it isn't, so I'm going to believe it whatever the evidence to the contrary. This is a variation on Lewis's "argument from Joy," the assertion that the human hunger for God is enough to demonstrate that God really does exist; if you want it enough, it's as good as true. You might as well decide that you prefer the medieval universe to the Newtonian one, and adjust the physics textbooks accordingly.

Like the Green Lady's underground kingdom, the medieval universe had its ceiling, its (false) limits. Did Lewis ever feel that he was running around in circles? He shared my attraction to "twilight" and "undiscovered byways," wayward forces that eluded the moral polarities of the great monotheistic religions born in the Middle East. But to admit such things into his picture of the world would undermine the very quality that made that picture so comforting: its comprehensive, celestial harmony. Fairies, neither angels nor men, neither good nor evil, have no place in God's plan. That is the real source of their appeal and their threat, and the reason why fundamentalists object to witches, wizards, and other occult elements in children's books. It's not that these figures lure readers to Satanism, but that they introduce the possibility that God and Satan are not your only options. Whether or not you believe in fairies, they stand for that choice, for the third road.

Lewis certainly felt the appeal of such figures, the imaginary companions of his boyhood's secret life and the native spirits of his homeland, so much more captivating than men in sandals and robes. Perhaps he felt sometimes that his own trumpeted faith was a bit claustrophobic. Otherwise, why include a whole chapter on the Longaevi in *The Discarded Image,* and why characterize them as a source of relief? Lewis's delight in the subject is evident in the reading of that chapter, but his own enthusiasm may also have troubled him a little. When he wrote a fairy into the Chronicles, she had to be made to embody all the most perilous spiritual traps—sensuality, the dominance of the female, materialism, pride.

But even the Green Witch's subterranean kingdom has its own otherworld, an alternate reality, a third road. It is the "Really Deep Land," known to the gnomes as Bism. When Rilian kills the witch, the floor of her kingdom cracks open, and the way to Bism is revealed. This, as the gnome Golg explains, is the true homeland of the Green Witch's former slaves, and our heroes snatch a glimpse from the brink of the chasm:

> They could make out a river of fire, and, on the banks of that river, what seemed to be fields and groves of an unbearable, hot brilliance—though they were dim compared to the river. There were blues, reds, greens and whites all jumbled together: a very good stained-glass window with the tropical sun staring straight through it at midday might have something of the same effect...."Yes," said Golg, "I have heard of those little scratches in the crust that you Topdwellers call mines. But that's where you get dead gold, dead silver, dead gems. Down in Bism we have them alive and growing. There I'll pick you bunches of rubies that you can eat and squeeze you a cupful of diamond juice."

In Bism, salamanders, "too white-hot to look at," swim in the fire river and talk to the gnomes. They are "wonderfully clever with their tongues: very witty and eloquent." The prince and Eustace can barely restrain themselves from accepting the gnome's invitation to adventure there (at this moment, Eustace recalls the example of Reepicheep), but duty to Narnia restrains them, as it does Caspian at the end of *The Voyage of the Dawn Treader*. "I fear it must be so," says Rilian, when he agrees to return to the overworld. "But I have left half my heart in the land of Bism."

So did I, and so, I believe, did Lewis. Bism remains one of Narnia's tantalizing loose threads, the dozen or so untold stories that he alludes to from time to time. How did Doctor Cornelius obtain Queen Susan's horn? How did the Lone Islands become a Narnian protectorate? Why was the star Coriakin demoted to mere magician status and why does he hang, in his hallway, a little mirror with hair on the top and a beard on the bottom? How did Fair Olvin turn the giant Pire to stone? And so on. These hints are part of what creates the impression that Narnia, as Neil Gaiman puts it, is "an infinite number of stories waiting to happen." It is permeable and fluid, a realm where anything might occur.

Narnia is itself, of course, a vision of Faerie, as evidenced in the way Narnian time passes differently from the time of our world. Like Faerie, it mostly consists of a great forest. Where the imagery of the Bible is Mediterranean — vineyards, roads, and villages — the landscape of Narnia is northern, thick with trees. The wilderness of the Middle East is the desert, an empty, harsh, barren place; trees there are few and carefully nurtured, the obedient bearers of figs and olives. In northern Europe the wild is woods; the very world itself, according to Norse mythology, is a tree: Yggdrasil, the World Ash. There, the uncivilized world is not empty but full, populated by any number of strange creatures and people going about their unfathomable, ancient business. The biblical wilderness offers little more than death and deprivation; the tribes of Israel wandered there, their lives and history in suspension. But the British wilderness is where stories begin, where the old gods live, where young men go to seek their fortunes, where nature and humanity resume a long and exciting conversation.

"Wildness" is what Lewis names the welcome note that fairies introduce to the medieval universe, and "wild" is a word to conjure with in Narnia. Aslan, we're repeatedly told, is "not a tame lion," the music the fauns play is wild, and so are the red dwarves and everything else Narnian that the Telmarines are at war with at the beginning of *Prince Caspian*. Wildness is Bacchus and his rampaging girl followers, so joyful, so untrammeled, and ultimately so enticing that Lewis knew he'd gotten carried away and felt obliged to have Susan nervously remind his readers (and possibly himself) that they aren't very safe.

This is not the real wildness of, say, the backcountry of California's Sierra Nevada, the woods of my own girlhood, beautiful but vast, harsh, and inhospitable; that is not wildness but *wilderness*. Lewis never set foot in such a place. Narnia's wildness is the wildness of Rostrevor Forest, where I got lost in the fog on one miserable and eventually rainy afternoon. I tramped around in soggy circles before I finally found my way out, but at no point was I as truly frightened as I would have been if I were in Yosemite. I knew that the woods were so small that if I walked long enough I'd come to the edge. I would meet neither bears nor mountain lions; large predators vanished along with all the substantial forests in England many centuries ago. You can die in the wilderness where I come from; hikers do all the time. In Britain, you might catch a bad cold.

But the wildness of Lewis's Britain is no less vivid for being notional and poetic. It is an *idea* about the natural world, not nature itself, the product of the Britons' long, interpenetrating relationship with their environment. The people got into the land—draining it, plowing it, shaping it, tending the woods almost as diligently as they tended the fields—and the land got into the people. The memory of the lost forest is all the more potent because it is a memory and has graduated into the realm of myth. It has become the emblem of the oldest of the old religions, which, as every Briton knows, worshipped the trees. So, in *Puck of Pook's Hill,* a book in which the eponymous fairy acquaints two children with England's historical roots, Rudyard Kipling includes a song:

> Oh, do not tell the Priest our plight,
> Or he would call it a sin;
> But — we have been out in the woods all night,
> A-conjuring Summer in!
> And we bring you news by word of mouth —
> Good news for cattle and corn —
> Now is the Sun come up from the South,
> With Oak and Ash and Thorn!

Ostensibly, Lewis chose the priest in this standoff, but he was a great fan of *Puck of Pook's Hill,* too. Half his heart, and much of Narnia, would always belong to the woods and the road that runs through them.

CHAPTER TWENTY-SIX

A Formula of Power over Living Men

Stories leave themselves open to a much wider spectrum of interpretation than theology does. As the Iranian academic and writer Azar Nafisi, author of *Reading Lolita in Tehran,* once observed, "Stories are wayward. They never remain within the control even of their own creators." This is a problem for the orthodox, but Lewis felt that certain important truths could be fully communicated only via stories. What was captured, or was meant to be captured, was ineffable. "To be stories at all," Lewis wrote, "they must be series of events; but it must be understood that this series—the plot, as we call it—is only really a net whereby to catch something else. The real theme may be, and perhaps usually is, something that has no sequence in it, something other than a process and much more like [a] state or quality."

Everyone is available, is *susceptible,* to the spell of story. That is one reason critics have generally found it unworthy of study; Lewis observed that the more story predominates in a book, the less intellectuals think of it. The appetite for and appreciation of story requires no training or cultivation; it is a common denominator lower even than titillating descriptions of sex, because children are usually not very interested in those. But it is potent. The word "spell," as Tolkien mentions in his essay "On Fairy Stories," once meant "both a story told, and a formula of power over living men." Where does this power come from and what is it made of? Tolkien thought that to ask this question was to speculate about the very origins of language and the mind.

Not long ago, I heard an ornithologist on the radio, explaining that for birds, singing is a learned behavior. Young larks, for example, listen to adult larks sing and then practice until they perfect the skill. The scientist then played recordings of two birds singing to illustrate his point. The mature lark ran confidently through a succession of repeating, fully developed motifs, while the youngster's song skittered around, jumbling together fragments of different songs in patterns that didn't resolve. The ornithologist called this "babbling," and to illustrate his point further, he played a recording of his own eighteen-month-old daughter babbling in baby talk, that is, making sounds that approximated language without quite being language. Human children, it seems, learn to speak in much the same way that birds learn to sing. The ornithologist's daughter rattled off a series of nonsense syllables, mimicking the inflections of adult speech, occasionally tossing in familiar phrases from nursery rhymes: "Wee, wee, wee, all the way home."

When my friends Desmond and Corinne were learning to talk, they too went through a babbling phase. Corinne is a particularly canny impressionist, and before she could command many useful real words, she would fix a nearby adult with a confiding look and chatter in her pretend language, perfectly reproducing the cadences of real conversation. Eventually, after she acquired more words, she and her brother learned how to use and arrange them properly: "this" for an object close at hand; "that" for the thing on the other side of the room you want the grown-up to bring to you. For a while, they both stopped answering yes-or-no questions with a "yes" or a "no" and responded only in full sentences: "Did you like the circus?" "I did." "Is the Cat in the Hat making a mess?" "He is!" It was as if, having finally sussed out a few of the occult powers of grammar, they wanted to exercise them as often as possible.

Now that the twins are three, they seem to be practicing another kind of grammar. Just as they absorb the words they hear every day and learn to make sense of the patterns they form, so they are soaking up stories. Corinne has begun to spin out what I think of as story babble, buttonholing sympathetic adults à la Coleridge's Ancient Mariner, and treating them to endless, rambling narratives that all seem to run together into a single infinite saga. (Since Corinne's nickname is Nini, her parents call this epic the Niniad.) Her characters are lifted from Beatrix Potter and Dr. Seuss, from the people and animals in her world and from the figures that populate the imaginary life she has built with her brother. At present, these characters don't do much more than eat, hide, and throw things out the window, but every so often, a shard of fully formed story language pops into the narrative. A turtle and a tadpole will be engaged in a perpetual cycle of looking for food and dodging the predatory "big fish" when suddenly "the moon came up and shone on the quiet fields of snow and they got into their warm, soft beds and fell fast asleep."

Whenever Corinne summons one of these fragments of story talk, she lowers her voice and slips into a hushed, singsong rhythm that is, of course, her imitation of the special voice that adults use when reading or telling a story to children. In my experience, there is no better way to seize the attention of distracted children than to start speaking in this voice. They will drop the fought-over stuffed animal or the annoying toy drum and drift over to your knee with the faces of the hypnotized—attentive and pliable as long as you keep it coming. It is the kind of power that can go to your head.

Adults don't become immune to this power, either; they just learn to respond to different cues. Instead of "Once upon a time," we latch onto "It is a truth universally acknowledged, that a single man in possession of a good fortune, must be in want of a wife," perhaps the most famous first sentence in the history of the English novel. Equally effective is the grand, sweeping, and old-fashioned "It was the best of times, it was the worst of times," from Dickens's *Tale of Two Cities.* Or we might acquire a taste for laconic leaps into the middle of the action, such as Mickey Spillane's opener for *I, the Jury:* "I shook the rain from my hat and walked into the room." A simple, even mundane sentence, that one, but it does the trick; it makes you wonder what happens next. You're hooked.

Who can catalog the myriad ways that human beings use to signal, "Now, I am telling you a story"? The speaker leaves off ordinary talk, the listener recalibrates her attention, and both enter into a relationship older than the memory of our race. A story takes us, for a while, out of time and the particularities of our own existence. The initiation into this ritual might come as a pause, a change of tone, or even as the apparition of a studio logo shining on the screen in a darkened movie theater. This tells us that a special kind of language, the language of story, has begun.

Human beings speak thousands of languages, but most linguists agree with the theory, first advanced by Noam Chomsky, that there is a "universal grammar," a common structural basis underlying all human languages. Despite the great variety of tongues, they all work in the same fundamental way. Our brains, it is thought, have an innate response to languages that employ this structure and we are particularly attuned to it during childhood, when we learn languages quickly and easily. An infant's babbling sounds like adorable nonsense, but it's really the evidence of a powerful information processor assembling itself, rifling through sounds and sequences of sounds and figuring how all the pieces fit together to form meanings.

Could stories work the same way? Could Corinne, when she corners me and launches into yet another installment of the Niniad, be practicing the grammar of storytelling, arranging and rearranging the components, trying out different kinds of voices, experimenting with repetitions, with dramatic conflict and its resolution, if not yet, alas, with endings? I think so. But while everyone learns to speak, not everyone learns how to tell stories, or at least not how to tell them successfully.

Most of us recognize a fully formed story when we hear or read or see it; this, to me, seems almost as universal as our ability to distinguish, in our own language, between a grammatically correct sentence—"John watched the dog chase the ball"—and a grammatically broken one—"The chase John ball watched the dog." But, as Chomsky famously pointed out, a sentence can be grammatically correct but still nonsensical: his example was "Colorless green ideas sleep furiously." Even a story with the requisite components of beginning, middle, and end can seem essentially meaningless.

Lewis suspected that, at base, story is difficult to analyze because it really can't be taken apart, and myth was the prime example of story's deep roots in the human mind. To Lewis, the word "myth" meant something more than just a tale from an obsolete religion; it was a unit of meaning. Sometimes it was only a sketch of a narrative; a myth might be no more than the image of a beautiful youth falling in love with his own reflection in a pond. Not all old stories qualified as myth in his opinion, and some new ones did. You could identify them not so much by their common characteristics as by how people responded to them.

Lewis considered Franz Kafka to be one modern genius in the creation of myth; reading *The Trial* and *The Castle,* he felt "a profound significance, but it emanates from the whole story and is not built up by understanding the parts, nor could I state it except by retelling the story." There was something irreducible in the kind of story he called myth. We might come up with a thousand explanations for what it "stands for," but none of them will ever be complete or sufficient. It's impossible to say what the myth of Orpheus is *about;* it is exactly itself. The only way to convey its significance fully is to tell the story one more time. We might claim that the ordeals of Kafka's K. symbolize the individual's struggle against the modern state or some such theme, but we know that's only one facet of its significance. When hassling with some red-tape nightmare, we call it Kafkaesque, not because Kafka wrote about bureaucracy but because bureaucracy often seems to be *about* Kafka's myth.

Myth troubles critics, Lewis believed, because its value is "extra-literary." The power of a myth doesn't arise from the particular words used to convey it; it can be felt even when no words at all are used. A myth might be told in pantomime, silent film, or a "pictorial series" (such as a comic book) and still impress its audience with the sensation that "something of great moment has been communicated to us." There is only one version of, say, *Madame Bovary* or Keats's "Ode on Melancholy"; it would make no sense to talk of an equally legitimate version of either work that used different words. But what is the definitive version of the Orpheus myth? Aren't each of the renditions—Ovid's verse, Monteverdi's opera, the film *Black Orpheus,* Tennessee Williams's play *Orpheus Descending*—equally valid and recognizably Orpheus? Although lyric poetry sometimes avails itself of mythic material, it is in a sense the opposite of myth, because "in poetry the words are the body and the 'theme' or 'content' is the soul. But in myth the imagined events are the body and something inexpressible is the soul; the words, or mime, or film, or pictorial series are not even clothes."

This conception of myth comes in part from Owen Barfield, one of Lewis's closest friends and a fellow Inkling; *The Lion, the Witch and the Wardrobe* is dedicated to Barfield's daughter, Lucy, and *The Allegory of Love* is dedicated to Barfield himself. In 1928, Barfield published a book, *Poetic Diction,* based on his Oxford B.Litt. thesis, and it had an influence on both Lewis and Tolkien. Barfield suggested that myth is a remnant of an early stage of both language and understanding or consciousness, a time of "unitary, concrete meanings." At this stage, for example, the story of Demeter and Persephone was not just associated with the experience of winter, it *contained* the very idea of winter—along with the concepts of waking and sleeping and life and death, among other things—in a single, dense unit of meaning. Such meanings, according to Barfield, "could not be *known,* but only experienced or lived."

Very small children often think in this way, Barfield believed. When Desmond was just beginning to learn the names of people, I asked him to tell me who I was. He studied me for a while, and replied tentatively, "Mommy?" He knew I was not his mother, but because I sometimes cared for him, I was subsumed in the concept of Mommy-ness, along with the mother animals pictured in his board books and, possibly, physical warmth and food—the experience of being cared for itself. All of this was "Mommy." Perhaps he regarded me as a minor manifestation of his own mother in the way the Romans considered the Celtic goddess Sulis to be one of the lesser faces that their goddess Minerva presented to the backward provincials of the world.

As languages develop, Barfield speculated, they begin to divide these larger units of meaning into smaller parts. This makes language more modular, and therefore easier to manipulate and more useful, but it also saps the intensity out of individual words and concepts. When, for Desmond, I became Laura, I was easier to think about as a distinct person who looked and behaved differently from the distinct person who is his mother, Leslie. But in becoming an individual, I also lost my place as part of the wondrous continuum of nurturing presence that was "Mommy." Desmond knows that I am like his mother because we're both female grown-ups, but that category does not have the potency it once did; it is disenchanted. Now I am my own woman, but I used to be a goddess.

When human beings learn to generalize and abstract, to label oaks, elms, and birches as "trees," for example, they arrive at a new type of unity that is practical and sterile, in Barfield's eyes—very different from the kind of consciousness that understood the world to be an ash tree or an oak to be a god. Barfield believed that in metaphor in particular and in poetry in general, we recover a little of the old, lost unity; metaphor rejoins what has been split apart. This is the source of the sensation of illumination, of recognition that a powerful metaphor delivers. For, as much as our minds like to *analyze,* to break things down into their constituent parts in order to examine and manipulate them, we also long for *synthesis,* the sensation that our words and our world are connected and infused with "intrinsic life." It is in myths that we find that life, that meaning, in its most intact form (although even here it is "mummified," according to Barfield). Myth defies intellect—if by "intellect" we mean analytical, logical thought—because it predates it. An echo of this old, preanalytical unity is the "something inexpressible" that Lewis felt myth imparts.

Lewis read omnivorously and had ecumenical tastes, but fiction that conveyed this "something" had always been and always would be his favorite. A pulp novelist like H. Rider Haggard, he thought, exemplified the "mythopoetic" (mythmaking) art in isolation from all other literary gifts. A book didn't always have to be *good* in any sense that matters to literary critics—in its prose, its construction of believable characters, its ideas, or its originality—to pack a mythopoetic wallop. Lewis knew that Haggard wasn't a very good writer, but he also knew that he felt strangely swayed and captivated by books like *She* and *King Solomon's Mines.* In Haggard, it was made apparent how the "daemon," or mythopoetic genius, "triumphs over all obstacles and makes us tolerate all faults. It is quite unaffected by any foolish notions which the author himself, after the daemon has left him, may entertain about his own myths. He knows no more about them than any other man."

To Lewis's mind, no writer channeled this "daemon" better than his "master," the Victorian novelist George MacDonald. Lewis had bought a copy of MacDonald's *Phantastes* in a railway station bookstall when he was sixteen years old and far from home, boarding with his tutor in Surrey. Reading it, he was transported. The book somehow bridged a gulf within him, between his imagination, that "many-islanded sea of poetry and myth," and the banal stuff of everyday life. He felt that MacDonald had shown him how Joy, an aura he once attached only to grand and distant things, to faraway mountains and Nordic heroes, might also be found in the nearby and the humble. "Up till now," Lewis wrote in *Surprised by Joy,* "each visitation of Joy had left the common world momentarily a desert." In *Phantastes,* he saw "the bright shadow coming out of the book into the real world and resting there, transforming all common things and yet itself unchanged." His imagination had been, "in a certain sense, baptized."

Phantastes, like *The Prelude,* would remain a touchstone book for Lewis, perhaps the single most powerful literary experience of his life — his Magician's Book, you could say. Nevertheless, Lewis was a literary critic, and his critical judgment told him that MacDonald, like Haggard, was not a technically good writer. "If we define Literature as an art whose medium is words," he wrote in the introduction to a 1946 collection of MacDonald's writings, "then certainly MacDonald has no place in its first rank — perhaps not even in its second."

It seems impossible to define literature as anything *but* an art whose medium is words. The term "literature," from the French *littera,* for "letter," seems to dictate that it can be nothing else. *Phantastes* itself was, of course, written in words, and not particularly felicitous ones. But there was something else in it, too, some other property that transcended words, a quality of story and image that Lewis would, years later, come to call by a name that Tolkien had invented, mythopoeia. As far as Lewis was concerned, MacDonald was "the greatest genius" at mythopoeia he had ever encountered.

Phantastes is, like Charles Williams's *The Place of the Lion,* a very strange book. A young man, Anodos — a name signifying "the way up" in Greek — describes the events following his twenty-first birthday, when he inherits an old desk with a secret compartment. A tiny, beautiful lady emerges from that compartment, and before vanishing, she zooms up to normal size, claims to be his great-grandmother, and promises him a trip to "Fairy Land." He awakens the next morning to find a brook flowing through his bedroom and all the floral patterns on his carpet, furniture, and curtains turned to living plants and flowers. He then follows a footpath into a dense forest, where, during twenty-one days of wandering, he encounters flower fairies, evil and benevolent tree spirits, a fabulous book-filled castle whose inhabitants he can't quite see, a statue of a woman that he brings to life, a penitent knight, a cottage whose several doors open onto entirely different regions of Fairy Land as well as into his own past, and more. In the course of this "faerie romance for men and women" (as MacDonald subtitled the book), the hero progresses from a selfish desire to be loved to a redeemed state of self-sacrificing altruism.

Like William Morris's romances, *Phantastes*, first published in 1858, was innovative. Anodos, despite his allegorical name, is more or less a contemporary person, and no one else had yet hit upon the idea of setting a Victorian gentleman loose in the land customarily roamed by the Redcrosse Knight or Snow-White. (*Alice's Adventures in Wonderland* hadn't appeared yet; MacDonald, who later became a friend of Lewis Carroll's and whose children read and loved an early draft of Alice's story, played a significant role in getting *Alice* published.) In letters he wrote to Arthur Greeves upon first reading *Phantastes*, Lewis enthused about the book's phantasmagorical and uncanny elements—the magnificent fairy palace and an eerie tale that Anodos recounts of a young man who falls in love with a lady imprisoned in a mirror. It was only later that Lewis decided that the story was not merely a parade of marvels, that the "quality which had enchanted me in [MacDonald's] imaginative works turned out to be the quality of the real universe, the divine, magical, terrifying, and ecstatic reality in which we all live."

This statement bewilders me. I know that how Lewis felt about *Phantastes* resembles how I feel about the Chronicles. True, I admire Lewis's prose as he could never admire MacDonald's, but that's not

the fundamental source of his books' appeal. It was exactly the mythopoeic quality in *The Lion, the Witch and the Wardrobe* that caused
me to hand it back to Mrs. Belden, effectively speechless. By all
rights, the book that had had the same effect on Lewis ought to
move me deeply, but it doesn't. I have friends who feel differently,
about MacDonald's children's fiction (*The Princess and the Goblin* and
At the Back of the North Wind, for example), and I've come to appreciate the sweetness (it is never cloying) that pervades his books.
Nevertheless, *Phantastes* seemed little more to me than an interesting, even trippy curiosity; the tremors that shot through Lewis when
he first read it did not electrify me.

This was the difficulty with mythopoeia as Lewis defined it, that
is, by the profundity of a reader's response: not everyone recognizes it
in the same books. Lewis knew this all too well. He could hardly fail
to notice how many of his peers turned up their noses at his favorites.
"It is plain," he wrote, "that...the same story may be a myth to one
man and not another." If so, then how can we be sure that it's really a
myth? He had a passing interest in anthropological and psychological theories about where the recurring motifs in the world's religions
and legends might have come from, and was intrigued enough by
Carl Jung's theory of archetypes to look into it. Ultimately, though,
Lewis concluded that what Jung had to say was not so much a theory
of myth as yet *another* myth. Jung's description of the collective unconscious was magnificent, written in the quasi-mystical language of
"good poetry," but it wasn't supported with sufficiently solid material
evidence to merit the status of science. "Surely the analysis of water
should not itself be wet?" Lewis quipped.

And, after all, Lewis didn't need a theory of the collective unconscious—or of narrative "grammar" embedded in the neurological
workings of the human brain. If he wanted to explain why we feel
we recognize certain stories even when we're encountering them
for the first time, or why the same types of story seem to arise again
and again in every culture, he had a perfectly adequate reason: they

were facets of a truth that transcended the individual self. Myths were God's way of calling us home.

But how can the skeptic understand such things? How to explain why certain stories exert a power that feels virtually biological over me, while leaving other readers cold? Fire will burn any human body it touches, and starvation will waste it, but stories are not so predictable in their effects. During the time I was working on this book, the information that I was writing about Narnia elicited very different responses in conversation. Some people would give me a look of politely blank puzzlement; if they'd read the Chronicles at all, they hadn't especially liked them. Others would exclaim, "Oh, I loved those books!" and for a moment their gaze would drift off to some distant prospect, remembering. One woman, the proprietor of a bed and breakfast I stayed at in Ireland, came up to me holding seven frayed paperbacks, the old Puffin editions of the Chronicles published in Britain, pressed between her two flattened hands like sacred objects; she'd kept them safe for nearly forty years. I wasn't sure she'd even let me touch them, and then hardly knew what to say about them when she did. These weren't the editions I'd read, of course, but I'd seen similar ones before, so they weren't a novelty to me. They were just paperback books, really. But I knew what they meant to her.

In his memoir of his own childhood reading, *The Child That Books Built,* Francis Spufford describes the effect that the Chronicles had on him when he first read them:

The book in my hand sent jolts and shimmers through my nerves. It affected me bodily. In Narnia, C. S. Lewis invented objects for my longing, gave forms to my longing, that I would never have thought of, and yet they seemed exactly right: he had anticipated what would delight me with an almost unearthly intimacy. Immediately I discovered them, they became the inevitable expressions of my longing. So from the moment I first encountered *The Lion, the Witch and the Wardrobe* to when I was eleven or twelve, the seven Chronicles of Narnia represented essence-of-book to me. They were the Platonic Book of which other books were more or less imperfect shadows.

Which is spookier: that Spufford has so perfectly articulated my own childhood feelings about Narnia, or that Lewis was able to achieve this "unearthly intimacy" with me, Spufford, my Irish hostess, and millions of other young readers? We have very little commentary directly from Lewis himself about what he thought he was doing when he first sat down to write *The Lion, the Witch and the Wardrobe*. Later in life, he could offer no more illumination than that he was in the grip of an old image (a faun walking through a snowy wood) cherished for decades, and that a "fairy tale" seemed the best form for what he wanted to say. But what exactly he meant by that image, or by any of the rest of it until, rather late in the process, he hit upon the idea of rewriting the Passion of Christ, he could never entirely explain. He wrote the Chronicles in a pell-mell rush, at a time in his life when he was distracted, emotionally taxed, and physically exhausted, in an effort that seems almost haphazard. But just as we sometimes dance best when we are not consciously thinking about the steps, it was in writing the Chronicles of Narnia that Lewis finally managed to do what he had admired for so long in others: create myths.

CHAPTER TWENTY-SEVEN

Further Up and Further In

Of all Lewis's inventions in the Chronicles, the one that comes closest to his conception of myth is the Wood Between the Worlds in *The Magician's Nephew*. Digory's scheming, vainglorious uncle Andrew tricks Polly into picking up a magic yellow ring that transports her out of our universe, and Digory has no choice but to follow her, carrying the green rings that can bring them both back. The rings are made from the contents of an otherworldly box of dust Uncle Andrew inherited from his godmother ("one of the last mortals in this country who had fairy blood in her"), but he has always been too much of a coward to try them out himself. Uncle Andrew has no appetite for adventure, although he was willing to undergo "disagreeable" experiences with "devilishly queer people" in order to obtain his expertise in magic. He regards sorcery not as romance but as a kind of technology. Like all bad magicians, he is "dreadfully practical" (never a term of praise coming from Lewis).

The yellow ring takes Digory to the Wood Between the Worlds. In this quiet forest, there are small pools beneath the trees every few yards as far as the eye can see. It is warm and bright, although leaves obscure the sky. Digory steps out of one of the pools and finds Polly safe, lying on the grass "just between sleeping and waking." Eventually, they discover that each pool is a passage to a different world. If you jump into any one of them while wearing a green ring, you will find yourself in another universe; touching the yellow rings takes you back to the Wood.

Before they figure this out, however, the children almost get lost forever. The Wood isn't a dangerous place, exactly. (Digory and Polly come across one of Uncle Andrew's previous experimental subjects, a guinea pig, and decide to leave it there, since the magician will only do "something horrid" to it if they bring it back.) But, once in the Wood, people find it easy to forget who they are and where they came from. The narrator speculates that Digory, if asked, would have replied that he had always been there. At first, he and Polly just barely recognize each other and can't recall why. They are like people trying to remember a dream that is slipping away, but in this case, the dream is real life. The guinea pig is the trigger that brings it all back, but even after they recover themselves, Polly argues against lingering in the Wood, "or we shall just lie down and drowse forever and ever."

The Wood Between the Worlds owes a little to the "wood where things have no names" in Lewis Carroll's *Through the Looking-Glass*. Wandering through that forest, Alice meets a fawn, and for a while they walk together, Alice with her arm around the fawn's soft neck, until they reach an open field. Out of the wood, the fawn suddenly recalls that it is indeed a fawn, and runs away, leaving Alice on the verge of tears at losing "her dear little fellow-traveler," but somewhat comforted at having regained her own name. This interlude, a sojourn through that preverbal land where child and beast are reunited, feels like an afterthought and takes less than a page. Perhaps for a writer as fond of wordplay as Carroll, the idea of a wood without words was uninteresting, merely empty.

Although Lewis's wood has a similar effect on people's memories, it represents a qualitatively different primeval state. Stories may not happen here, but this is where they are born. Looking around, Digory feels not only as if he "had always been in that place," but also that he'd "never been bored although nothing had ever happened." There are no animals or insects, yet the Wood seems charged with vitality: "When he tried to describe it afterward Digory always said, 'It was a *rich* place; rich as plumcake.'" This becomes manifest after the children have made an exploratory visit to the world of Charn. Charn's last empress, the sorceress Jadis, succeeds in hitching a ride back with them, only to find that the air in the Wood—"this horrible place," as she calls it—suffocates her. If the Wood is dense with life, Jadis, who has killed every other living thing in her own world rather than submit to being conquered by her sister, is an avatar of death; she can't survive there.

The Wood Between the Worlds shares some traits with other liminal spaces, way stations and thresholds like the bardo of Tibetan Buddhism or the door-lined hallway that Alice tries so hard to get out of in *Alice's Adventures in Wonderland*. But unlike other "between" places in myth and fiction, the Wood is both empty *and* full. It is a unitary moment, containing everything, the pause before a story is told, in which nothing has happened and so anything might. It is not the point of embarkation, but the embarkation itself, the feeling we all experience when we understand that a story is about to begin, the reading mind rendered geographical, like the allegorical medieval self. The pools open into entire worlds, and this, too, is what stories do. They build a world around us as they go along.

On a less abstract level, the Wood is also a library. For someone like Lewis, who lived so much through his reading, each book was potentially a portal to another world. This is one of the chief differences between a child's experience of a favorite book and an educated adult's. For the adult, a book may be a work of art, possibly a very great one, but for the child reader, certain books are universes. If we are lucky, we retain some of that capacity to be immersed in a story; Lewis seems to have held on to it better than most, and in this sense, those who describe him as a man who remained a "child at heart" are right. Nevertheless, the adult awareness that a book is a *made* thing—the work of a human being who, however talented he or she may be, is still only human, and flawed—always takes up some of the imaginative space formerly occupied by total belief. At seven, Neil Gaiman believed the events in the Chronicles to be "true"; now he knows they are "made up."

The made-up-ness of Narnia has always seemed particularly glaring to certain well-read adults who never encountered the books as children. Lewis's mythic syncretism—fauns and dragons and dwarves and Arabian Nights exoticism all jumbled together—undermines the Chronicle's religious integrity for readers like John Goldthwaite, and the Christian subtext spoils the imaginative freedom for readers like my own teenage self. For Tolkien, these undigested borrowings and the lack of coherent, unified world-building make Narnia a flimsy, derivative concoction that spits in the eye of true sub-creation. The idea that the Chronicles are allegories—a supposedly crude, reductive, pedantic form of literature—as well as a collection of insufficiently original tidbits, offends against the premium that contemporary critics place on naturalism and novelty. "Narnia is all pieces of other fullnesses," complains Goldthwaite, "hastily thrown together like stage props retrieved from a warehouse. The only law of consistency Lewis observed was the law of his own fancy."

Perhaps children are just too ignorant to recognize this as a flaw, but I think not. Here at least is one case where the naive reader knows better. When Goldthwaite describes "his own fancy" as the "only law" Lewis obeys, he underestimates the potency of that fancy. The Chronicles *are* unified, not by anything resembling the exhaustive cultural *stuff* that Tolkien invented for Middle-earth, not by a single aesthetic or style, and not even, really, by a cogent religious vision, but by readerly desire. Lewis poured into his imaginary world everything that he had adored in the books he read as a child and in the handful of children's books he'd enjoyed as an adult. And there is more, too: treasures collected from Dante, from Spenser, from Malory, from Austen, from old romances and ballads and fairy tales and pagan epics. Everything that Lewis had ever read and loved went into Narnia, and because he was a great reader, these things were as deeply felt by him as actual experiences. In his own way, Lewis, too, believed that everything in the Chronicles was true, and this conviction is what he communicates to his young readers.

The Chronicles resemble the Wood Between the Worlds in this way: they, too, are a portal to other worlds, literary worlds. I was probably the only undergraduate in my junior-year seminar on Edmund Spenser who felt perfectly at home with *The Faerie Queene,* although at the time I couldn't have told you why. The "troupe of Faunes and Saytres...daucing in a rownd / Whiles old Sylvanus slept in shady arber sound," who come to the lady Una's rescue when she is menaced by the knight Sansloy, were old friends of mine, people whose company I had missed. The marvel-filled woods that Spenser's heroes roamed, Prospero's Island, the lands Odysseus visited, and the Underworld traversed by Aeneas—all these were like old haunts to me. I would even catch flashes of a familiar figure like Uncle Andrew ("Men like me, who possess hidden wisdom, are freed from common rules just as we are cut off from common pleasures") in the characters of Raskolnikov and Dr. Frankenstein. For the rest of my life as a reader, I will no doubt be meeting again the characters, places, and events that I first encountered in Narnia.

Lewis not only provided my first introduction to these wonders, he also taught me how to understand them, by which I mean that he showed me how a story can work in several different registers at once. I learned to read ironically with the excerpts from Eustace's diary in *The Voyage of the Dawn Treader;* that meant looking past a character's own descriptions of events to get to a more impartial version of what had actually happened. I learned to read morally by recognizing my own flaws in the ignoble impulses of Edmund Pevensie and Jill Pole. Both are styles of reading I would need once I became old enough for *Lolita* and *Crime and Punishment.* But Lewis also showed me how to read in another way: allegorically, or as he would later come to call it, symbolically.

Lewis traced a familial connection between allegory and literary myth in *The Allegory of Love.* Allegory, he thought, was a stage that religious stories passed through on their way to becoming the mythic elements used by poets, romancers, and novelists. It is a big leap from faith to art. As long as people believe in a god, they will most likely want something from him, regard him with what Lewis called an "urgent practical interest" and subject him to "selfish prayer." But, given time, an unworshipped god can "come to light in the imagination" as a symbol pure and simple. Only when the last vestiges of belief have faded can he attain the full imaginative power of what Lewis called myth. This can take centuries. While those years pass, a god or a hero is always in danger of being simply forgotten. The idea of that god or hero, like the bottled juice of grapes fermenting into wine, "must be stored up somewhere, not wholly dead, but in winter sleep, waiting its time. If it is not so stored up, if it is allowed to perish, then the imagination is impoverished. Such a sleeping-place was provided for the gods by allegory."

Demeter, for example, was the goddess of the harvest to her ancient worshippers, a deity who walked the earth, replete with all the meanings that Barfield described as residing in a full-fledged, primordial myth — motherhood, fruitfulness, grief, deprivation, pilgrimage, recovery. She is now a "myth" in Lewis's sense of the word, a figure who exists only in stories. She still contains most of the old meanings, and even some newer ones, but artists can now do whatever they like with her without fearing either divine retribution or irate believers. (This is a freedom that no one today enjoys with either Muhammad or Jesus.) At some point, between the days when people all over the ancient world convened in Greece to celebrate the rites of the Eleusinian Mysteries in Demeter's honor and the moment in the nineteenth century when Alfred Lord Tennyson sat down to write the poem "Demeter and Persephone," the goddess underwent an imaginative sea change. Lewis believed that she (and Orpheus and Aphrodite and the rest) spent the first part of those long centuries of metamorphosis in the "sleeping-place" of allegory.

In the 1940s, after he'd written *The Allegory of Love* but before he started the Chronicles, Lewis sometimes used the word "symbol" interchangeably with "myth" in order to distinguish it from allegory. He had not lost his interest in the allegory as a form, but it did have its limits. He still thought that a good allegory must be read skill-fully—by giving equal status to the images of the sparkling fountain and the lady's eyes in *The Romance of the Rose,* for example—and by recognizing that the character's behavior and actions are often a way of representing what we now regard as entirely internal conflicts. Modern readers who lack these skills misperceive allegories as no more than a pointlessly labored narrative code. But if allegory is not really as reductive as contemporary readers usually think, it is still constrained. An allegorical figure labeled "Patientia," for example, is permitted to stand for only one thing: the virtue of patience.

Many people today also talk about "symbols" in this way, as sim-ple equations; the farm in *Animal Farm* stands for the Soviet Union, and so on. As Lewis used the word "symbol," it could not be so eas-ily pinned down or exhausted. For him a symbol, like a myth, was "a story out of which ever-varying meanings will grow for different readers and in different ages." A strict allegory is harnessed, more or less subject to its creator's conscious control. A myth or symbol is less obedient. "Into an allegory," Lewis explained to one correspondent, "a man can put only what he already knows: in a myth he puts what he does not yet know and could not come to know in any other way." Like the images on the alethiometer in Philip Pullman's Dark Materi-als trilogy, like literature itself, its meaning can never be exhausted.

In the Chronicles, Lewis endeavored to create symbols like this; so, too, did Tolkien with *The Lord of the Rings.* That contemporary

readers often mistook those books for allegories only served to illustrate for Lewis the degree to which readerly sophistication and
versatility had atrophied in modern times. People really only knew
how to read realistic fiction. Lewis (unlike Tolkien) appreciated
quite a few realistic novels, but that was merely one arrow in literature's quiver! As a writer, he could move easily in and out of various literary modes in the course of a single book. In *The Magician's
Nephew,* for example, the confrontation between Jadis and Digory's
aunt Letty in Letty's London parlor is farce, with Aunt Letty assuming that the tall, outlandishly dressed Jadis is a circus performer
and her Charnian incantations the mutterings of a drunk. Tolkien,
had he read the book, would probably have regarded this scene as
unconscionable levity—Jadis, after all, is Lewis's villain; it's hard to
imagine the creator of Sauron allowing *him* to appear so ridiculous,
however briefly.

This doesn't keep Jadis from serving as a credible menace later on,
insinuating and manipulative when she tempts Digory in the garden.
Aunt Letty's parlor, where mattresses are mended and adults make
remarks alluding to an alternate, Trollopian narrative taking place offstage ("Andrew, I wonder *you* are not ashamed to ask *me* for money")
coexists in the same story as the Wood Between the Worlds and the
mystical creation of Narnia. The fracas Jadis causes on the streets of
London when she commandeers a hansom cab is Dickensian comedy; the scene in the garden is dreamlike and allegorical. Today, I
wonder how Lewis managed to make all this feel as if it belongs
together, in the same book. As a child I took it for granted, though
if asked I might have said that *The Magician's Nephew* was as rich as
plumcake.

This is the other side of Neil Gaiman's boyhood intimation that
Narnia is an infinite number of stories waiting to happen. Countless
stories went into it, and countless stories come out of it. Narnia is
the country of literature, of books, and of reading, a territory so vast

that it might as well be infinite. This is why the conclusion of *The Last Battle* feels like such a mistake, and no doubt why everyone I interviewed for this book described it as their least favorite Chronicle. After the destruction of the world, it is revealed that the Narnia we have known in the previous six Chronicles is "only a shadow of a copy of something in Aslan's real world." Everyone of merit is ushered into the "real Narnia," a Platonic paradise where colors are brighter, the fruits are infinitely richer and sweeter, and "every rock and flower and blade of grass looked as if it meant more."

This is a far cry from the voice that told of trees stirred by "a hushing, ruffling sort of wind which meant that rain was coming soon." Lewis, reaching for celestial beauty, attains only a hallucinatory hyperrealism that unstitches Narnia from the humble, medieval details that made it live. *The Last Battle* was the one Chronicle I didn't reread very often. The ending left me feeling empty and gloomy instead of satisfied.

Jonathan Franzen calls *The Last Battle* a "weak finish" that "quickly turns into that which [Lewis] has amazingly avoided" in the previous six books; that is, a story overwhelmed by its preacherly and philosophical elements. For Neil Gaiman, the book "has got a few good bits in: it's got the dwarves, it's got 'further up and further in,' and yes, we've gotten to see a couple of characters we'd loved who are dead."

"Although," I interjected, "have you noticed that one of the best, Puddleglum, doesn't get any lines? That really disappointed me, but at the same time I know Lewis could never have let Puddleglum be his usual self, that pessimistic Marsh-wiggle we all loved, because how could he say something Puddleglummish in that completely perfect and therefore completely dull Narnia?"

"That *astonishingly* dull Narnia! I can't imagine that any kid who read the books and wanted to go to Narnia — and I assume that any kid who'd read the books would want to go — ever wanted to go to *that* Narnia. As a kid, you edit out *The Last Battle* in a way because it's not *true*."

The perfected Narnia that Lucy and her friends arrive at can never actually *be* Narnia, because it is a place without conflict, without danger, without error, without change. Without any of those things, you can't have a story. And without stories, there is no Narnia.

If you read enough, and C. S. Lewis certainly did that, you come to see that every great story contains elements — talking beasts and brave orphans, lonely girls and dying gods, trackless forests and perilous cities — that can and have been used and reused over and over again, without becoming exhausted. If anything, they grow denser, richer, more potent with each new telling. Every great storyteller contributes a little to this patina, but storytellers are human, and inevitably those contributions have flaws. Myths and stories are repositories of human desires and fears, which means that they contain our sexual anxieties, our preoccupation with status, and our xenophobia as well as our heroism, our generosity, and our curiosity. A perfect story is no more interesting or possible than a perfect human being.

A long time ago, I opened a book, and this is what I found inside: a whole new world. It isn't the world I live in, although sometimes it looks a lot like it. Sometimes, though, it feels closest to my world when it doesn't look like it at all. This world is enormous, yet it all fits inside an everyday object. I don't have to keep everything I find there, but what I choose to take with me is more precious than anything I own, and there is always more where that came from. The world I found was inside a book, and then that world turned out to be made of even more books, each of which led to yet another world. It goes on forever and ever. At nine I thought I must get to Narnia or die. It would be a long time before I understood that I was already there.

ACKNOWLEDGMENTS

Among the many people who shared their memories with me, I would like to thank in particular those individuals who agreed to be interviewed for this book: Wilanne Belden, Tiffany Lee Brown, Susanna Clarke, Jonathan Franzen, Neil Gaiman, and Pam Marks. The Marion E. Wade Center at Wheaton College proved invaluable in my research into the life of C. S. Lewis, especially the efforts of Laura Schmidt, archivist. In Headington, Oxfordshire, Chelsea Carter and Theresa Kipp of the C. S. Lewis Foundation gave me a welcoming and informative tour of the Kilns and its grounds, and in San Diego, Nancy Miller helped me reconnect with the past.

Several people took the time to discuss various aspects of this book with me. Thanks to Michael Chabon, John Clute, Richard Dienst, Jennifer Egan, Gavin Grant, Colin Greenland, P. J. Marks, Jennifer Reese, and Gary Wolfe. For general encouragement, I'm very grateful to Mignon Khargie, Jonathan Lethem, Daniel Mendelsohn, and Lorin Stein. Lydia Wills helped me wrestle a mass of ideas into coherence, and Michael Pietsch brought the whole thing into focus.

A few people provided inspiration without realizing it. One is Philip Pullman, whose intelligence, curiosity, and good humor are well worth emulating. Two more are Corinne and Desmond O'Hehir, who I hope will someday read about themselves here and forgive me for it. Special thanks to their parents, Leslie Kauffman and Andrew O'Hehir.

INDEX

on individualism, 95; informal nature writing, 188–89; Irishness of, 155–57, 186–87, 203, 204, 251–52, 272–73; and irony, 242; on joy, 6, 183–85, 220, 289; as literary critic, 5, 126–27, 210, 259–64, 267, 268, 289; and masculinity, 69–71, 76; and medieval literature, 45–48, 133, 154, 233, 248, 259–65, 270–72, 279; on modernism, 155, 157, 224–25; on myth, 48, 240, 244, 285–93, 294, 299–300; and occultism, 111–12; prejudices of, 123, 124–28; privacy of, 38, 41–42, 50, 70, 76, 80, 96, 116; productivity of, 222–23, 293; on reading, 5–6, 10, 13, 115–16, 288, 291, 297–301; and romances, 227, 228, 231, 248, 259, 266, 297; on rural Britain, 123; and sexuality, 36, 130, 163–66, 242–43; smoking of, 122, 135; on Stonehenge, 250; on stories, 91–92, 281–82, 285; on symbol, 299, 300; on "the Tao," 64–65. *See also specific works*

Lewis, Flora, 38, 49, 50, 57, 111
Lewis, Warren: alcoholic binges of, 137, 222; on cookery, 120–21; and Kilns, 135, 187; on landscape of Narnia, 180; on Albert Lewis, 38–41; military service of, 59, 121; on Janie Moore, 136, 137, 138; as nostalgic bachelor, 142; relationship with C. S. Lewis, 31–32, 42, 50, 58, 68, 72, 75, 138; smoking of, 122; social success of, 148–49
L'Heureux, John, 170
Liddell, Alice, 253
Lion, the Witch and the Wardrobe, The (Lewis): as allegory, 45, 112; Christian symbolism of, 6, 87, 90, 96, 98–99, 101, 104, 247–48; destiny in, 235; early writing on, 67–68; evil in, 43; female villain of, 132, 162, 275; friendship in, 73, 75; illustrations of, 194–95, 252; landscape of Narnia in, 181–82, 184, 187, 191, 194, 203; Lucy's role in, 67–72, 76, 78–79; metaphors of, 23–24; mythical creatures in, 28; mythopoeic quality of, 291; parents in, 52, 74; rereading of, 22–23; school depicted in, 151; scruples of children in, 53–54, 74–75; Tolkien on, 241, 244; Tumnus's storytelling in, 72–73; vindication in, 64; violence in, 58–59

Lion, the Witch and the Wardrobe, The (2005 film), 73–75
literary criticism: Freudian literary criticism, 161; of Lewis, 5, 126–27, 210, 259–64, 267, 268, 289; purpose of, 98, 116–17; reading as critic, 5, 6, 9
literary value, 10, 14
Loki Bound (Lewis), 150
Longfellow, Henry Wadsworth, 202
Lord of the Flies (Golding), 112, 113, 115
Lucan, 267
Lurie, Alison, 61, 63, 64

MacDonald, George, 113, 288–91
Magician's Nephew, The (Lewis): and animal language, 27; female villain in, 43–44, 132, 275, 296, 301; friendship in, 44; garden in, 43–44, 48–49; illustrations for, 195; landscape of Narnia in, 184, 193; literary modes in, 301; vanity in, 131; Wood Between the Worlds in, 294–97, 298, 301
Malory, Thomas, 45, 232, 248, 253, 268, 297
Marks, Pam, 101–3, 110
Mary Poppins (Travers), 26–27, 29, 30
McCloskey, Robert, 33
Mere Christianity (Lewis), 126, 223
metaphor, 23–24, 44, 108–9, 287–88
Miller, H. R., 195
Milton, John, 171, 173, 183, 261, 264
misogyny, 124, 137, 140, 141, 144, 242
Moore, Janie "Minto": deterioration in health, 136, 137, 162, 188, 222; and Kilns, 135, 187; Lewis's relationship with, 135–38, 139, 141, 142, 155, 157, 165, 166
Moore, Patrick, 135
Morris, William, 45, 228–32, 236, 238, 290
Murdoch, Iris, 215
myth: of Ireland, 273; Lewis on, 48, 217, 240, 244, 248, 285–93, 294, 299–300; mythical creatures, 28; and ritual, 91; Tolkien on, 235, 269. *See also* Norse mythology

Nabokov, Vladimir, 264
Nafisi, Azar, 281
narratives. *See* stories
Nesbit, E., 52, 69, 195, 236, 248
Nietzsche, Friedrich, 29

Castelreagh Hills, 183; on Christianity,
99–100, 111; on female dominance,
133–34, 137; on gardens, 42–43; on
homeliness, 204; on interruptions, 137;
on Albert Lewis, 39; on MacDonald,
289; on mother's death, 38, 49–50;
on Norse mythology, 202, 203; on
reading, 115–16; on social structure,
148, 149, 150; on Tolkien, 200–201;
and Wordsworth's influence, 220; on
World War I, 57–58
survival, 51–52, 54–57, 234
Sykes, Bryan, 255

Tennyson, Alfred Lord, 45, 299–300
That Hideous Strength (Lewis), 148, 246
Through a Glass Darkly (film), 80
Tolkien, Christopher, 204
Tolkien, Hilary, 206
Tolkien, J. R. R.: on allegory, 45–46; on
Arthurian tradition, 253, 255–56; and
Barfield, 286; botanical interests of,
189; and Catholic Church, 90, 157, 201,
205–7, 245; on Celtic culture, 253–57,
268; *The Children of Húrin,* 230; on
communion with living things, 27;
dislike of Chronicles of Narnia, 76,
158, 241, 244, 247, 297; and dissonances in myths, 269; and Dunsany,
162; on escapism, 101; on fairies, 272,
273; on fairy tales, 161, 215–17, 236,
241, 244, 282; *Farmer Giles of Ham,*
194, 249; *The Fellowship of the Ring,*
212; friendship with Lewis, 9, 14, 75,
157, 187, 200–201, 210–11, 215, 216,
218–19, 220, 221–24, 226, 238, 243–
48; *The Hobbit,* 9, 21, 212–13, 223,
236, 238, 239, 244–45; on Jews, 125;
landscape of Middle-earth, 180, 181,
191, 199, 206, 209, 211–12, 213, 244,
258, 259; and language, 201, 205–8,
211, 212, 214, 227, 236, 243, 254, 255,
259; *The Lord of the Rings,* 45, 58, 75,
98, 198, 210, 211, 213–15, 221–22, 223,
227–28, 235–38, 239, 241, 242, 243–
44, 273, 297, 300; "Mythopoeia," 218–
19, 289; national identity of, 204–6,
208, 209, 253; and Norse mythology,

200–201, 204, 208–9, 249, 250; and
romances, 227–28, 231, 235–36, 248;
on rural Britain, 123; and sexuality, 242–44; *The Silmarillion,* 212, 214,
235, 237–38, 250, 253–54; on Williams,
245, 246
Tolkien, Mabel, 205–6
Tolkien, Michael, 207
Travers, P. L., 26–27, 29, 30
Turner, William, 196

universalism, 106–7

Van Allsburg, Chris, 77
vanity, 131, 145
Voyage of St. Brendan the Navigator, The,
266–67
Voyage of the Dawn Treader, The (Lewis):
Calormenes in, 119; Christian symbolism in, 99, 267, 268; and duty
to Narnia, 278; elitism in, 145–46;
friendship in, 79–82, 84; illustrations
of, 193–94; irony in, 298; and magician's book, 11–12, 139–40; and medieval literature, 267–68, 274; reform
in, 64; and "right books," 53, 55, 57,
83–84, 145; and romances, 266; setting
of, 184; vividness in language, 265–66;
worldliness of, 241–42

Wagner, Richard, 50, 201, 202–3, 236
Wells, H. G., 24, 225
Wilder, Laura Ingalls, 51–52
Williams, Charles, 245–46, 289
Wilson, A. N.: on Freud, 160–61; on
Griffiths, 76; on Lewis, 39, 70, 99–100,
126; on Warren Lewis, 68; on Janie
Moore, 136, 138
Wilson, Edmund, 214, 227, 235
Wind in the Willows, The (Grahame), 9, 33,
155, 225
Wolfe, Gary, 258–59
Woolf, Virginia, 171, 225, 268
Wordsworth, Dorothy, 219–20
Wordsworth, William, 29, 218–24, 226,
247, 289

Yeats, William Butler, 13

Reading Group Guide

the

Magician's Book

A SKEPTIC'S
ADVENTURES
in
NARNIA

by

LAURA MILLER

A conversation with the author of *The Magician's Book*

Laura Miller talks with Rebecca Traister of Salon.com

How did you first encounter Narnia?

I was given *The Lion, the Witch, and the Wardrobe* by my second-grade teacher, Wilanne Belden, whom I worshipped and am still in touch with. I interviewed her for *The Magician's Book*. When I asked how she came to give me this thing that would become the whole center of my inner world, she said, "You were just a kid who needed to read this book." What surprised me was that she had had *The Lion, the Witch, and the Wardrobe* for quite a while, probably around ten years, before she actually tried giving it to one of her students to read. I was the first one. And it was a huge success.

Your obsession with the Chronicles did not stop at one reading?

I became obsessed and read them so many times that I practically have them memorized—except for *The Last Battle,* because, as with many people, that is my least favorite of the seven. I saved up my money to buy my own copies. My mother gave me a paperback set, but I wanted the hardcovers. And I'm not a collector; this was the only thing about which I've ever said, "I have to have it."

Then, when I was thirteen and in the process of trying to track down other books that would give me the same kind of thrill, I discovered [in a book of literary criticism] that there was all this Christian symbolism in the Chronicles. That completely shocked me. I was so horrified, because I had been raised as a Catholic—not a superstrict or guilt-heavy Catholic, but nevertheless Catholic—and

I wasn't really a believer. I wasn't into church or religion in any way. For me, Narnia was everything I would want life to be, and none of the things I disliked, such as church and religion and the Bible. The idea that this thing I was trying to get away from was secretly lurking in my place of refuge, in my most private, cherished thing—I remember feeling physically nauseated by that, deceived and betrayed.

But you did believe in Narnia, if not Christianity.

Yes, when I was small. It's like Neil Gaiman told me: he had no doubt that this was true and that these things had happened. I particularly loved the creatures of classical mythology—I thought the centaurs were so cool! And the trees that were people. But these are things that have nothing to do with Christianity. They come from Lewis's background as a literary scholar. He had read everything and had been strongly influenced by *The Faerie Queene* and many more obscure narratives, including material that is older than Christianity and is pervasive in Western culture. A lot of what we're responding to in Narnia, for example, is the ideal of Arcadia, from classical mythology.

With *The Magician's Book,* I wanted to pull that stuff out from the background because it tends to get overwhelmed by everyone's perception of the Christian message. Lewis was trying to integrate all of it in his imagination. Some of his critics, especially Tolkien, would complain that it was a random crazy patchwork—Santa Claus is there, and Norse mythology—and Tolkien felt it wasn't consistent. But it *is* consistent in that it held everything meaningful to its author. That's what hits child readers. What I said to my teacher was, "I didn't realize anyone else had an imagination like mine." That has come up again and again: it's as if the author of this book had reached into my head and found the things I wanted most, and made them into a story.

Your path—of ardent belief in Narnia, and then a rejection and repudiation of your childhood devotion, and then your return and reckoning—actually mimics what many people consider a religious journey.

Yes, and very consciously so. The story of naive faith, and then loss of faith, and then the recuperation of something that is not faith, because it's not unquestioning. . . . It's what Philip Pullman, who is a guiding light in some ways for this project, would call "experience." It's not just a loss of innocence: it's a different path to grace. My belief in the power of books is embodied in these seven books, with their ability to have an infinite number of meanings, to have meanings that the author didn't intend, or that the author put in there without being aware of it.

My feeling of being cut off from that wellspring of my imagination during the adolescence of my reading life, which is the middle of the book, is like a loss of faith. Then there is the later process of working through how and why I loved these books as a child and continued to love them as an adult, to get to something much bigger than my early belief in them.

Can you talk a bit about Philip Pullman's influence on that final stage of your journey?

In Pullman's trilogy His Dark Materials, Lyra, the young heroine, has been able to read a divination instrument without really trying, thanks to the grace of being unself-conscious. When she becomes self-aware with puberty, she loses that grace and can no longer read it. A character comes to her and explains that there is another kind of grace you can find through experience. If she devotes herself to studying the instrument, she can reach a point where she'll be able to read it even better than she did before.

When you're writing children's books, or writing about children's books, there is this feeling that the loss of innocence is only a loss. Lots of the great children's authors were obsessed with childhood and their desire to go back to childhood. But there's something adolescent about just being disillusioned. Many people, in any situation—it could be a love relationship, or how you feel about Barack Obama—get stuck at the stage of disillusionment. Pullman is saying that you have to persevere, to put effort into it. If you do that, you can come to an enlarged understanding that is, in its own way, a kind of grace.

And you pursued that enlarged understanding, in part, by pursuing Lewis himself?

One treasure I discovered was his literary criticism. He wrote two major works, *The Allegory of Love* and his volume of *The Oxford History of English Literature,* which is mostly about Spenser. Those inspiring books show an enthusiasm and appetite for the literary experience that you rarely see in any academic, and in precious few literary critics. They helped me to reengage with Lewis as a writer. I also tried to track down everything in biographies, in his letters, his diaries, and other writings that would tell me what had contributed to Narnia.

I came to see how my own relationship with the Chronicles continued without my realizing it. As an English major, I read a lot of the books that Lewis loved and I also loved them — Dante, Milton, Spenser, Austen. I've been *recognizing* them all along because Lewis put all of them into Narnia. His books made a reader out of me by preparing my mind and heart for an imaginative experience that would last for the rest of my life.

When I was in college, very strict realism was the only thing to do in American literature, and it was hard to explain why you would want to read a book that had magic in it. In *The Allegory of Love,* one of the things Lewis explains is that a story that's not strictly realistic can nevertheless be profoundly truthful. [An author may use] witches or centaurs in order to tell a story about a human experience that transcends realism. It can be universal in a way that realism can't.

There's also something religious in your desire to move beyond your naive faith in Narnia to a world in which you could pick apart books. Your experience of reading Animal Farm, *alongside learning of Lewis's Christian message, is tantamount to biting the apple and getting thrown out of Eden.*

I wanted to know more, I wanted to understand more, I wanted to read more, I wanted to be a grown-up, to have the knowledge and power and responsibility that comes with that. Part of that knowledge was admitting to myself that there was no Narnia, that it had been invented by a man. I had been like Neil Gaiman, thinking, "This has to be true; this is too good not to be true," which is actually how Lewis felt about God. He wanted God too much for God not to be real.

Then I discovered the idea that a story can have a secret meaning, that it doesn't just describe events. As a child, when you think that stories are things that happened to people who actually existed, that's all you need to know. But when you come to see a story as created by a person who has intentions, the story itself can have intentions, such as the intention to teach you something. That's the most rudimentary criticism you learn as a beginning student: What does this symbolize? These pigs stand for certain revolutionaries and Boxer the horse stands for the proletariat. Once you see stories as having some purpose, they cease to exist simply for the sake of their wonderfulness.

Adapted from an interview originally posted at Salon.com on December 6, 2008. Reprinted with permission.

Questions and topics
for discussion

1. Laura Miller was introduced to the Chronicles of Narnia by her teacher and was immediately swept into their magical world. Describe your own discovery and reaction to them.

2. When Miller writes about her most powerful reading experiences while growing up, she cites *Island of the Blue Dolphins, Five Children and It,* and the *Little House on the Prairie* series. Name some of the formative books of your childhood and discuss why they were important to you. What about them has stayed with you into adulthood?

3. In the excerpt that opens *The Magician's Book,* Lucy encounters the best story she has ever read. Afterward, she is unable to remember what happened in the story or to reread it. Have you ever lost yourself in a story as Lucy did? What were you reading? How old were you? Discuss why you think you were able to forget yourself so completely. How do our daily lives affect the way we read? What does this say about the role readers play in the creation of a story's meaning?

4. Neil Gaiman and Jonathan Franzen note the importance of C. S. Lewis's books in their own lives and work. Discuss the similarities and differences between their books and the Chronicles of Narnia. Have you noticed Lewis's influence on other writers? If so, which writers? And why does their work remind you of the Pevensie children's adventures?

5. Does Miller's description of C. S. Lewis's life and personality alter your view of his novels? In what ways? Have your opinions of other books changed after discovering personal details about the author? Why does biographical information affect our interpretation?

6. Laura Miller writes that she will not address the religious symbolism in the Chronicles, focusing instead on the stories and their creator. Do you agree with her decision? Are there other aspects of the books you would have liked Miller to address?

7. When Miller discovered Narnia's Christian messages, her feeling of betrayal drove her away. Eventually, she returned and reexamined the books as an adult. Why was she upset by her new understanding? Discuss the role that the passage from innocence to understanding played in her reaction. Is one experience more valid than another?

8. Part memoir, part biography, and part literary criticism, *The Magician's Book* touches on the many factors that shaped the author's relationship with the novels. Discuss the extent to which each reader's knowledge informs and shapes his or her interpretations of stories.

9. At its core, *The Magician's Book* is the story of Laura Miller's attempt to regain her childhood enchantment with the Chronicles. Have you reread the Chronicles of Narnia as an adult? If so, how has your enjoyment or understanding of them changed? Do you think it is possible to regain the childhood experience of reading? Why?

Laura Miller's suggestions for further reading

While I was writing *The Magician's Book,* I often found myself talking with parents whose kids adored Narnia. A few of them asked me to recommend similar titles for their children. Since I remember how eagerly I searched for such books when I was a girl, it's a request I take very seriously.

Beyond the best-known classics — *The Wizard of Oz,* the Harry Potter series, *Charlie and the Chocolate Factory, The Wind in the Willows, The Hobbit,* etc. — here are a few suggestions. Some of these books I loved as a child; others I've discovered since. You can find more information about these books and additional recommendations, as well as a full bibliography for *The Magician's Book* and related materials, at www.magiciansbook.com.

Joan Aiken, *The Serial Garden*
Lloyd Alexander, The Prydain Chronicles, beginning with *The Book of Three*
Susan Cooper, The Dark Is Rising series, beginning with *Over Sea, Under Stone*
Edward Eager, *Half Magic*
Neil Gaiman, *Coraline*
Tove Jansson, *Finn Family Moomintroll*
Norton Juster, *The Phantom Tollbooth*
Andrew Lang, editor, *The Red Fairy Book*
Madeleine L'Engle, *A Wrinkle in Time*
Ursula K. Le Guin, *A Wizard of Earthsea*
George MacDonald, *The Princess and Curdie*

China Miéville, *Un Lun Dun*

E. Nesbit, *Five Children and It*

Garth Nix, *Sabriel*

Philip Pullman, His Dark Materials trilogy, beginning with *The Golden Compass*

Lemony Snicket, A Series of Unfortunate Events series

P. L. Travers, *Mary Poppins*

Ysabeau S. Wilce, *Flora Segunda*

Diana Wynne Jones, The Chronicles of Chrestomanci, beginning with *Charmed Life*

Laura Miller is a journalist and critic. She is a cofounder of Salon .com, where she is currently a staff writer, and is the editor of *The Salon.com Readers Guide to Contemporary Authors*. She contributes regularly to the *New York Times Book Review*, and her work has also appeared in *The New Yorker*, the *Los Angeles Times*, *Time*, and other publications. She lives in New York.

For more information, visit www.magiciansbook.com.